SEARCHING

in

Illinois

A REFERENCE
GUIDE TO
PUBLIC AND
PRIVATE RECORDS

by
Gayle Beckstead
and
Mary Lou Kozub

PRINTED IN THE UNITED STATES OF AMERICA

Library of Congress Catalog Card Number: 84-80217

ISBN: 0-942916-05-0

ACKNOWLEDGEMENTS

Special thanks is expressed to Leslie Dustin for
her editing services and to Beverly Mosman, Jerry
Placeres, and Rita Samuiloff for their help in
compiling, typing, and proofing.

ISC PUBLICATIONS
Post Office Box 10857
Costa Mesa, CA 92627

CONTENTS

INTRODUCTION

This book is a guide to locating and utilizing the many types of reference and source materials, both public and private, that are available for review and inspection by researchers.

SECTION I

STATE-WIDE INFORMATION

ILLINOIS
COUNTIES

7

ILLINOIS COUNTIES AND COUNTY SEATS

COUNTY	CITY	ZIP CODE	COUNTY	CITY	ZIP CODE
ADAMS	Quincy	62301	LEE	Dixon	61021
ALEXANDER	Cairo	62914	LIVINGSTON	Pontiac	61764
BOND	Greenville	62246	LOGAN	Lincoln	62656
BOONE	Belvidere	61008	MC DONOUGH	Macomb	61455
BROWN	Mt. Sterling	62353	MC HENRY	Woodstock	60098
BUREAU	Princeton	61356	MC LEAN	Bloomington	61701
CALHOUN	Hardin	62047	MACON	Decatur	62523
CARROLL	Mt. Carroll	61053	MACOUPIN	Carlinville	62626
CASS	Virginia	62691	MADISON	Edwardsville	62025
CHAMPAIGN	Urbana	61801	MARION	Salem	62881
CHRSITIAN	Taylorville	62568	MARSHALL	Lacon	61540
CLARK	Marshall	62441	MASON	Havana	62644
CLAY	Louisville	62858	MASSAC	Metropolis	62960
CLINTON	Carlyle	62231	MENARD	Petersburg	62675
COLES	Charleston	61920	MERCER	Aledo	61231
COOK	Chicago	60606	MONROE	Waterloo	62298
CRAWFORD	Robinson	62454	MONTGOMERY	Hillsboro	62049
CUMBERLAND	Toledo	62468	MORGAN	Jacksonville	62650
DE KALB	Sycamore	60178	MOULTRIE	Sullivan	61951
DE WITT	Clinton	61727	OGLE	Oregon	61061
DOUGLAS	Tuscola	61953	PEORIA	Peoria	61601
DU PAGE	Wheaton	60187	PERRY	Pinckneyville	62274
EDGAR	Paris	61944	PIATT	Monticello	61856
EDWARDS	Albion	62806	PIKE	Pittsfield	62363
EFFINGHAM	Effingham	62401	POPE	Golconda	62938
FAYETTE	Vandalia	62471	PULASKI	Mound City	62963
FORD	Paxton	60957	PUTNAM	Hennepin	61327
FRANKLIN	Benton	62812	RANDOLPH	Chester	62233
FULTON	Lewistown	61542	RICHLAND	Olney	62450
GALLATIN	Shawneetown	62984	ROCK ISLAND	Rock Island	61201
GREENE	Carrollton	62016	ST. CLAIR	Belleville	62220
GRUNDY	Morris	60450	SALINE	Harrisburg	62946
HAMILTON	McLeansboro	62859	SANGAMON	Springfield	62701
HANCOCK	Carthage	62321	SCHUYLER	Rushville	62681
HARDIN	Elizabethtown	62931	SCOTT	Winchester	62694
HENDERSON	Oquawka	61469	SHELBY	Shelbyville	62565
HENRY	Cambridge	61238	STARK	Toulon	61483
IROQUOIS	Watseka	60970	STEPHENSON	Freeport	61032
JACKSON	Murphysboro	62966	TAZEWELL	Pekin	61554
JASPER	Newton	62448	UNION	Jonesboro	62952
JEFFERSON	Mt. Vernon	62864	VERMILION	Danville	61832
JERSEY	Jerseyville	62052	WABASH	Mt. Carmel	62863
JO DAVIESS	Galena	61036	WARREN	Monmouth	61462
JOHNSON	Vienna	62995	WASHINGTON	Nashville	62263
KANE	Geneva	60134	WAYNE	Fairfield	62837
KANKAKEE	Kankakee	60901	WHITE	Carmi	62821
KENDALL	Yorkville	60560	WHITESIDE	Morrison	61270
KNOX	Galesburg	61401	WILL	Joliet	60431
LAKE	Waukegan	60085	WILLIAMSON	Marion	62959
LA SALLE	Ottawa	61350	WINNEBAGO	Rockford	61101
LAWRENCE	Lawrenceville	62439	WOODFORD	Eureka	61530

8

CITY/COUNTY CROSS REFERENCE

CITY	COUNTY
ABINGDON	KNOX
ADAIR	MC DONOUGH
ADDISON	DU PAGE
ADELINE	OGLE
ADRIAN	HANCOCK
AKIN	FRANKLIN
ALBANY	WHITESIDE
ALBERS	CLINTON
ALBION	EDWARDS
ALDEN	MC HENRY
ALEDO	MERCER
ALEXANDER	MORGAN
ALEXIS	WARREN, MERCER
ALGONQUIN	MC HENRY, KANE
ALHAMBRA	MADISON
ALLENDALE	WABASH
ALLENVILLE	MOULTRIE
ALLERTON	VERMILION, CHAMPAIGN
ALORTON	ST. CLAIR
ALPHA	HENRY
ALSIP	COOK
ALTIERBERRY	MENARD
ALTON	MADISON
ALTONA	KNOX
ALTO PASS	UNION
ALVIN	VERMILION
AMBOY	LEE
ANCONA	LIVINGSTON
ANDALUSIA	ROCK ISLAND
ANNA	UNION
ANNAPOLIS	CRAWFORD
ANNAWAN	HENRY
ANTIOCH	LAKE
ARCOLA	DOUGLAS
ARENZVILLE	CASS
ARGENTA	MACON
ARGO	COOK
ARLINGTON	BUREAU
ARLINGTON HEIGHTS	COOK, LAKE
ARMINGTON	TAZEWELL
ARMSTRONG	VERMILION
AROMA PARK	KANKAKEE
ARROWSMITH	MC LEAN
ARTHUR	MOULTRIE, DOUGLAS
ASHKUM	IROQUOIS
ASHLAND	CASS
ASHLEY	WASHINGTON
ASHMORE	COLES
ASHTON	LEE
ASSUMPTION	CHRISTIAN
ASTORIA	FULTON
ATHENS	MENARD
ATHENSVILLE	GREENE
ATKINSON	HENRY
ATLANTA	LOGAN
ATTERBERRY	MENARD
ATWOOD	PIATT, DOUGLAS
AUBURN	SANGAMON
AUGUSTA	HANCOCK
AURORA	KANE, DU PAGE
AVA	JACKSON
AVISTON	CLINTON

CITY	COUNTY
AVON	FULTON
BAILEYVILLE	OGLE
BALDWIN	RANDOLPH
BANNOCKBURN	LAKE
BARDOLPH	MC DONOUGH
BARRINGTON	LAKE, COOK
BARRINGTON HILLS	COOK, LAKE, KANE MC HENRY
BARRY	PIKE
BARTLETT	COOK, DU PAGE
BARTONVILLE	PEORIA
BATAVIA	KANE, DU PAGE
BATH	MASON
BEARDSTOWN	CASS
BEASON	LOGAN
BEAUCOUP	WASHINGTON
BEAVERVILLE	IROQUOIS
BECKEMEYER	CLINTON
BEDFORD PARK	COOK
BEECHER	WILL
BEECHER CITY	EFFINGHAM
BELGIUM	VERMILION
BELKNAP	JOHNSON
BELLE RIVE	JEFFERSON
BELLEVILLE	ST. CLAIR
BELLFLOWER	MC LEAN
BELLMONT	WABASH
BELMONT	IROQUOIS
BELLWOOD	COOK
BELVIDERE	BOONE
BEMENT	PIATT
BENLD	MACOUPIN
BENSENVILLE	DU PAGE, COOK
BENSON	WOODFORD
BENTON	FRANKLIN
BERKELEY	COOK
BERLIN	SANGAMON
BERWICK	WARREN
BERWYN	COOK
BETHALTO	MADISON
BETHANY	MOULTRIE
BIBLE GROVE	CLAY
BIGGSVILLE	HENDERSON
BISMARK	VERMILION
BLANDINSVILLE	MC DONOUGH
BLOOMINGTON	MC LEAN
BLUE ISLAND	COOK
BLUE MOUND	MACON
BLUFF CITY	FAYETTE
BLUFFS	SCOTT
BOGOTA	JASPER
BOLINGBROOK	WILL, DU PAGE
BONE GAP	EDWARDS
BONNIE	JEFFERSON
BOURBON	DOUGLAS
BOURBONNAIS	KANKAKEE
BOWEN	HANCOCK
BOYLESS	PIKE
BRACEVILLE	GRUNDY
BRADFORD	STARK
BRADLEY	KANKAKEE
BRAIDWOOD	WILL

9

CITY	COUNTY
BREESE	CLINTON
BREMEN	RANDOLPH
BRIDGEPORT	LAWRENCE
BRIDGEVIEW	COOK
BRIGHTON	MACOUPIN, JERSEY
BRIMFIELD	PEORIA
BRISTOL	KENDALL
BROADFIELD	POPE
BROADLANDS	CHAMPAIGN
BROADVIEW	COOK
BROCTON	EDGAR
BROOKFIELD	COOK
BROOKPORT	MASSAC
BROWNFIELD	POPE
BROWNS	EDWARDS
BROWNSTOWN	FAYETTE
BRUSSELS	CALHOUN
BUCKLEY	IROQUOIS
BUDA	BUREAU
BUFFALO	SANGAMON
BUFFALO PRAIRIE	ROCK ISLAND
BUNCOMBE	JOHNSON
BUNKER HILL	MACOUPIN
BUREAU	BUREAU
BURNHAM	COOK
BURNSIDE	HANCOCK
BURR RIDGE	COOK, DU PAGE
BUSHNELL	MC DONOUGH
BUSHTON	COLES
BYRON	OGLE
CAHOKIA	ST. CLAIR
CAIRO	ALEXANDER
CALHOUN	CALHOUN, RICHLAND
CALUMET CITY	COOK
CAMBRIA	WILLIAMSON
CAMBRIDGE	HENRY, LAKE
CAMDEN	SCHUYLER
CAMERON	WARREN
CAMPBELL HILL	JACKSON
CAMP GROVE	MARSHALL
CAMP POINT	ADAMS
CAMPUS	LIVINGSTON
CANTON	FULTON
CAPRON	BOONE
CARBON CLIFF	ROCK ISLAND
CARBONDALE	JACKSON
CARBON HILL	GRUNDY
CARLINVILLE	MACOUPIN
CARLOCK	MC LEAN, WOODFORD
CARLYLE	CLINTON
CARMI	WHITE
CARPENTERSVILLE	KANE
CARRIERS MILL	SALINE
CARROLLTON	GREENE
CARTERVILLE	WILLIAMSON
CARTHAGE	HANCOCK
CARY	MC HENRY
CASEY	CLARK, CUMBERLAND
CASEYVILLE	ST. CLAIR
CATLIN	VERMILION
CEDAR POINT	LA SALLE
CEDARVILLE	STEPHENSON
CENTRAL CITY	MARION
CENTRALIA	CLINTON, MARION
CENTREVILLE	ST. CLAIR
CERRO GORDO	PIATT

CITY	COUNTY
CHADWICK	CARROLL
CHAMPAIGN	CHAMPAIGN
CHANA	OGLE
CHANDLERVILLE	CASS
CHANNAHON	WILL
CHANUTE AFB	CHAMPAIGN
CHAPIN	MORGAN
CHARLESTON	COLES
CHATHAM	SANGAMON
CHATSWORTH	LIVINGSTON
CHEBANSE	IROQUOIS
CHEMUNG	MC HENRY
CHENOA	MC LEAN
CHERRY VALLEY	WINNEBAGO
CHESTER	RANDOLPH
CHESTERFIELD	MACOUPIN
CHESTNUT	LOGAN
CHICAGO	COOK, DU PAGE
CHICAGO HEIGHTS	COOK
CHICAGO RIDGE	COOK
CHILLICOTHE	PEORIA
CHRISMAN	EDGAR
CHRISTOPHER	FRANKLIN
CICERO	COOK
CISCO	PIATT
CISNE	WAYNE
CISSNA PARK	IROQUOIS
CLAREMONT	RICHLAND
CLARENDON HILLS	DU PAGE
CLARK CENTER	CLARK
CLAY CITY	CLAY
CLAYTON	ADAMS
CLAYTONVILLE	IROQUOIS
CLIFTON	IROQUOIS
CLINTON	DE WITT
COAL CITY	GRUNDY
COALTON	MONTGOMERY
COAL VALLEY	ROCK ISLAND, HENRY
COBDEN	UNION
COFFEEN	MONTGOMERY
COLCHESTER	MC DONOUGH
COLFAX	MC LEAN
COLLINSVILLE	MADISON, ST. CLAIR
COLLISON	VERMILION
COLUMBIA	MONROE
COLUSA	HANCOCK
COMPTON	LEE
CONCORD	MORGAN
CONGERVILLE	WOODFORD
COOKS MILLS	COLES
COOKSVILLE	MC LEAN
CORDOVA	ROCK ISLAND
CORTLAND	DE KALB
COTTAGE HILLS	MADISON
COULTERVILLE	RANDOLPH
COUNTRY CLUB HILLS	COOK
COUNTRYSIDE	COOK, KANE, KENDALL, LAKE
COWDEN	SHELBY
CREAL SPRINGS	WILLIAMSON
CRESCENT CITY	IROQUOIS
CREST HILL	WILL
CRESTON	OGLE
CRESTWOOD	COOK
CRETE	WILL
CREVE COEUR	TAZEWELL

10

CITY	COUNTY	CITY	COUNTY
CROSSVILLE	WHITE	ELIZABETHTOWN	HARDIN
CRYSTAL LAKE	MC HENRY	ELK GROVE VILLAGE	COOK, DU PAGE
CUBA	FULTON	ELKHART	LOGAN
CULLOM	LIVINGSTON	ELKVILLE	JACKSON
CURRAN	SANGAMON	ELLISGROVE	RANDLOPH
CUSTER PARK	WILL	ELLISVILLE	FULTON
CUTLER	PERRY	ELLSWORTH	MC LEAN
CYPRESS	JOHNSON	ELMHURST	DU PAGE
DAHINDA	KNOX	ELMWOOD	PEORIA
DAKOTA	STEPHENSON	ELMWOOD PARK	COOK
DALLAS CITY	HANCOCK	EL PASO	WOODFORD
DALZELL	BUREAU	ELSAH	JERSEY
DANA	LA SALLE	ELWOOD	WILL, VERMILION
DANFORTH	IROQUOIS	EMDEN	LOGAN
DANVERS	MC LEAN	EMINGTON	LIVINGSTON
DANVILLE	VERMILION	EMMA	WHITE
DAYTON	LA SALLE	ENERGY	WILLIAMSON
DECATUR	MACON	ENFIELD	WHITE
DEER CREEK	TAZEWELL	EQUALITY	GALLATIN
DEERFIELD	LAKE, COOK	ERIE	WHITESIDE
DEER GROVE	WHITESIDE	ESMOND	DE KALB
DE KALB	DE KALB	EUREKA	WOODFORD
DE LAND	PIATT	EVANSTON	COOK
DELAVAN	TAZEWELL	EVANSVILLE	RANDOLPH
DENVER	HANCOCK	EVERGREEN PARK	COOK
DEPUE	BUREAU	FAIRBURY	LIVINGSTON
DE SOTO	JACKSON	FAIRDALE	DE KALB
DES PLAINES	COOK	FAIRFIELD	WAYNE
DEWEY PARK	MADISON	FAIR GRANGE	COLES
DIVERNON	SANGAMON	FAIRMONT CITY	ST. CLAIR, MADISON
DIX	JEFFERSON, FORD	FAIRMOUNT	PIKE, MADISON
DIXMOOR	COOK		MASSAC, VERMILION
DIXON	LEE	FAIRVIEW	FULTON
DOLTON	COOK	FAIRVIEW HEIGHTS	ST. CLAIR
DONNELLSON	ADAMS	FARINA	FAYETTE
DONGOLA	UNION	FARMER CITY	DE WITT
DONOVAN	IROQUOIS	FARMERSVILLE	MONTGOMERY
DOVER	BUREAU	FARMINGTON	FULTON
DOWNERS GROVE	DU PAGE	FENTON	WHITESIDE
DOWNS	MC LEAN	FIATT	FULTON
DUBOIS	WASHINGTON	FILLMORE	MONTGOMERY
DUNDEE	KANE	FINDLAY	SHELBY
DUNLAP	PEORIA	FISHER	CHAMPAIGN
DU QUOIN	PERRY	FITHIAN	VERMILION
DURAND	WINNEBAGO	FLANAGAN	LIVINGSTON
DWIGHT	LIVINGSTON, GRUNDY	FLORA	CLAY
EARLVILLE	LA SALLE	FLORENCE	PIKE
EAST ALTON	MADISON	FLOSSMOOR	COOK
EAST DUBUQUE	JO DAVIESS	FOOSLAND	CHAMPAIGN
EAST DUNDEE	KANE	FOREST CITY	MASON
EAST GALESBURG	KNOX	FOREST HOMES	MADISON
EAST MOLINE	ROCK ISLAND	FOREST PARK	COOK
EAST PEORIA	TAZEWELL	FOREST VIEW	COOK
EAST ST. LOUIS	ST. CLAIR	FORREST	LIVINGSTON
EATON	CRAWFORD	FORRESTON	OGLE
EDELSTEIN	PEORIA	FORSYTHE	MACON
EDGEWOOD	EFFINGHAM	FORT SHERIDAN	LAKE
EDINBURG	CHRISTIAN	FOUNTAIN GREEN	HANCOCK
EDWARDSVILLE	MADISON	FOWLER	ADAMS
EFFINGHAM	EFFINGHAM	FOX LAKE	LAKE, MC HENRY
EGAN	OGLE	FOX RIVER GROVE	MC HENRY
ELBURN	KANE	FRANKFORT	WILL
ELDORADO	SALINE	FRANKLIN	MORGAN
ELDRED	GREENE	FRANKLIN GROVE	LEE
ELGIN	KANE, COOK	FRANKLIN PARK	COOK
ELIZABETH	JO DAVIESS	FREEBURG	ST. CLAIR

11

CITY	COUNTY	CITY	COUNTY
FREEPORT	STEPHENSON	HANOVER	JO DAVIESS
FRIENDSVILLE	WABASH	HARDIN	CALHOUN
FULTON	WHITESIDE	HARDINVILLE	CRAWFORD
FULTS	MONROE	HARMON	LEE
GALATIA	SALINE	HARRISBURG	SALINE
GALE	ALEXANDER	HARTFORD	MADISON
GALENA	JO DAVIESS	HARTSBURG	LOGAN
GALESBURG	KNOX	HARVARD	MC HENRY
GALVA	HENRY	HARVEY	COOK
GARDEN PRAIRIE	BOONE	HARWOOD HEIGHTS	COOK
GARDNER	GRUNDY	HAVANA	MASON
GARRETT	DOUGLAS	HAZEL CREST	COOK
GENESEO	HENRY	HEBRON	MC HENRY
GENEVA	KANE	HEGELER	VERMILION
GENOA	DE KALB	HENDERSON	KNOX
GEORGETOWN	VERMILION	HENNEPIN	PUTNAM
GERMANTOWN	CLINTON	HENRY	MARSHALL
GERMAN VALLEY	STEPHENSON	HERRICK	SHELBY
GIBSON CITY	FORD	HERRIN	WILLIAMSON
GIFFORD	CHAMPAIGN	HERSCHER	KANKAKEE
GILBERTS	KANE	HEYWORTH	MC LEAN
GILLESPIE	MACOUPIN	HICKORY HILLS	COOK
GILMAN	IROQUOIS	HIGHLAND	MADISON
GILSON	KNOX	HIGHLAND PARK	LAKE
GIRARD	MACOUPIN	HIGHWOOD	LAKE
GLADSTONE	HENDERSON	HILLCREST	OGLE
GLASFORD	PEORIA	HILLSBORO	MONTGOMERY
GLEN CARBON	MADISON	HILLSDALE	ROCK ISLAND
GLENCOE	COOK	HILLSIDE	COOK
GLENDALE HEIGHTS	DU PAGE	HINCKLEY	DE KALB
GLEN ELLYN	DU PAGE	HINDSBORO	DOUGLAS
GLENVIEW	COOK	HINES	COOK
GLENWOOD	COOK	HINSDALE	DU PAGE, COOK
GODFREY	MADISON	HODGKINS	COOK
GOLCONDA	POPE	HOFFMAN	CLINTON
GOLDEN	ADAMS	HOMER	CHAMPAIGN
GOODFIELD	WOODFORD, TAZEWELL	HOMETOWN	COOK
GOOD HOPE	MC DONOUGH	HOMEWOOD	COOK
GOREVILLE	JOHNSON	HOOPESTON	VERMILION
GRAFTON	JERSEY	HOPEDALE	TAZEWELL
GRAND DETOUR	OGLE	HOYLETON	WASHINGTON
GRAND RAPIDS	LA SALLE	HUDSON	MC LEAN
GRAND TOWER	JACKSON	HULL	PIKE
GRANDVIEW	SANGAMON	HUNTLEY	MC HENRY
GRANITE CITY	MADISON	HURST	WILLIAMSON
GRANTFORK	MADISON	HUTSONVILLE	CRAWFORD
GRANT PARK	KANKAKEE	ILLINOIS CITY	MERCER
GRANVILLE	PUTNAM	ILLIOPOLIS	SANGAMON
GRAYSLAKE	LAKE	INA	JEFFERSON
GRAYVILLE	WHITE, EDWARDS	INDUSTRY	MC DONOUGH
GREAT LAKES	LAKE	INGALLS PARK	WILL
GREENFIELD	GREENE	INGLESIDE	LAKE
GREEN ROCK	HENRY	IPAVA	FULTON
GREENUP	CUMBERLAND	IROQUOIS	IROQUOIS
GREEN VALLEY	TAZEWELL	IRVING	MONTGOMERY
GREENVIEW	MENARD	ISLAND LAKE	LAKE, MC HENRY
GREENVILLE	BOND	ITASCA	DU PAGE, COOK
GRIDLEY	MC LEAN	JACKSONVILLE	MORGAN
GRIGGSVILLE	PIKE	JANESVILLE	CUMBERLAND
GULF PORT	HENDERSON	JEROME	SANGAMON
GURNEE	LAKE	JERSEYVILLE	JERSEY
HAMBURG	CALHOUN	JOHNSON CITY	WILLIAMSON
HAMILTON	HANCOCK	JOLIET	WILL
HAMPSHIRE	KANE	JONESBORO	UNION
HAMPTON	ROCK ISLAND	JOPPA	MASSAC
HANNA CITY	PEORIA	JOY	MERCER

12

CITY	COUNTY
JUSTICE	COOK
KANEVILLE	KANE
KANKAKEE	KANKAKEE
KANSAS	EDGAR
KARBERS RIDGE	HARDIN
KARNAK	PULASKI
KASKASKIA	RANDOLPH
KEITHSBURG	MERCER
KELL	MARION
KEMPTON	FORD
KENILWORTH	COOK
KEWANEE	HENRY
KINCAID	CHRISTIAN
KINDERHOOK	PIKE
KINGS	OGLE
KINMUNDY	MARION
KIRKLAND	DE KALB
KIRKWOOD	WARREN
KNOXVILLE	KNOX
LACON	MARSHALL
LADD	BUREAU
LA FAYETTE	STARK, RANDOLPH
LA GRANGE	COOK, BROWN
LA HARPE	HANCOCK
LAKE BLUFF	LAKE
LAKE CATHERINE	LAKE
LAKE FOREST	LAKE
LAKE VILLA	LAKE
LAKE ZURICH	LAKE
LA MOILLE	BUREAU
LANARK	CARROLL
LANSING	COOK
LA SALLE	LA SALLE
LAWNDALE	LOGAN
LAWRENCEVILLE	LAWRENCE
LEAF RIVER	OGLE
LEBANON	ST. CLAIR
LELAND	LA SALLE
LEMONT	COOK, DU PAGE
LENA	STEPHENSON
LE ROY	MC LEAN
LEWISTOWN	FULTON
LEXINGTON	MC LEAN
LIBERTY	ADAMS, SALINE, WHITE
LIBERTYVILLE	LAKE
LINCOLN	LOGAN, LAKE, WILL
LINCOLNSHIRE	LAKE, WILL
LINCOLNWOOD	COOK
LINDENHURST	LAKE
LISLE	DU PAGE
LITCHFIELD	MONTGOMERY
LITTLETON	MC DONOUGH
LIVERPOOL	FULTON
LIVINGSTON	MADISON, CLARK
LOCKPORT	WILL
LODA	IROQUOIS
LOMAX	HENDERSON
LOMBARD	DU PAGE
LONDON MILLS	FULTON, KNOX
LONG GROVE	LAKE
LOSTANT	LA SALLE
LOUISVILLE	CLAY
LOVEJOY	ST. CLAIR
LOVES PARK	WINNEBAGO
LOVINGTON	MOULTRIE

CITY	COUNTY
LYNDON	WHITESIDE
LYNWOOD	COOK
LYONS	COOK, VERMILION
MC CLURE	ALEXANDER
MC COOK	COOK
MC CULLOM LAKE	MC HENRY, LAKE
MC HENRY	MC HENRY
MC LEAN	MC LEAN
MC LEANSBORO	HAMILTON
MACKINAW	TAZEWELL
MACOMB	MC DONOUGH
MACON	MACON
MADISON	MADISON
MAHOMET	CHAMPAIGN
MAKANDA	JACKSON
MALTA	DE KALB
MANCHESTER	SCOTT
MANHATTAN	WILL
MANITO	MASON
MANSFIELD	PIATT
MANTENO	KANKAKEE
MAPLE PARK	KANE, DE KALB
MAQUON	KNOX
MARENGO	MC HENRY
MARINE	MADISON
MARION	WILLIAMSON
MARISSA	ST. CLAIR
MARKHAM	COOK, MORGAN
MAROA	MACON
MARQUETTE HEIGHTS	TAZEWELL
MARSEILLES	LA SALLE
MARSHALL	CLARK
MARTINSVILLE	CLARK
MARYVILLE	MADISON
MASCOUTAH	ST. CLAIR
MASON CITY	MASON
MATHERVILLE	MERCER
MATTESON	COOK
MATTOON	COLES
MAYWOOD	COOK
MAZON	GRUNDY
MEADOWBROOK	MADISON
MEDORA	MC DONOUGH, MACOUPIN
MELROSE PARK	COOK
MELVIN	FORD
MENDON	ADAMS
MENDOTA	LA SALLE
MEREDOSIA	MORGAN
MERRIONETTE PARK	COOK
METAMORA	WOODFORD
METROPOLIS	MASSAC
MIDDLETOWN	LOGAN
MIDLOTHIAN	COOK
MILAN	ROCK ISLAND
MILFORD	IROQUOIS
MILLEDGEVILLE	CARROLL
MILLSTADT	ST. CLAIR
MILTON	PIKE
MINERAL	BUREAU
MINIER	TAZEWELL
MINONK	WOODFORD
MINOOKA	GRUNDY, WILL
MODESTO	MACOUPIN
MOKENA	WILL
MOLINE	ROCK ISLAND

13

CITY	COUNTY	CITY	COUNTY
MOMENCE	KANKAKEE	NORTH RIVERSIDE	COOK
MONEE	WILL	NORTH UTICA	LA SALLE
MONMOUTH	WARREN	OAK BROOK	DU PAGE, COOK
MONTGOMERY	KANE	OAK FOREST	COOK
MONTICELLO	PIATT	OAKLAND	COLES
MOOSEHART	KANE	OAK LAWN	COOK
MORO	MADISON	OAK PARK	COOK
MORRIS	GRUNDY	OAKWOOD	VERMILION, PEORIA
MORRISON	WHITESIDE		DU PAGE
MORRISONVILLE	CHRISTIAN	OBLONG	CRAWFORD
MORRISTOWN	WINNEBAGO, HENRY	OCONEE	SHELBY
MORTON	TAZEWELL	ODELL	LIVINGSTON
MORTON GROVE	COOK	ODIN	MARION
MOUND CITY	PULASKI	O'FALLON	ST. CLAIR
MOUNDS	PULASKI	OGDEN	CHAMPAIGN
MT. CARMEL	WABASH	OGLESBY	LA SALLE
MT. CARROLL	CARROLL	OHIO	BUREAU
MT. HARRIS	OGLE	OKAWVILLE	WASHINGTON
MT. MORRIS	OGLE	OLIVE BRANCH	ALEXANDER
MT. OLIVE	MACOUPIN	OLNEY	RICHLAND
MT. PROSPECT	COOK	OLYMPIA FIELDS	COOK
MT. PULASKI	LOGAN	OMAHA	GALLATIN
MT. STERLING	BROWN	ONARGA	IROQUOIS
MT. VERNON	JEFFERSON	ONEIDA	KNOX
MT. ZION	MACON	OPDYKE	JEFFERSON
MOWEAQUA	SHELBY, CHRISTIAN	OQUAWKA	HENDERSON
MULLBERRY GROVE	BOND	ORANGEVILLE	STEPHENSON
MUNDELEIN	LAKE	OREANA	MACON
MURPHYSBORO	JACKSON	OREGON	OGLE
MURRAYVILLE	MORGAN	ORION	HENRY
NAPERVILLE	DU PAGE, WILL	ORLAND PARK	COOK
NAPLATE	LA SALLE	OSWEGO	KENDALL
NASHVILLE	WASHINGTON	OTTAWA	LA SALLE
NAUVOO	HANCOCK	OWANECO	CHRISTIAN
NEBO	PIKE	PALATINE	COOK
NEOGA	CUMBERLAND	PALESTINE	CRAWFORD
NEPONSET	BUREAU	PALMER	CHRISTIAN
NEWARK	KENDALL	PALMYRA	MACOUPIN
NEW ATHENS	ST. CLAIR	PALOS PARK	COOK
NEW BADEN	CLINTON, ST. CLAIR	PANA	CHRISTIAN
NEW BEDFORD	BUREAU	PARIS	EDGAR
NEW BERLIN	SANGAMON	PARKERSBURG	RICHLAND
NEW BOSTON	MERCER	PARK FOREST	COOK, WILL
NEW BURNSIDE	JOHNSON	PARK RIDGE	COOK
NEW DOUGLAS	MADISON	PATOKA	MARION
NEW HAVEN	GALLATIN	PAWNEE	SANGAMON
NEW LENOX	WILL	PAW PAW	LEE
NEWMAN	DOUGLAS	PAXTON	FORD
NEW SALEM	PIKE	PAYSON	ADAMS
NEWTON	JASPER	PEARL	PIKE
NEW WINDSOR	MERCER	PEARL CITY	STEPHENSON
NIANTIC	MACON	PECATONICA	WINNEBAGO
NILES	COOK	PEKIN	PEORIA, TAZEWELL
NOBLE	RICHLAND	PEORIA	PEORIA
NOKOMIS	MONTGOMERY	PEORIA HEIGHTS	PEORIA, TAZEWELL,
NORMAL	MC LEAN		WOODFORD
NORRIDGE	COOK	PEOTONE	WILL
NORRIS CITY	WHITE	PERCY	RANDOLPH
NORTH AURORA	KANE	PERRY	PIKE
NORTHBROOK	COOK	PESOTUM	CHAMPAIGN
NORTH CHICAGO	LAKE	PETERSBURG	MENARD
NORTHFIELD	COOK	PHILO	CHAMPAIGN
NORTHLAKE	COOK	PHOENIX	COOK
NORTH HENDERSON	MERCER	PINCKNEYVILLE	PERRY
NORTH PARK	WINNEBAGO	PIPER CITY	FORD
NORTH PEKIN	TAZEWELL	PITTSFIELD	PIKE

14

CITY	COUNTY	CITY	COUNTY
PLAINFIELD	WILL	ROYALTON	FRANKLIN
PLANO	KENDALL	RUSHVILLE	SCHUYLER
PLEASANT HILL	PIKE, MC LEAN, DU PAGE	RUTLAND	LA SALLE
		ST. ANNE	KANKAKEE
PLEASANT PLAINS	SANGAMON	ST. AUGUSTINE	FULTON
PLYMOUTH	HANCOCK	ST. CHARLES	KANE, DU PAGE
POCAHONTAS	BOND	ST. DAVID	FULTON
POLO	OGLE	ST. ELMO	FAYETTE
PONTIAC	LIVINGSTON	ST. FRANCISVILLE	LAWRENCE
POPLAR GROVE	BOONE, ROCK ISLAND	ST. JACOB	MADISON
PORT BYRON	ROCK ISLAND	ST. JOSEPH	CHAMPAIGN
POSEN	COOK, WASHINGTON	SALEM	MARION
POTOMAC	VERMILION	SANDOVAL	MARION
PRAIRIE CITY	MC DONOUGH	SANDWICH	DE KALB, KENDALL
PRAIRIE DU ROCHER	RANDOLPH	SAN JOSE	MASON, LOGAN
PRAIRIE VIEW	LAKE	SAUK VILLAGE	COOK
PREEMPTION	MERCER	SAVANNA	CARROLL
PRINCETON	BUREAU	SAVOY	CHAMPAIGN
PRINCEVILLE	PEORIA	SAYBROOK	MC LEAN
PROPHETSTOWN	WHITESIDE	SCHAUMBURG	COOK, DU PAGE
PROSPECT HEIGHTS	COOK	SCHILLER PARK	COOK
QUAD CITIES	ROCK ISLAND	SCIOTA	MC DONOUGH
QUINCY	ADAMS	SCOTTVILLE	MACOUPIN
RAMSEY	FAYETTE	SCRHAM CITY	MONTGOMERY
RANKIN	VERMILION	SENECA	LA SALLE, GRUNDY
RANTOUL	CHAMPAIGN	SESSER	FRANKLIN, JEFFERSON
RAPIDS CITY	ROCK ISLAND		
RARITON	HENDERSON	SEYMOUR	CHAMPAIGN
RAYMOND	MONTGOMERY	SHABBONA	DE KALB
RED BUD	RANDOLPH	SHANNON	CARROLL
REDDICK	KANKAKEE, LIVINGSTON	SHAWNEETOWN	GALLATIN
REYNOLDS	ROCK ISLAND, MERCER	SHEFFIELD	BUREAU
RICHMOND	MC HENRY	SHELBYVILLE	SHELBY
RICHTON PARK	COOK	SHELDON	IROQUOIS
RICHVIEW	WASHINGTON	SHERIDAN	LA SALLE
RIDGE FARM	VERMILION	SHERRARD	MERCER
RIDGWAY	GALLATIN	SHILOH	ST. CLAIR
RIVERDALE	COOK, WINNEBAGO	SHOREWOOD	WILL, KANKAKEE
RIVER FOREST	COOK	SIDELL	VERMILION
RIVER GROVE	COOK	SIDNEY	CHAMPAIGN
RIVERSIDE	COOK	SILVIS	ROCK ISLAND
RIVERTON	SANGAMON	SKOKIE	COOK
ROANOKE	WOODFORD	SMITHTON	ST. CLAIR
ROBBINS	COOK	SOMONAUK	DE KALB, LA SALLE
ROBINSON	CRAWFORD	SORENTO	BOND
ROCHELLE	OGLE	SOUTH BELOIT	WINNEBAGO
ROCHESTER	SANGAMON	SOUTH ELGIN	KANE
ROCK CITY	STEPHENSON	SOUTH HOLLAND	COOK
ROCKDALE	WILL	SOUTH JACKSONVILLE	MORGAN
ROCK FALLS	WHITESIDE	SOUTH PEKIN	TAZEWELL
ROCKFORD	WINNEBAGO	SOUTH WILMINGTON	GRUNDY
ROCK ISLAND	ROCK ISLAND	SPARLAND	MARSHALL
ROCKTON	WINNEBAGO	SPARTA	RANDOLPH
ROLLING MEADOWS	COOK, MC DONOUGH	SPRINGFIELD	SANGAMON
ROME	PEORIA	SPRING VALLEY	BUREAU
ROMEOVILLE	WILL	STANFORD	MC LEAN
ROODHOUSE	GREENE	STAUNTON	MACOUPIN
ROSCOE	WINNEBAGO	STEELEVILLE	RANDOLPH
ROSELLE	DU PAGE, COOK	STEGER	COOK, WILL
ROSEMONT	COOK, ST. CLAIR	STERLING	WHITESIDE
ROSEVILLE	WARREN	STEWARD	LEE
ROSEWOOD HEIGHTS	MADISON	STEWARDSON	SHELBY
ROSECLARE	HARDIN	STICKNEY	COOK
ROSSVILLE	VERMILION	STILLMAN VALLEY	OGLE
ROUND LAKE	LAKE	STOCKTON	JO DAVIESS
ROXANA	MADISON	STONE PARK	COOK

CITY	COUNTY	CITY	COUNTY
STONINGTON	CHRISTIAN	WARRENSBURG	MACON
STREAMWOOD	COOK	WARRENVILLE	DU PAGE
STREATOR	LA SALLE, LIVINGSTON	WARSAW	HANCOCK
STRONGHURST	HENDERSON	WASHBURN	WOODFORD, MARSHALL
SUGAR GROVE	KANE, MERCER	WASHINGTON	TAZEWELL
SULLIVAN	MOULTRIE	WASHINGTON PARK	ST. CLAIR
SUMMIT	COOK	WATAGA	KNOX
SUMNER	LAWRENCE	WATERLOO	MONROE
SWANSEA	ST. CLAIR	WATERMAN	DE KALB
SYCAMORE	DE KALB	WATSEKA	IROQUOIS
TABLE GROVE	MC DONOUGH	WAUCONDA	LAKE
TALLULA	MENARD	WAUKEGAN	LAKE
TAMAROA	PERRY	WAVERLY	MORGAN
TAMMS	ALEXANDER	WAYNE CITY	WAYNE
TAMPICO	WHITESIDE	WAYNESVILLE	DE WITT
TAYLOR RIDGE	ROCK ISLAND	WELDON	DE WITT
TAYLOR SPRINGS	MONTGOMERY	WENONA	MARSHALL
TAYLORVILLE	CHRISTIAN	WESTCHESTER	COOK
TENNESSEE	MC DONOUGH	WEST CHICAGO	DU PAGE
TEUTOPOLIS	EFFINGHAM	WEST CITY	FRANKLIN
THAYER	SANGAMON	WESTERN SPRINGS	COOK
THOMASBORO	CHAMPAIGN	WESTFIELD	CLARK, WILL
THOMSON	CARROLL	WEST FRANKFORT	FRANKLIN
THORNTON	COOK	WESTMONT	DU PAGE
TILDEN	RANDOLPH	WEST SALEM	EDWARDS
TILTON	VERMILION	WESTVILLE	VERMILION
TIMEWELL	BROWN	WHEATON	DU PAGE
TINLEY PARK	COOK, WILL	WHEELING	COOK, LAKE
TISKILWA	BUREAU	WHITE HALL	GREENE
TOLEDO	CUMBERLAND	WILLIAMSFIELD	KNOX
TOLONO	CHAMPAIGN	WILLIAMSVILLE	SANGAMON
TOLUCA	MARSHALL	WILLISVILLE	PERRY
TONICA	LA SALLE	WILLOW SPRINGS	COOK, DU PAGE
TOULON	STARK	WILMETTE	COOK
TOWANDA	MC LEAN	WILMINGTON	WILL
TOWER HILL	SHELBY	WILSONVILLE	MACOUPIN
TREMONT	TAZEWELL, MADISON	WINCHESTER	SCOTT
TRENTON	CLINTON	WINDSOR	SHELBY, MERCER
TROY	MADISON	WINFIELD	DU PAGE
TUSCOLA	DOUGLAS	WINNEBAGO	WINNEBAGO
ULLIN	PULASKI	WINNETKA	COOK
UNION	MC HENRY, LOGAN	WINSLOW	STEPHENSON
URBANA	CHAMPAIGN	WINTHROP HARBOR	LAKE
UTICA	LA SALLE	WITT	MONTGOMERY
VALIER	FRANKLIN	WOOD DALE	DU PAGE
VALMEYER	MONROE	WOODHULL	HENRY
VANDALIA	FAYETTE	WOODLAWN	JEFFERSON
VENICE	MADISON	WOODRIDGE	DU PAGE
VERMONT	FULTON	WOOD RIVER	MADISON
VERNON	MARION	WOODSTOCK	MC HENRY
VICTORIA	KNOX	WORDEN	MADISON
VIENNA	JOHNSON	WORTH	COOK
VILLA GROVE	DOUGLAS	WYANET	BUREAU
VILLA PARK	DU PAGE	WYOMING	STARK
VILLA RIDGE	PULASKI	YATES CITY	KNOX
VIOLA	MERCER	YORKVILLE	KENDALL
VIRDEN	MACOUPIN, SANGAMON	ZIEGLER	FRANKLIN
VIRGINIA	CASS	ZION	LAKE
WADSWORTH	LAKE		
WAGGONER	MONTGOMERY		
WALNUT	BUREAU		
WALTONVILLE	JEFFERSON		
WAMAC	MARION, CLINTON, WASHINGTON		
WAPELLA	DE WITT		
WARREN	JO DAVIESS		

16

ILLINOIS ADOPTION LAWS AND PRACTICES

Jurisdiction

In Illinois, the Circuit Court has jurisdiction over adoption proceedings. A minimum of 6 months is required between filing a petition to adopt and the final decree, except for the adoption of a related child or with agency consent. The adoption petition is to be filed within 30 days after placement except for a related child or an adult.

Records

The Court may order the file of any adoption proceeding to be impounded by the Clerk of the Court. The file can be opened for examination only on the specific order of the Court. Chapter 40, Domestic Relations, 1522, Section 18, states:

> "Upon motion of any party to an adoption proceeding the court shall, or upon the court's own motion the court may, order that the file relating to such proceeding shall be impounded by the clerk of the court and shall be opened for examination only upon specific order of the court, which order shall name the person or persons who are to be permitted to examine such file. Certified copies of all papers and documents contained in any file so impounded shall be made only on like order."

Adoptees' birth certificates have been amended since an unspecified year prior to 1935. Illinois is a closed state: Illinois Annotated Statutes, Chapter 111-1/2, Section 73-17(4)(Supp. 1972). This section was amended in August 1971 to permit the use of a false birthplace on amended birth certificates.

17

The sealing of birth records began in the late 1930s and early 1940s and was dependent on the method of adoption used--private or agency.

Agency Adoptions

The agencies, state or independent, performed the home study for the proposed adoption. For easy reference, State Adoptions Agencies are listed on Page 20 and Independent Agencies on Page 24.

Private Adoptions

Private adoptions are handled at the county level. Many of the Illinois counties shared these services with one or more other counties. It is the responsibility of this office to perform the home study and give a recommendation to the Court. This office will provide background information to adoptees and birthparents upon written request. It is always recommended to have a request of this nature notorized.

Cook County private adoptions are handled by the Department of Supportive Services, which was formulated in 1945. Their services may extend outside the county if one of the parties to the adoption resides in another county. Their address is:

Department of Supportive Services
118 N. Clark Street, Room 618
Chicago, IL   60602
(312) 443-4703

Nonidentifying Information

Most agencies, state and independent, will provide the adoptee, birthparent(s), and adoptive parents with "nonidentifying information" upon receipt of a notarized letter. This information may include:

National origin of parents
Ages of parents
States of birth of parents
Educational level achieved
Occupations
Medical history
Religion
Physical descriptions
Circumstances of relinquishment
Background of adopting family
Background of birthparent(s) family

Nonidentifying information for private adoptions is obtainable from the Department of Supportive Services in Cook County and from the Circuit Court in the remaining counties. Prior to 1945, this type of information is usually found with the doctor, lawyer, minister or pastor who arranged the adoption.

STATE ADOPTION AGENCIES

The Department of Children and Family Services in Illinois provides a full range of child welfare services including adoption services. The delivery of adoption services is supervised and coordinated in eight regional offices. There is no fee charged by the state adoption agencies in Illinois.

State Office:

> Department of Children and Family Services
> 1 North Old State Capital Plaza
> Springfield, Illinois 62706
> (217) 785-2519

Office of Adoptions:

> Associate Deputy Director
> 510 North Dearborn Street, Suite 400
> Chicago, Illinois 60601
> (312) 793-6894

Regional Offices of Illinois Department of Child and Family Services:

Aurora Region
1470 North Farnsworth, Room 300
Aurora, Illinois 60505
(312) 898-7800

Counties
Served:

Du Page	Kankakee	Mc Henry
Grundy	Kendall	Will
Kane	Lake	

Champaign Region
2125 South First Street
Champaign, Illinois 61820
(217) 333-1037

Counties
Served:

Champaign	Douglas	Macon
Clark	Edgar	Mc Lean
Coles	Ford	Moultrie
Cumberland	Iroquois	Piatt
De Witt	Livingston	Shelby
		Vermilion

Chicago Region
510 North Dearborn Street, Suite 400
Chicago, Illinois 60612
(312) 793-6800

Counties
Served: Cook

East St. Louis Region
10 Collinsville Avenue, Suite 102
East St. Louis, Illinois 62201
(618) 875-9300

Counties
Served:

Bond	Monroe	Washington
Clinton	Randolph	
Madison	St. Clair	

Marion Region
2209 West Main Street
Marion, Illinois 62959
(618) 997-4371

Counties
Served:

Alexander	Hardin	Pope
Clay	Jackson	Pulaski
Crawford	Jasper	Richland
Edwards	Jefferson	Saline
Effingham	Johnson	Union
Fayette	Lawrence	Wabash
Franklin	Marion	Wayne
Gallatin	Massac	White
Hamilton	Perry	Williamson

Peoria Region
5415 North University Avenue
Peoria, Illinois 61614
(309) 691-2200

Counties
Served:

Bureau	La Salle	Putnam
Fulton	Marshall	Rock Island
Henderson	Mc Donough	Stark
Henry	Mercer	Tazewell
Knox	Peoria	Warren
		Woodford

Rockford Region
4302 North Main Street
Post Office Box 915
Rockford, Illinois 61105

Counties
Served:

Boone	Jo Daviess	Stephenson
Carroll	Lee	Whiteside
De Kalb	Ogle	Winnebago

Springfield Region
4500 South 6th Street
Springfield, Illinois 62706
(217) 786-6830

Counties
Served:

Adams	Jersey	Pike
Brown	Logan	Sangamon
Calhoun	Macoupin	Schuyler
Cass	Mason	Scott
Christian	Menard	
Green	Montgomery	
Hancock	Morgan	

INDEPENDENT ADOPTION AGENCIES

	Other Counties Served
County	

Champaign

Children's Home & Aid of Illinois
East Central Office
307 W. University
Champaign, IL   61820
(217) 359-8815

Cook

Abbott Adoption Agency   Entire state
230 N. Michigan Ave.
Chicago, IL   60611
(312) 236-6240

Afro-American Family &   Chicago only
  Community Services
440 W. Division St.
Chicago, IL 60610
(312) 943-5900

Bensenville Home Society
331 S. York Rd.
Bensenville, IL   60106
(312) 766-5800

Casa Central
2222 N. Kedzie Ave.
Chicago, IL   60647
(312) 276-0500, Ext. 44

Catholic Charities of Chicago   Lake
126 N. Des Plaines St.
Chicago, IL   60606
(312) 236-5172

Chicago Child Care Society   Du Page
5467 S. University
Chicago, IL 60615
(312) 643-0452

Children's Home and   Du Page, Kane,
  Aid Society of Illinois   Mc Henry, Will
1122 N. Dearborn
Chicago, IL 60610
(312) 944-3313

Children's Home and Aid   Du Page, Kane,
  Society of Illinois   Mc Henry, Will
2106 W. 95th St.
Chicago, IL 60643
(312) 238-3203

The Cradle Society   Du Page, Kane,
2049 Ridge Ave.   Mc Henry, Will
Evanston, IL 60204
(312) 475-5800

Easter House   Entire state
111 N. Wabash
Chicago, IL 60601
(312) 372-1254

Family Care Services   Du Page, Kane,
234 S. Wabash   Mc Henry, Will
Chicago, IL 60604
(312) 427-8790

Jewish Children's Bureau   Entire state
1 S. Franklin
Chicago, IL 60606
(312) 346-6700

Lake Bluff/Chicago Homes
   for Children
1661 N. Northwest Hwy.
Park Ridge, IL 60068
(312) 298-1610
(312) 694-2727

Lutheran Child and Family   Metro Chicago,
   Services   Downstate
7620 Madison St.
River Forest, IL 60305
(312) 287-4848

Lutheran Social Services   Entire state
   of Illinois
Chicago Metropolitan Services
4840 W. Byron
Chicago, IL 60641
(312) 282-7800

St. Mary's Services   Du Page, Lake
5725 N. Kenmore Ave.
Chicago, IL 60626
(312) 561-5288

Travelers Aid Society of   Entire state
   Metro Chicago
127 S. La Salle St.
Suite 1500
Chicago, IL 60606
(312) 435-4500

Woodlawn Child Care Institute
1180 E. 63rd St.
Chicago, IL 60637
(312) 288-5840

Du Page

Catholic Charities   Kendall
26 N. Park
Lombard, IL 60148
(312) 495-9850

LDS Social Services of Illinois   Entire state,
1809 N. Mill St.   Minnesota
Naperville, IL 60540
(312) 369-8406

Sunny Ridge Family Center   Entire state
2 South 426 Orchard Rd.
Wheaton, IL 60187
(312) 668-5117

TAG, Inc.
1415 Hill St.
Wheaton, IL 60187
(312) 690-9430

Evangelical Child and   Metro Chicago
   Family Services
1530 N. Main St.
Wheaton, IL 60187
(312) 653-6400

Kankakee

Kankakee Catholic Charities   Ford, Iroquois
187 S. Schuyler
Kankakee, IL 60901
(815) 933-7791

Lake

Family Counseling Clinic, Inc.   Cook, Du Page,
Route 1, Box 228   Kane, Mc Henry
Grayslake, IL 60030
(312) 223-8107

Macon

Family Service of Decatur   Christian, De Witt,
151 E. Decatur St.   Logan, Moultrie,
Decatur, IL 62521   Piatt, Shelby
(217) 429-5216

Madison

Children's Home and Aid Society   Jersey, St. Clair
1002 College Ave.
Alton, IL 62002
(618) 462-2714

Mc Lean

The Baby Fold   54 area
Box 327   counties
108 E. Willow St.
Normal, IL 61761
(309) 452-1170

Peoria

Catholic Social Service   25 area
   of Peoria   counties
2900 W. Heading Ave.
P. O. Box 817
Peoria, IL 61652
(309) 671-5700

The Children's Home   Central
2130 N. Knoxville   Illinois
Peoria, IL 61603
(309) 685-1047

Counseling and Family Service   Tazewell,
1821 N. Knoxville Ave.   Woodford
Peoria, IL 61603
(309) 685-5287

Rock Island

Bethany Home   13 area
220 11th Ave.   counties
P. O. Box 638
Moline, IL 61265
(309) 797-7700

Interagency Adoption Committee   Henry, Mercer
c/o Bethany Home
220 11th Ave.
P. O. Box 638
Moline, IL 61265
(309) 797-7700

Sangamon

Catholic Charities   28 area
108 E. Cook St.   counties
Springfield, IL 62704
(217) 523-4551

Family Service Center of
  Sangamon County
1308 S. Seventh St.
Springfield, IL 62703
(217) 528-8406

Will

Catholic Charities of the   Grundy
  Diocese of Joliet
411 Scott St.
Joliet, IL   60432
(815) 723-3405

Winnebago

Catholic Charities of the   Boone, Carroll,
  Diocese of Rockford   De Kalb, Jo
Catholic Social Service   Daviess, Kane,
921 W. State St.   Lee, Mc Henry,
Rockford, IL   61102   Ogle, Whiteside,
(815) 965-0623   Stephenson

Children's Home and Aid Society   Boone, Carroll,
  of Illinois   De Kalb, Ogle,
730 N. Main   Stephenson
Rockford, IL   61103
(815) 962-1043

MATERNITY HOMES AND HOSPITALS AND ORPHANAGES

The following is a list of maternity homes and hospitals and orphanages, by county, open and closed. The information is a result of research compiled through 1977. Those closed prior to 1900 have been omitted. If closed, the approximate year closed and city location is noted. If the name has been changed, the current name and address are referenced.

Adams

Catholic Charities	510 Jersey St.	Quincy	62301
Chaddock Boys' School	205 South 24th St.	Quincy	62301
Detention Home	Quincy (1933)		
Family Service Agency	915 Vermont	Quincy	62301
IL Dept. of Children & Family Services	410 N. 9th St.	Quincy	62301
Quincy Humane Society	Quincy (1923)		
St. Aloysius' Orphanage	Quincy (1933)		
Woodland Home	2707 Maine St.	Quincy	62301

Alexander

Cairo Childrens Home	Cairo (1933)	

Bureau

Covenant Children's Home	502 Elm St.	Princeton	61356

Champaign

Catholic Social Service	500 Robeson Building	Champaign	61820
Champaign Co. Dept. of Public Aid	405 S. State St.	Champaign	61820
Champaign Co. Youth Home	1601 E. Main St.	Urbana	61801
Children's Home & Aid Society	113 N. Neil St.	Champaign	61820
Cunningham Children's Home	1301 N. Cunningham	Urbana	61801
IL Dept. of Children & Family Services	2125 S. 1st St.	Champaign	61820
Huling Memorial	106 N. Chanute St.	Rantoul	61866

Christian

Kemmerer Village	R. R. 1	Assumption	62510

Coles

Baby Fold	2202 South 4th	Charleston	61920

Afro-American Family Community Services	440 W. Division St.	Chicago	60610
Anchorage (see Crittenton Comprehensive Care Centers)			
Angel Guardian Orphanage	2001 W. Devon Ave.	Chicago	60659
Audy Home for Children	2245 W. Ogden Ave.	Chicago	60612
Augustana Nursery	400 W. Dickens Ave.	Chicago	60614
Bartelme Homes	542 S. Dearborn St.	Chicago	60605
Beulah Home	Chicago (1929)		
Bishop Quarter's School	Oak Park (1922)		
Bohemian Home	Chicago (1933)		
Booth Memorial Hospital	5040 N. Pulaski Rd.	Chicago	60630
Boys' Home of Evanston	3116 Hartzell St.	Evanston	60201
C.A.M. Adoption Service of IL	3932 W. Madison St.	Chicago	60624
Catholic Charities	126 N. Des Plaines	Chicago	60606
Catholic Home Bureau	645 W. Randolph St.	Chicago	60606
Catholic Home Finding Assn. of IL	Chicago (1926)		
Central Baptist Children's Home	Maywood (1933)		
Chandler House (see Cradle Society)	Evanston (1966)		
Chapin Hall for Children	2801 W. Foster Ave.	Chicago	60625
Chicago Child Care Society	5467 S. University	Chicago	60615
Chicago Comprehensive Care Center (see Crittenton Comprehensive Care Centers)			
Chicago Foundlings' Home	1725 W. Harrison St.	Chicago	60612
Chicago Home for the Friendless	Chicago (1948)		
Chicago Home for Girls	Chicago (1948)		
Chicago Home for Jewish Orphans	Chicago (1933)		
Chicago Industrial Home for Children	Woodstock (1933)	(see Des Plaines)	
Chicago Industrial School for Girls (see St. Mary's Training School)		Des Plaines	60016
Chicago Industrial Training School for Jewish Girls	Chicago (1933)		
Chicago Lying-In Hospital	5845 S. Maryland	Chicago	60637
Chicago Manual Training School for Jewish Boys	Chicago (1933)		
Chicago Maternity Hospital and Training School	Chicago (1929)		
Chicago Nursery & Half Orphan Asylum	2801 W. Foster Ave.	Chicago	60625
Chicago Orphan Asylum	Chicago (1947)		
Chicago Refuge for Girls	Chicago (1948)		
Chicago Women's Shelter	Chicago (1926)		
Chicago Youth Centers	611 W. Adams St.	Chicago	60606
Child & Family Services	234 S. Wabash Ave.	Chicago	60604
Child & Family Services	828 Davis St.	Evanston	60201
Child & Family Services	1011 Lake St.	Oak Park	60301
Children's Aid of La Rabida	17 N. Wabash Ave.	Chicago	60602
Children's Home & Aid Society (see IL Children's Home and Aid Society)			
Children's Home of the Croation Fraternal Union	Des Plaines (1933)		
Children's Receiving Home	Maywood (1933)		
Christian Action Ministry (see C.A.M. Adoption Service)			
Church Mission of Help	Chicago (1933)		
Churches United, Inc.	3900 S. Michigan	Chicago	60653
Community Family Service Center	1338 W. Flournoy St.	Chicago	60607
Cook Co. Dept. of Public Aid & Welfare	624 S. Michigan	Chicago	60605
Cook Co. Hospital	1825 W. Harrison St.	Chicago	60612
Cradle Society	2049 Ridge Ave.	Evanston	60204
Crittenton Comprehensive Care Centers	3639 S. Michigan	Chicago	60653
Cuneo Hospital	750 W. Montrose Ave.	Chicago	60613
Danish Evangelical Lutheran Church's Orphan Home	Chicago (1933)		
Daughters of Jacob	Chicago (1933)		
Daughters of Zion	Chicago (1933)		
Deborah Home for Jewish Boys	Chicago (1923)		
Douglas Park Day & Night Nursery	Chicago (1933)		

Name	Address	City	ZIP
Easter House Adoption Agency	11 North Wabash	Chicago	60602
Eleanor Association	16 N. Wabash	Chicago	60602
Evangelical Child & Family Agency	127 N. Dearborn St.	Chicago	60602
Evangelical Hospital of Chicago	5421 S. Morgan St.	Chicago	60621
Evangelical Lutheran Home Findings Soc. (see Lutheran Welfare Services)			
Evanston Children's Home	826 Ridge Ave.	Evanston	60202
Evanston Hospital	2650 Ridge Ave.	Evanston	60202
Evanston King's Daughters' Home	Evanston (1933)		
Family Living Center (see Crittenton)			
Federated Home for Dependent Colored Children	Chicago (1933)		
Foundlings' Home (see Chicago Foundlings' Home)			
Frances Juvenile Home Association	Chicago (1926)		
German Evangelical Deaconess Hospital (see Evangelical Hospital of Chicago)			
Glenwood School for Boys	187th and Halsted	Glenwood	60425
Hephzibah Children's Home	946 W. North Blvd.	Oak Park	60301
Homes for Children	77 W. Washington St.	Chicago	60602
Homes for Children	1661 N. N.W. Hwy.	Park Ridge	60068
Homes Now Program	10801 S. Halsted St.	Chicago	60628
Hospital of St. Anthony De Padula	2875 W. 19th St.	Chicago	60623
House of the Good Shepherd	1126 W. Grace St.	Chicago	60613
Hyde Park Jewish Community Center	5307 S. Hyde Pk Blvd.	Chicago	60615
IL Children's Home & Aid Society	(see Evanston Children's Home)		
IL Children's Home & Aid Society	1122 N. Dearborn St.	Chicago	60610
IL Masonic Children's Home	Post Office Box 429	La Grange	60525
IL Masonic Hospital	834 W. Wellington	Chicago	60657
IL Missionary Children's Home	2016 W. Evergreen	Chicago	60622
IL Protestant Children's Home	Chicago (1933)		
IL Tech. School for Colored Girls	Chicago (1944)		
Jewish Children's Bureau	120 W. Eastman	Arlington Hgts	60004
Jewish Children's Bureau	5050 Church St.	Skokie	60076
Jewish Children's Bureau of Chicago	1 S. Franklin St.	Chicago	60606
Jewish Home Finding Society	Chicago (1933)		
Jewish Orphan Society	Chicago (1919)		
Jewish Social Service Bureau of Chicago	Chicago (1923)		
Joint Services Bureau	Chicago (1933)		
Juvenile Detention Home	Chicago (1944)		
Juvenile Protection Association	12 E. Grand Ave.	Chicago	60611
Juvenile Service League	Chicago (1926)		
Kasper Industrial School (see Angel Guardian Orphanage)	Chicago (1964)		
Ketteler Manual Training School for Boys	Chicago (1964)		
Klingberg Children's Home	Chicago (1933)		
Lake Bluff/Chicago Home (see Homes for Children)			
Lawrence Hall	4833 N. Francisco	Chicago	60625
Lewis Memorial Maternity Hospital	Chicago (1958)		
Lutheran Deaconess Home & Hospital	Chicago (1958)		
Lutheran Child & Family Services	7620 Madison St.	River Forest	60305
Lutheran Home Finding Society (see Lutheran Welfare Services)			
Lutheran Welfare Services	59 E. Van Buren St.	Chicago	60605
Lydia Children's Home	4300 W. Irving Pk Rd.	Chicago	60641
Lying-In Hospital	(see Chicago Lying-In Hospital)		
Marks Nathan Jewish Orphan Home	Chicago (1933)		
Mary Thompson Hospital	140 N. Ashland	Chicago	60614
Maryville Academy	1150 N. River Rd.	Des Plaines	60016
Mercy Hospital	2510 King Drive	Chicago	60616
Methodist Youth Services	542 S. Dearborn St.	Chicago	60605
Misericordia Home	2916 W. 47th St.	Chicago	60632
Mission of Our Lady of Mercy	1142 W. Jackson Blvd.	Chicago	60607
Morgan Park Schools	Chicago (1933)		
Mount Carmel	Clyde (1923)		
Mount Sinai Hospital	2750 W. 15th Pl.	Chicago	60608
National Children's Home Society (see IL Children's Home and Aid Society)			
Neumayer Maternity Home	Brookfield (1926)		
Norwegian Lutheran Children's Home	Edison Park (1933)		
Norwegian Lutheran Children's Home	Chicago (1933)		

```
Our Lady of Mercy Mission (see Mission of Our Lady of Mercy)
Park Ridge School for Girls            733 N. Prospect       Park Ridge      60068
Passavant Memorial Hospital            303 E. Superior St.   Chicago         60611
Polish Manual Training School for Boys  Chicago (1944)
Protestant Child Haven Association     Chicago (1933)
Protestant Children's Aid              Chicago (1926)
Protestant Women's National Association Chicago (1926)
Reese Hospital, see Michael Reese      E. 29th/Ellis Ave.    Chicago         60616
Ruth Club                              Chicago (1933)
St. Ann's Department (see House of the Good Shepherd)
St. Anne's Hospital                    4950 W. Thomas St.    Chicago         60651
St. Anthony De Padula (see Hospital of St. Anthony De Padula)
St. Bernard's Home                     Chicago (1923)
St. Bernard's Hospital                 6337 S. Harvard Ave.  Chicago         60621
St. Elizabeth's Hospital               1435 N. Claremont     Chicago         60622
St. Hedwig's Industrial School         Chicago (1944)
St. Hedwig's Industrial School and
   Polish Manual Training School       Edison Park (1944)
St. Hedwig's Industrial School         7135 N. Harlem Ave.   Chicago         60631
St. Joseph's Home for the Friendless   739 E. 35th St.       Chicago         60616
St. Joseph's Orphan Home               Chicago (1923)
St. Joseph's Hospital                  2900 N. Lake Shore    Chicago         60657
St. Margaret's Home                    Chicago (1941)
St. Mary of Nazareth Hospital          2233 W. Division St.  Chicago         60622
St. Mary's Services                    5725 N. Kenmore Ave.  Chicago         60660
St. Mary's Training School (see Chicago
   Industrial School for Girls)        Des Plaines (1944)
St. Mary's Training School (see Chicago
   Industrial School for Girls)                              Feehanville     60656
St. Vincent's Infant Asylum            Chicago (1972) (See Catholic Charities)
Salvation Army Home (see Booth Memorial Hospital)
Service Council for Girls              Chicago (1933)
State Dept. of Children/Family Services 160 N. La Salle St.  Chicago         60601
State Society for Prevention of Cruelty Chicago (1923)
Stevenson Home (see Chicago Maternity Hospital) Chicago (1929)
Travelers Aid Society                  327 S. La Salle St.   Chicago         60604
Tzyrl Foundation (see Easter House)
Uhlich Children's Home                 3737 N. Mozart St.    Chicago         60618
United Evangelical Lutheran Orphan Asylum Chicago (1933)
United Hebrew Relief Association  (see Michael Reese Hospital)
Wesley Memorial Hospital               2449 S. Dearborn St.  Chicago         60614
West Suburban Hospital                 518 N. Austin Blvd.   Oak Park        60302
Women's & Children's Hospital          140 N. Ashland Ave.   Chicago         60607
Working Boys' Home (see Mission of Our Lady of Mercy)


De Kalb

Family Service Agency                  Post Office Box 831   De Kalb         60115


Du Page

Addison Industrial School for Girls    Addison (1933)
Addison Manual Training School for Boys Addison (1933)
Bensenville Home Society               331 S. York Rd.       Bensenville     60106
Catholic Charities                     420 Glenwood Ave.     Glen Ellyn      60137
Catholic Charities                     Wheaton (1964)
Du Page Co. Dept. of Public Aid        146 W. Roosevelt Rd.  Villa Park      60181
Evangelical Child & Family Agency      105 N. Maple St.      Elmhurst        60126
Evangelical Home for Children          Bensenville (1933)
Life Boat Rescue Home                  Hinsdale (1929)
Lisle Industrial School for Girls      Lisle (1944)
Lisle Manual Training School for Boys  Lisle (1944)
Lutheran Child and Family Services     343 W. Lake St.       Addison         60101
St. Mary's Home for Children           Elmhurst (1925)
Sunnyridge Home for Children           25426 Orchard Rd.     Wheaton         60187
West Suburban Home for Girls           Hinsdale (1937)
```

Edgar

Edgar Co. Children's Home	300 Eads Ave.	Paris	61944

Grundy

Dena J. Erickson Maternity Home	Morris (1926)
Eliza Britt Maternity Home	Morris (1926)

Hancock

Children's Memorial Home	Carthage (1933)

Henry

Lutheran Home for Children	Lynn Center (1933)
Lutheran Home and Farm School	Andover (1926)

Jackson

Huber's Boys' Home	R. R. 1	Carbondale	62901

Jefferson

United Methodist Children's Home	2023 Richview Road	Mount Vernon	62664

Kane

Catholic Charities	556 W. Galena Blvd.	Aurora	60506
Catholic Social Service	566 Dundee Ave.	Elgin	60120
Fox Hill Group Home	569 W. Galena Blvd.	Aurora	60506
Fox Hill Home, Inc.	333 S. Jefferson	Batavia	60510
IL Dept. of Children & Family Services	1470 N. Farnsworth	Aurora	60505
Juvenile Protective Association	301 W. Park Ave.	Aurora	60506
Kane Co. Dept. of Public Aid	361 Old Indian Trail	Aurora	60507
Larkin Home for Children	1212 Larkin Ave.	Elgin	60120
Mooseheart		Mooseheart	60539
St. Charles School for Boys			
IL State Training School for Boys		St. Charles	60174
Smith Home	301 W. Park Ave.	Aurora	60506
State Training School for Girls		Geneva	60134
Yeoman City of Childhood	Elgin (1933)		

Kankakee

Alfred Fortin Villa	Bourbonnais (1964)		
Catholic Charities	187 S. Schuyler Ave.	Kankakee	60901

Knox

Catholic Social Service	2401 N. Broad St.	Galesburg	61401
Galesburg and Knox Counties Free			
Kindergarten Home	W. Simmons/Cedar Sts.	Galesburg	61401
Harrington Home (Louise T.)	91 W. Simmons St.	Galesburg	61401
Knox Co. Detention Home	Galesburg (1926)		
Knox Co. Home and Maternity Hospital	Knoxville (1926)		
McKnight Industrial Home	Galesburg (1933)		

Lake

Allendale School for Boys	Post Office Box 277	Lake Villa	60046
Arden Shore Home for Boys	Post Office Box 278	Lake Bluff	60044
Catholic Charities	4 S. Genesee St.	Waukegan	60085
Central Baptist Children's Home	Post Office Box 218	Lake Villa	60046
Dorcas Home	Deerfield (1933)		

35

IL Children's Home & Aid Society	4 S. Genesee St.	Waukegan	60085
IL Dept. of Children & Family Services	4 S. Genesee St.	Waukegan	60085
IL Missionary Children's Home	420 N. Old Rand Rd.	Lake Zurich	60047
Jewish Children's Bureau	210 Skokie Valley Rd.	Highland Park	60035
Judson Industrial School	Lake Bluff (1933)		
Lake Co., Department of Public Aid	114 S. Genesee St.	Waukegan	60085
Lake Bluff Children's Home	200 Scranton Ave.	Lake Bluff	60044
Methodist Deaconess Orphanage	Lake Bluff (1933)		
Meyer Manual Training School	Lake Bluff (1933)		
Miss Wiseman's Home	Barrington (1926)		

La Salle

Catholic Social Service	535 3rd St.	La Salle	61301
IL Dept. of Children & Family Services	633 La Salle	Ottawa	61350
La Salle Co. Dept. of Public Aid	401 W. Washington St.	Ottawa	61350
La Salle Co. Youth Service Bureau, Inc.	1306 E. 77th St.	La Salle	61301

Lee

| Angear Hospital | Sublette (1937) | | |
| Lutheran Welfare Service of IL | | Nachusa | 61507 |

Livingston

| Hansen Maternity Hospital | Dwight (1926) | | |
| Salem Children's Home | | Flanagan | 61740 |

Logan

| Odd Fellows' Children's Home | 721 Wyatt Ave. | Lincoln | 62656 |

Macon

Catholic Charities	247 W. Prairie Ave.	Decatur	62523
Decatur and Macon Co. Opportunity Home for Boys	Decatur (1933)		
Decatur & Macon Co. Welfare Home for Girls	Decatur (1933)		
Family Service of Decatur	151 E. Decatur St.	Decatur	62521
IL Dept. of Children & Family Services	119 W. William St.	Decatur	62523
IL Pythian Home for Children	Decatur (1933)		
Macon Co. Department of Public Aid	3122 N. Water St.	Decatur	62526
Millikin Home	Decatur (1933)		
Pythian Home (see IL Pythian Home for Children)			
Webster-Cantrell Hall	1942 E. Cantrell St.	Decatur	62521

Macoupin

| The Home | Girard (1926) | | |

Madison

Assembly of God Children's Home of IL	Post Office Box 201	Maryville	62062
Catholic Charities	1120 E. 6th St.	Alton	62002
Catholic Children's Home	1400 State St.	Alton	62002
Catholic Charities of Quad Cities	2012 Delmar Ave.	Granite City	62040
IL Children's Home & Aid Society	1002 College Ave.	Alton	62002
Madison Co. Department of Public Aid	No. 16 Nameoki	Granite City	62040
Nazareth Home	Alton (1923)		
Wood River Maternity Hospital	Wood River (1926)		

Marion

| Hudelson Baptist Children's Home | 1400 E. 2nd St. | Centralia | 62801 |
| IL Dept. of Children & Family Services | 205 E. Locust St. | Salem | 62881 |

Mc Donough

Baby Fold	1212 W. Calhoun	Macomb	61455
Mc Donough Co. Orphanage	Macomb (1933)		
Mc Donough Co. Youth Services Bureau	110 East Davis	Bushnell	61422
Salvation Army	505 N. Randolph St.	Macomb	61455

Mc Henry

Chicago Industrial Home for Children	Woodstock (1933)		
Mc Henry Co., Dept. of Public Aid	1316 N. Madison St.	Woodstock	60098

Mc Lean

Baby Fold	108 E. Willow St.	Normal	61761
Catholic Social Service	106 W. Chestnut St.	Bloomington	61701
Girls Industrial Home	Bloomington (1926)		
IL Soldiers & Sailors' Children's School	600 E. Lincoln St.	Normal	61761
Mc Lean Co. Dept. of Public Aid	719 W. Chestnut St.	Bloomington	61701
Mc Lean Co. Home for Colored Children	Bloomington (1933)		
Morgan Home	403 S. State St.	Bloomington	61701
National Children's Home/Welfare Assn.	Bloomington (1936)		
Victory Hall	904 Hovey Ave.	Normal	61761
Washington Home	403 State St.	Bloomington	61701

Morgan

Catholic Charities of Jacksonville	306 E. State St.	Jacksonville	62650

Ogle

Old People's & Orphans' Home	Mount Morris (1923)
Peek Home	Polo (1933)

Peoria

Bridgeman Lying-In Home	Chillicothe (1926)		
Cabrini Hall Maternity Home	413 N.E. Monroe St.	Peoria	61603
Catholic Social Service	413 N.E. Monroe St.	Peoria	61603
Child & Family Service (see Counseling and Family Service)			
Child Welfare League of Peoria	Peoria (1933)		
Children's Home of Peoria	2130 Knoxville Ave.	Peoria	61603
Counseling & Family Service	1821 N. Knoxville	Peoria	61603
Crittenton Home	2619 W. Heading Ave.	Peoria	61604
Detention Home	Peoria (1933)		
Guardian Angel Home	2900 W. Heading Ave.	Peoria	61604
Home for the Friendless	Peoria (1933)		
Home of the Good Shepherd	Peoria (1941)		
IL Dept. of Children & Family Services	5415 N. University	Peoria	61614
IL Lutheran Welfare Association (see Lutheran Child Welfare)			
Lutheran Child Welfare Association	815 N. Western St.	Peoria	61604
Methodist Hospital	221 N.E. Glen Oak	Peoria	61603
Peoria Children's Home	(see Children's Home of Peoria)		
Peoria Co. Department of Public Aid	605 N.E. Jefferson	Peoria	61656
St. Francis Hospital	530 N.E. Glen Oak	Peoria	61603
Schlarman Children's Home	Peoria (1964)		
South Side Mission	311 Olive St.	Peoria	61650
Youth Farm, Inc.	7225 W. Plank Rd.	Peoria	61604

Perry

IL Children's Home & Aid Society	Du Quoin (1931)

Rock Island

Bethany Home	Rock Island (1933)		
Bethany Home	220 11th Ave.	Moline	61265
Catholic Social Service	816 20th St.	Rock Island	61201
IL Dept. of Children & Family Services	2810 41st St.	Moline	61265
Lutheran Welfare Services	1518 5th Ave.	Moline	61265
Prince Hall Masonic Home	Rock Island (1923)		
Rock Island Co. Dept. of Public Aid	2821 5th St.	Rock Island	61201
Rock Island Family Life Bureau (see Catholic Social Service)			

Saint Clair

Catholic Social Service	16 S. Illinois St.	Belleville	62220
Catholic Social Service	8315 State St.	East St. Louis	62203
IL Children's Home & Aid Society	East St. Louis (1963)		
IL Dept. of Children & Family Services	10 Collinsville Ave.	East St. Louis	62201
Lutheran Child and Family Services	2408 Lebanon Ave.	Belleville	62221
Pentecost Children's Home	East St. Louis (1933)		
St. Clair Co. Dept. of Public Aid	320 N. 9th St.	East St. Louis	62201
St. Clair Co. Detention Home	10501 W. Main St.	East St. Louis	62203
St. Clair Co. Humane Society	East St. Louis (1923)		
St. John's Children's Home	2620 Lebanon Ave.	Belleville	62221

Sangamon

Catholic Charities	108 E. Cook St.	Springfield	62704
Child Care Assn. of IL	2101 W. Lawrence Ave.	Springfield	62704
Child & Family Service	1411 E. Jefferson	Springfield	62703
Children's Service League	East Springfield (1948)		
Children's Service League	Springfield (1948)		
Detention Home	Springfield (1933)		
Family Service Center	1308 S. 7th St.	Springfield	62703
IL Dept. of Children & Family Services	1 N. Old State		
IL Soldiers/Sailors' Children's School	Springfield (1933)		
Lincoln Colored Home	Springfield (1926)		
Lutheran Child & Family Services	1229 S. 6th St.	Springfield	62703
Maternity Hospitals	Springfield (1933)		
Orphanage of the Holy Child	Springfield (1933)		
St. John's Hospital	800 E. Carpenter St.	Springfield	62702
St. Monica Hall	107 E. Lawrence Ave.	Springfield	62704
Sangamon Co. Dept. of Public Aid	1604 S. Grand Ave.	E. Springfield	62703
Service Bureau for Colored Children	Springfield (1959)		
Springfield Home for the Friendless	Springfield (1926)		
Springfield Redemption Home	Springfield (1933)		

Stephenson

Emma Eder Maternity Home	Freeport (1926)		
King's Daughters' Homes for Children	222 W. Exchange	Freeport	61032
St. Vincent's Home for Children	659 E. Jefferson	Freeport	61021

Tazewell

Tazewell Co. Dept. of Public Aid	2816 Court St.	Pekin	61554

Vermilion

Children's Home of Vermilion Co.	702 North Logan	Danville	61832
IL Children's Home & Aid Society	120 E. Williams St.	Danville	61832
IL Children's Home & Aid Society	Potomac (1923)		
Lee's Colored Children's Home	Danville (1923)		
Vermilion Co. Department of Public Aid	110 E. Williams St.	Danville	61832

38

Washington

Evangelical Orphans' Home	Hoyleton (1933)		
Hoyleton Children's Home	Post Office Box 218	Hoyleton	62803
Hudelson Baptist Orphanage	Irvington (1933)		

White

Baptist Children's Home	R. R. 4, Box 379	Carmi	62821

Whiteside

Catholic Social Service	212 E. 4th	Sterling	61081
Mount Carmel Orphanage	Morrison (1933)		

Will

Catholic Charities	310 Bridge St.	Joliet	60435
Catholic Charities	756 Luther Dr.	Romeoville	60441
Guardian Angel Home	Plainfield/Theodore	Joliet	60435
IL Dept. of Children & Family Services	58 N. Chicago St.	Joliet	60431
Lutheran Home for Children			
(see Swedish Lutheran Orphans' Home)	Joliet (1933)		
Swedish Lutheran Orphans' Home			
(see Lutheran Home for Children)	Joliet (1925).		
Will Co. Dept. of Public Aid	101 S. Larkin St.	Joliet	60436

Williamson

Catholic Social Service	1100-1/2 Tower Plaza	Marion	62959
IL Dept. of Children & Family Services	2209 W. Main St.	Marion	62959
So. IL Children's Service Center	Bush St.	Hurst	62949

Winnebago

Catholic Charities	921 W. State St.	Rockford	61102
Children's Home of Rockford	4450 N. Rockton Ave.	Rockford	61103
IL Children's Home & Aid Society	304 N. Main St.	Rockford	61101
IL Dept. of Children & Family Services	4302 N. Main St.	Rockford	61105
McFarlane Home for Children	Rockford (1933)		
Rosecrance Memorial Home	1505 N. Alpine Rd.	Rockford	61107
Rosecrance Rural Campus	Route 1	Durand	61024
Winnebago Co. Dept. of Public Aid	111 N. Avon St.	Rockford	61103
Winnebago Farm School	Durand (1933)		

39

FEDERAL RECORDS AND SOURCES

IMMIGRATION AND NATURALIZATION SERVICE (INS)

Immigration and naturalization records are public; however, they cannot be photocopied. Searchers should contact the Immigration and Naturalization Service at the following address:

> INS
> Dirksen Federal Office Building
> 219 South Dearborn Street
> Chicago, Illinois 60604
> (312) 353-7344

Reportedly these files are kept from public view for 75 years; however, proceedings are recorded in a U.S. District Court.

NATIONAL (FEDERAL) ARCHIVES

The Illinois Branch of the National Archives is located at:

> National Archives & Records Center
> 7358 South Pulaski Road
> Chicago, Illinois 60629
> (312) 353-0161
> Hours: 8:00 a.m. - 4:30 p.m. M-F

The National Archives have immigration records, passport information, military records, Indian tribal records, and land dealings. Other sources for the above information are also listed.

Census Records

Census records from 1790 through 1910 are open to public inspection. Census records are available

through interlibrary loan. Information contained
in the census may vary from decade to decade and
may include:

> Names of all household members
> Month and year of birth of all household
>   members
> Place of birth of household members
> Place of birth of parents of each household
>   member
> Number of years married
> Number of children born to the marriage
> When immigrated
> When naturalized
> Occupation of members in household.

Indian Affairs

Indian and tribal information is available by
contacting:

> Bureau of Indian Affairs
> Department of the Interior
> 175 West Jackson Boulevard
> Chicago, Illinois 60604
> (312) 353-4480

Passport Information

The Passport Agency houses many types of passport
information and is located at:

> Passport Agency
> State Department Offices
> 230 South Dearborn
> Chicago, Illinois 60606
> (312) 353-5426 and/or 353-7155

Military Records

The National Archives has limited military records. Additional military information is available by contacting:

> National Personnel Records Center
> National Archives and Records Service
> 9700 Page Boulevard
> St. Louis, Missouri 63132
> (314) 263-3901

SELECTIVE SERVICE

Selective Service is a government agency which provides people for the Armed Forces in the event of a national emergency. Registration is done at the city level.

The selective service number contains a series of four numbers. Example: 11 28 34 10. Breakdown:

- 11 - State in which individual is registered
  (Note: 11 is Illinois)
- 28 - Local board number within the state
- 34 - Last two digits of year of birth of the registered individual
- 10 - Sequence number of individuals with same year of birth within local board.

The following is a list of the states and their corresponding number:

1. Alabama	20. Michigan	39. South Dakota
2. Arizona	21. Minnesota	40. Tennessee
3. Arkansas	22. Mississippi	41. Texas
4. California	23. Missouri	42. Utah
5. Colorado	24. Montana	43. Vermont
6. Connecticut	25. Nebraska	44. Virginia
7. Delaware	26. Nevada	45. Washington
8. Florida	27. New Hampshire	46. West Virginia
9. Georgia	28. New Jersey	47. Wisconsin
10. Idaho	29. New Mexico	48. Wyoming
11. Illinois	30. New York	49. District of Columbia
12. Indiana	31. North Carolina	50. New York City
13. Iowa	32. North Dakota	51. Alaska
14. Kansas	33. Ohio	52. Hawaii
15. Kentucky	34. Oklahoma	53. Puerto Rico
16. Louisiana	35. Oregon	54. Virgin Islands
17. Maine	36. Pennsylvania	55. Guam
18. Maryland	37. Rhode Island	56. Canal Zone
19. Massachusetts	38. South Carolina	

SOCIAL SECURITY

The Social Security Administration will not provide
names and addresses to anyone. A letter, if deter-
mined to be important and nonthreatening, will be
forwarded. Specific procedures and details are
available from the following office:

> Social Security Administration
> 320 West Washington Street
> Springfield, Illinois 62701
> (217) 492-4413

All Illinois-issued numbers begin with the numbers
318 through 361. The second two-digit number
indicates the area in which it was issued.

001-003	New Hampshire	440-448	Oklahoma
004-007	Maine	449-467	Texas
008-009	Vermont	468-477	Minnesota
010-034	Massachusetts	478-485	Iowa
035-039	Rhode Island	486-500	Missouri
040-049	Connecticut	501-502	North Dakota
050-134	New York	503-504	South Dakota
135-158	New Jersey	505-508	Nebraska
159-211	Pennsylvania	509-515	Kansas
212-220	Maryland	516-517	Montana
221-222	Delaware	518-519	Idaho
223-231	Virginia	520	Wyoming
232-236	West Virginia	521-524	Colorado
232, 237-246	North Carolina	525, 585	New Mexico
247-251	South Carolina	526-527	Arizona
252-260	Georgia	528-529	Utah
261-267	Florida	530	Nevada
268-302	Ohio	531-539	Ohio
303-317	Indiana	540-544	Oregon
318-361	Illinois	545-573	California
362-386	Michigan	574	Alaska
387-399	Wisconsin	575-576	Hawaii
400-407	Kentucky	577-579	District of Columbia
408-415	Tennessee	580	Virgin Islands
416-424	Alabama	580-585	Puerto Rico
425-428, 587	Mississippi	586	Guam, American Samoa,
429-432	Arkansas		Philippines
433-439	Louisiana	700-729	Railroad Employees*

*Number assigned to persons applying for a Social Security number between 1936 and 1963 while employed by the railroads. After 1963, the number was assigned according to the above chart.

Contact a local social security office for additional information.

Social Security Regional Offices

501 Belle St.	Alton	62002
120 W. Eastman St.	Arlington Hgts.	60004
122 W. Downer Pl.	Aurora	60507
218 W. Main St.	Belleville	62222
200 W. Front St.	Bloomington	61701
235 16th St.	Cairo	62914

250 W. Cherry	Carbondale	62901
1703 W. Springfield Ave.	Champaign	61820
4858 S. Ashland Ave.	Chicago	60609
8929 S. Harlem Ave.	Chicago	60455
6349 S. Cottage Grove Ave.	Chicago	60637
4370 W. 26th St.	Chicago	60623
175 W. Jackson St.	Chicago	60604
2100 N. California Ave.	Chicago	60647
500 S. Racine Ave.	Chicago	60607
2444 W. Lawrence Ave.	Chicago	60625
4415 N. Milwaukee Ave.	Chicago	60630
9730 S. Western Ave.	Chicago	60642
9020 S. Stony Island Ave.	Chicago	60619
5401 W. Chicago Ave.	Chicago	60651
1514 W. Division St.	Chicago	60622
102 N. Robinson	Danville	61832
355 N. Water	Decatur	62521
701 Lee St.	Des Plaines	60016
1121 Warren Ave.	Downers Grove	60515
112 W. Washington	Effingham	62401
1845 W. Grandstand Pl.	Elgin	60120
7220 W. Grand Ave.	Elmwood Park	60635
820 Church St.	Evanston	60204
50 W. Douglas St.	Freeport	61021
125 E. Main St.	Galesburg	61401
1920 Waukegan Rd.	Glenview	60025
325 E. Poplar	Harrisburg	62946
101 N. Joliet St.	Joliet	60434
300 N. Indiana Ave.	Kankakee	60901
1416 W. 55th St.	La Grange	60525
612 N. State St.	Litchfield	62056
3049 W. 159th St.	Markham	60426
105 S. 6th St.	Mount Vernon	62864
7222 W. Cermak Rd.	N. Riverside	60546
215 Court St.	Pekin	61554
2628 N. Knoxville	Peoria	61655
1530 Fourth St.	Peru	61354
2401 Lind St.	Quincy	62301
5115 18th St.	Rock Island	61201

612 N. Church St.	Rockford	61105
320 W. Washington St.	Springfield	62701
2315 E. 4th St.	Sterling	61081
146 W. Roosevelt Rd.	Villa Park	60181
1 N. Genesee	Waukegan	60085
1810 E. Main St.	W. Frankfort	62896
1090 Mc Connell Rd.	Woodstock	60098

VETERANS ADMINISTRATION

The Veterans' Administration's Freedom of Information Act (Section 1.502) states:

> "The monthly rate of pension, compensation, dependency and indemnity compensation, retirement pay, subsistence allowance, or educational allowance to any beneficiary shall be made known to any person who applies for such information."

All inquiries for veterans data should be directed to:

Veterans Administration Regional Office
536 South Clark Street
P. O. Box 8136
Chicago, IL   60680
(312) 663-5510

Veterans information may also be obtained by contacting:

Illinois Veterans Home
1707 N. 12th Street
Quincy, IL   62301
(217) 222-8641

The Approving Agencies for Veterans' Education are at the following two locations:

1229 S. Michigan Ave.　　　208 W. Cook St.
Chicago, IL　60605　　　　P. O. Box 5054
(312) 793-5530　　　　　　Springfield, IL　62705
　　　　　　　　　　　　　(217) 782-7837

The Veterans Administration Offices are listed here for easy reference.

County	Street	City	Zip Code
Adams	1707 N. 12th St.	Quincy	62301
Alexander	902 Poplar St.	Cairo	62914
Bond	Courthouse	Greenville	62246
Boone	Sheriff's Office	Belvidere	61008
Brown	Courthouse	Mt. Sterling	62353
Bureau	111 Park Ave. E.	Princeton	61356
Calhoun	Circuit Clerk	Hardin	62047
Carroll	Courthouse	Mt. Carroll	61053
	40 Jefferson St.	Savanna	61074
Cass	Golden Age Center	Beardstown	62618
	County Clerk	Virginia	62691
Champaign	4 Hensen Pl.	Champaign	61820
Christian	Sr. Citizens Hall	Pana	62557
	117 E. Market St.	Taylorville	62568

County	Address	City	ZIP
Clark	309 E. Main St. Courthouse	Casey Marshall	62420 62441
Clay	Am. Legion Home County Courthouse	Flora Louisville	62839 62881
Clinton	620 9th St.	Carlyle	62231
Coles	Courthouse 1000 Broadway	Charleston Mattoon	61920 61938
Cook #1	1229 S. Michigan 547 W. Roosevelt	Chicago Chicago	60605 60607
#2	950 E. 61st St. 4005 W. North Ave.	Chicago Chicago	60637 60639
#3	4328 N. Elston Ave. VFW Post 981 811 N. Yale	Chicago Arlington Heights	60641 60004
#4	3650 E. 112th St. 17355 68th Ct.	Chicago Tinley Park	60617 60477
#5	1601 Chicago Rd. 333 E. 162nd	Chgo Hgts. S. Holland	60411 60473
#6	3453 W. 111th St. Oak Forest Hosp. 155 S. Oak Park	Chicago Oak Forest Oak Park	60655 60452 60302
#7	6610 W. Cermak Rd. Hines VA Hospital Tuberculosis Sant.	Berwyn Hines Hindsdale	60402 60141 60521
Crawford	Courthouse	Robinson	62454
Cumberland	Town Hall Courthouse	Greenup Toledo	62428 62468
De Kalb	136 S. 2nd St.	De Kalb	60115
De Witt	119 S. Main	Clinton	61727

County	Location	City	ZIP
Douglas	Courthouse	Tuscola	61953
Du Page	VFW, RR #2, RT. 59	W. Chicago	60185
Edgar	149 E. Court St	Paris	61944
Edwards	Courthouse	Albion	62806
Effingham	Plaza Building	Effingham	62401
Fayette	129 N. Kennedy St.	Vandalia	62471
Ford	Sheriff's Office	Paxton	60957
Franklin	106 W. Church 604 W. Main	Benton W. Frankfort	62821 62896
Fulton	1200 S. 5th Ave.	Canton	61520
Gallatin	Am. Legion Home	Ridgeway	62979
Greene	Circuit Clerk Am. Legion Home	Carrollton White Hall	62016 62092
Grundy	201 Liberty	Morris	60450
Hamilton	Circuit Clerk	Mc Leansboro	62859
Hancock	County Courthouse	Carthage	62321
Hardin	Sheriff's Office	Eliz.town	62931
Henderson	Courthouse Fire Station	Oquawka Stronghurst	61469 61480
Henry	Courthouse Chamber of Commerce 306 W. 2nd St.	Cambridge Geneseo Kewanee	61238 61254 61443

County	Location	City	Zip
Iroquois	Value Village Mall	Watseka	60970
Jackson	300 S. Marion	Carbondale	62901
	1401 Walnut St.	Murphysboro	62966
Jasper	Sheriff's Office	Newton	62448
Jefferson	Courthouse	Mt. Vernon	62864
Jersey	Courthouse	Jerseyville	62052
Jo Daviess	310 N. Main St.	Galena	61036
	Village Hall	Hanover	61041
Johnson	Southside Ct. House	Vienna	62995
Kane	Watch City VFW	Elgin	60120
	322 W. State St.	Geneva	60134
Kankakee	187 S. Indiana Ave.	Kankakee	60901
Kendall	New Courthouse	Yorkville	60560
Knox	975 N. Henderson St.	Galesburg	61401
Lake	215 W. Water St.	Waukegan	60085
La Salle	745 2nd St.	La Salle	61301
	609 Columbus St.	Ottawa	61350
	Am. Legion Home	Streator	61364
Lawrence	606 13th St.	Lawrencevle	62439
Lee	Courthouse	Dixon	61021
Livingston	Courthouse	Pontiac	61764
	IL State Prison	Pontiac	61764
Logan	Courthouse	Lincoln	62656

Macon	132 S. Water St.	Decatur	62523
Macoupin	124 E. Main St.	Carlinville	62626
Madison	215 Piasa 1417 19th St.	Alton Granite City	62002 62040
Marion	200 E. Schwartz City Hall	Salem Centralia	62881 62801
Marshall	Courthouse	Lacon	61540
Mason	415 W. Adams	Havana	62644
Massac	City Hall	Metropolis	62960
Mc Donough	220 S. Randolph	Macomb	61455
Mc Henry	2200 Seminary	Woodstock	60098
Mc Lean	104 W. Washington	Bloomington	61701
Menard	No Service		
Mercer	Courthouse	Aledo	61231
Monroe	509 W. Mill St.	Waterloo	62298
Montgomery	ISEA Office	Litchfield	62056
Morgan	836 W. Morton	Jacksonville	62650
Moultrie	Courthouse	Sullivan	61951
Ogle	Courthouse	Oregon	61061
Peoria	228 N.E. Jefferson 605 N.E. Monroe St.	Peoria Peoria	61603 61615

Perry	25 N. Mulberry Ave.	DuQuoin	62832
	Courthouse	Pinckneyvle	62274
Piatt	County Building	Monticello	61856
Pike	Circuit Clerk	Pittsfield	62363
Pope	Courthouse	Golconda	62938
Pulaski	No Service		
Putnam	No Service		
Randolph	Courthouse	Chester	62233
	Menard Center	Menard	62259
Richland	120 S. Fair St.	Olney	62450
Rock Island	1504 3rd Ave.	Rock Island	61201
St. Clair	4807 W. Main St.	Belleville	62223
	10 Collinsville Ave.	E. St. Louis	62201
Saline	16 W. Poplar St.	Harrisburg	62946
Sangamon	208 W. Cook St.	Springfield	62705
Schuyler	Am. Legion Home	Rushville	62681
Scott	No Service		
Shelby	Courthouse	Shelbyville	62565
Stark	Courthouse	Toulon	61483
Stephenson	4 E. Stephenson	Freeport	61032
	Village Hall	Hanover	61041
Tazewell	11 N. 6th St.	Pekin	61554

Union	125 W. Davie	Anna	62906
Vermilion	110 E. Williams	Danville	61832
	200 E. Penn St.	Hoopeston	60942
Wabash	E. Third St.	Mt. Carmel	62863
Warren	203 S. "A" St.	Monmouth	61462
Washington	Courthouse	Nashville	62263
Wayne	Courthouse	Fairfield	62837
White	314 E. Robinson St.	Carmi	62821
Whiteside	Am. Legion Home	Fulton	61252
	611 1st Ave.	Rock Falls	61071
Will	4 E. Clinton	Joliet	60431
Williamson	2209 W. Main St.	Marion	62959
Winnebago	107 N. 3rd St.	Rockford	61110
Woodford	Courthouse	Eureka	61530

VA Cemeteries

Alton National
600 Pearl St.
Alton, IL 62003

Mound City National
P. O. Box 128
Mound City, IL 62963

Camp Butler
RFD No. 1
Springfield, IL 62707

Quincy National
36th & Maine St.
Quincy, IL 62301

Danville National
1900 E. Main St.
Danville, IL 61832

Rock Island National
Rock Island Arsenal
Rock Island, IL 61299

BUREAU OF VITAL STATISTICS

> Division of Vital Records
> State Department of Public Health
> 535 West Jefferson Street
> Springfield, Illinois 62701
> (217) 782-6553

> Birth & Deaths - January 1, 1916
> Marriages   - January 1, 1962
> Divorces   - January 1, 1962

Earlier records may be found on a county level at the County Clerk or Recorder's office.

Access - Section 73-24 ACCESS TO VITAL RECORDS

(1)   To protect the integrity of vital records, to insure their proper use, and to insure the efficient and proper administration of the vital records systems, access to vital records, and indexes thereof, including vital records in the custody of local registrars and county clerks originating prior to January 1, 1916, is limited to the custodian and his employees, and then only for administrative purposes, except that the indexes of those records in the custody of local registrars and county clerks, originating prior to January 1, 1916, shall be made available to members of Illinois genealogical societies. It is unlawful for any custodian to permit inspection of, or to disclose information contained in, vital records, or to copy or permit to be copied, all or part of any such record except as authorized by this Act or regulations adopted pursuant thereto.

(2) The State Registrar of Vital Records, or his
     agent, and any municipal, county, multicounty,
     public health district, or regional health
     officer recognized by the Department may
     examine vital records for the purpose only of
     carrying out the public health programs and
     responsibilities under his jurisdiction.

(3) The State Registrar of Vital Records may dis-
     close, or authorize the disclosure of data
     contained in the vital records when deemed
     essential for bona fide research purposes
     which are not for private gain. The amenda-
     tory Act of 1973 does not apply to any home
     rule unit.

Fees - In accordance with House Bill 1958, the
following fees for vital records service were
effective January 1, 1984:

Filing Delayed Record........................	$10
New Record by Adoption.......................	$10
New Record by Legitimation...................	$10
New Record by Paternity......................	$10
Amend Existing Record........................	$10

These fees include one certified copy of the new or
amended record. A $2 fee is required for each
additional copy.

Search for Birth, Death, or Fetal Death..... $10

If found, one certification issued at no additional
charge. If not found, one certification that no
record was found issued without additional charge.

Certified Copy of Birth, Death, or Fetal Death
..................................Additional $5
(Total of $10 fee for a certified copy)

A $2 fee is required for each additional certifica-
tion or certified copy of the same record.

Search for Death Record for Genealogical Research -
5-Year Search................................. $5
Each Additional Year Searched................ $1

The above fees include one UNCERTIFIED copy of the
record, if found.

Search and Verification of Marriage, Dissolution of
Marriage or Declaration of Invalidity of Marriage
.... $5

ILLINOIS STATE ARCHIVES

        Illinois State Archives
        State Archives Building
        Springfield, Illinois 62706
        (217) 782-2226

Regional Archives

  Booth Library   Morris Library
  Eastern Illinois Univ.   Southern Illinois Univ.
  Charleston, IL 61920   Carbondale, IL 62901
  (217) 581-6093   (618) 453-3040

  Brookens Library   Swen Parson Library
  Sangamon State Univ.   Northern Illinois Univ.
  Springfield, IL 62708   De Kalb, IL 60115
  (217) 786-6520   (815) 753-1779

  Milner Library   University Library
  Illinois State Univ.   Western Illinois Univ.
  Normal, IL 61761   Macomb, IL 61455
  (309) 438-5525   (309) 298-2411, Ext. 272

ILLINOIS STATE LIBRARY

Illinois State Library
Centennial Memorial Building
State Capitol Complex
Springfield, Illinois 62706
(217) 782-2994

Illinois State Historical Library
Old State Capitol Building
Springfield, Illinois 62706
(217) 782-4837

DEPARTMENT OF MOTOR VEHICLES

All inquiries pertaining to drivers' license
records and motor vehicle registrations should be
directed to:

Secretary of State
Motor Vehicles
State Capitol Building
Springfield, IL 62756
(217) 782-7766

The fee for this service is $2.00. This record
usually gives full name, address, if license is
current, any other names used (maiden, marriages),
and a brief driving record.

PROFESSIONAL ASSOCIATIONS

American Association of University Women
2037 15th Street
Moline, IL 61265   (309) 752-1684

American Bar Association
1155 E. 60th
Chicago, IL 60637   (312) 947-4000

American Board of Psychiatry & Neurology
    1 American Plaza
    Evanston, IL 60201   (312) 864-0830

American Dental Association
    55 E. Washington
    Chicago, IL 60602   (312) 726-4076

American Dental Hygienists Association
    444 N. Michigan Avenue
    Chicago, IL 60611   (312) 440-8900

American Hospital Association
    840 N. Lake Shore Drive
    Chicago, IL 60611   (312) 280-6000

American Legion/Department of Illinois
    13304 S. Baltimore Avenue
    Chicago, IL 60633   (312) 646-3272

American Medical Association
    515 N. Dearborn
    Chicago, IL 60610   (312) 670-2550

American Osteopathic Association
    212 E. Ohio
    Chicago, IL 60611   (312) 280-5800

Amvets State Headquarters
    2206 S. 6th Street
    Springfield, IL 62703   (217) 528-4713

Association of Teacher Educators
    Northern Illinois University
    Oak Lane Road
    De Kalb, IL 60115   (815) 895-5062

Associated Colleges of Illinois
    175 W. Jackson Boulevard
    Chicago, IL 60604   (312) 427-4129

Business and Professional Women's Club
    610 E. Vine Street
    Springfield, IL   62703   (217) 528-8985

Catholic War Veterans/Department of Illinois
    343 S. Dearborn
    Chicago, IL   60604   (312) 939-5480

Chicago Bar Association
    29 S. La Salle
    Chicago, IL   60603   (312) 332-1111

Civil Service Employees Association of Illinois
    108 N. State
    Chicago, IL   60602   (312) 782-5436

Cook County Physicians Association
    514 E. 50th Place
    Chicago, IL   60615   (312) 373-7145

Daughters of Union Veterans of the Civil War
    503 S. Walnut
    Springfield, IL   62702   (217) 544-0616

Federation of Independent Illinois Colleges and
Universities
    990 Grove Street
    Evanston, IL   60201   (312) 864-1000

Illinois Administrators of Special Education
    2110 Talcott Road
    Park Ridge, IL   60068   (312) 825-5234

Illinois Association for School, College, and
Universities Staffing
    Northern Illinois University
    De Kalb, IL   60115   (815) 753-1641

Illinois Association for Senior Citizens
    2466 E. Washington
    East Peoria, IL   61611   (309) 694-1606

Illinois Association of County Clerks and Recorders
    Winnebago County Courthouse
    Rockford, IL 61101   (815) 987-3055

Illinois Association of Ophthalmology
    55 E. Monroe
    Chicago, IL 60603   (312) 263-7150

Illinois Association of Osteopathic Physicians and
Surgeons
    900 E. Center Street
    Ottawa, IL 61350   (815) 434-5576

Illinois Association of School Administrators
    1201 S. 5th Street
    Springfield, IL 62703   (217) 522-4479

Illinois Association of School Boards
    1209 S. 5th Street
    Springfield, IL 62703   (217) 528-9688

Illinois Association of School Nurses
    903 Quince Lane
    Mt. Prospect, IL 60056   (312) 824-1945

Illinois Catholic Hospital Association
    300 E. Monroe Street
    Springfield, IL 62701   (217) 544-5888

Illinois Chiropractic Society
    200 E. Roosevelt
    Lombard, IL 60148   (312) 629-0988

Illinois Dental Hygienists Association
    728 E. Berkshire
    Lombard, IL 60148   (312) 629-0360

Illinois Education Association
    100 E. Edwards
    Springfield, IL 62704   (217) 544-0706

Illinois Elementary School Association
2703 McGraw
Bloomington, IL 61701   (309) 662-5741

Illinois Federation of Teachers
611 Enterprise
Oak Brook, IL 60521   (312) 986-0112

Illinois Funeral Directors Association
1045 Outer Park Drive
Springfield, IL 62704   (217) 787-8980

Illinois Hairdressers and Cosmetologists Association
911 W. Garfield
Bartonville, IL 61607   (309) 697-8599

Illinois High School Association
2715 McGraw Drive
Bloomington, IL 61701   (309) 663-6377

Illinois Hospital Association
1200 Jorie Boulevard
Oak Brook 60521   (312) 325-9040

Illinois Library Association
425 N. Michigan Avenue
Chicago, IL 60611   (312) 644-1896

Illinois Nurses Association
1 W. Old State Capitol Plaza
Springfield, IL 62701   (217) 523-0783

Illinois Nursing Home Administrators Association
200 5th Street
Lincoln, IL 62656   (217) 735-1507

Illinois Obstetrical and Gynecology Association
SIU School of Medicine
Springfield, IL 62708   (217) 782-8246

Illinois Public Health Association
1500 S. 7th Street
Springfield, IL 62706   (217) 522-5687

Illinois Retired Teachers Association
421 E. Capitol
Springfield, IL 62702   (217) 787-3357

Illinois State Bar Association
Illinois Bar Center
Springfield, IL 62701   (217) 525-1760

Illinois State Bar Association
332 N. Michigan
Chicago, IL 60601   (312) 726-8775

Illinois State Chamber of Commerce
215 E. Adams
Springfield, IL 62701   (217) 522-5512

Illinois State Dental Society
524 S. 5th
Springfield, IL 62705   (217) 525-1406

Illinois State Genealogical Society
P. O. Box 157
Lincoln, IL 62656   (217) 732-3988

Illinois State Historical Society
Old State Capitol
Springfield, IL 62701   (217) 782-4837

Illinois State Medical Society
701 S. 2nd Street
Springfield, IL 62704   (217) 528-5609

Illinois State Medical Society
55 E. Monroe
Chicago, IL 60603   (312) 782-1654

Illinois Telephone Association
300 E. Monroe Street
Springfield, IL 62706   (217) 525-1044

Illinois Terminal Railroad Historical Society
Illinois Central College
East Peoria, IL 61635   (309) 694-5309

Illinois Visually Handicapped Institute
1151 S. Wood
Chicago, IL 60612   (312) 996-1000

Independent Voters of Illinois
5 S. Wabash Avenue
Chicago, IL 60603   (312) 263-4274

League of Women Voters of Illinois
67 E. Madison
Chicago, IL 60603   (312) 236-0315

Licensed Practical Nurses Association of Illinois
3015 S. 6th Street
Springfield, IL 62702   (217) 522-8026

Student Nurses Association of Illinois
6 N. Michigan Avenue
Chicago, IL 60602   (312) 346-4369

Veterans of Foreign Wars Headquarters
2601 E. Stevenson Drive
Springfield, IL 62703   (217) 529-6688

Women's Bar Association of Illinois
20 N. Clark
Chicago, IL 60602   (312) 236-3866

COUNTY SOURCES

Assessor

Assessor's records are open to the public. Usually only a small copying fee is charged. The records may be found in log books, map books, on microfiche and microfilm, in sales ledgers, and in the master index. Ownership of property, both commerical and residential, by name(s), date of purchase, date of sale, cost and tax information on the said property are all available. Most counties have a complete history of each piece of property.

If a researcher is working with an address only, the Assessor's office will provide the name of the current owner and all previous owners. Since properties in the ledger books are listed by address, the researcher will have access to neighboring properties and the names of their owners. A visit to the long-time residents of the neighborhood can prove to be very beneficial as they may remember people who lived in the area years before.

County Clerk

In most Illinois counties, the County Clerk and the County Recorder are combined. In Cook County, the County Clerk and the County Recorder are independent of each other. The County Clerk houses birth, death, marriage, and other vital records.

Birth - Birth records are available for births within the specific county. Indexes and records are not open for public inspection. Requests can be in person or by mail and should include full name, date of birth, place of birth, and mother's maiden name. County Clerks will search a 3-year period if a birth date is unknown. Always include any alternate spellings of the last name on your request.

Marriages - Marriage certificates and sometimes marriage license applications are available at the county level.

Marriage license applications may contain the following information: full names, names of parents, ages and/or birthdates, addresses, occupations, birthplaces, maiden names of mothers, social security numbers, previous marriages, places of employment, highest grade in school, person performing marriage, and signatures of couple. As in all research, a request for a document should always be made in the event that it may be available.

Confidential Marriages - There is no provision in Illinois law for confidential marriages.

Death and Fetal Death Records - Death records may include any or all of the following: full name, date of death, place of death, cause of death, attending physician, names of parents including mother's maiden name, birthplace of parents, number of years in city, home address, length of time at that residence, social security number, military service if applicable, name of spouse, date of birth, place of birth, informant, funeral director, date of burial, name of cemetery, address of cemetery, and occupation. If death occurred in a hospital, the name and address of the hospital may also be listed.

County Recorder

The County Recorder records real estate deeds, wills, incorporations, and limited partnerships. All real estate records are on microfiche and stored in the Recorder's Office. They have no master index, so an address is required. Wills are stored in the Recorder's office only if will was recorded prior to death of the individual. They could also be stored in Probate Division of Circuit Court.

Courts

The State of Illinois is divided into Judicial Circuits, with the exception of Cook County which constitutes one Judicial Circuit. The Circuit Court shall have unlimited original jurisdiction of all cases, civil and criminal in law and in equity (Constitution Article VI, Section 9). The Circuit and the counties it serves are listed below.

Circuit	Counties Served
First	Alexander, Jackson, Johnson, Massac, Pope, Pulaski, Saline, Union, and Williamson
Second	Crawford, Edwards, Franklin, Gallatin, Hamilton, Hardin, Jefferson, Lawrence, Richland, Wabash, Wayne, and White
Third	Bond and Madison
Fourth	Christian, Clay, Clinton, Effingham, Fayette, Jasper, Marion, Montgomery, Shelby

Fifth	Clark, Coles, Cumberland, Edgar, and Vermilion
Sixth	Champaign, De Witt, Douglas, Macon, Moultrie, and Piatt
Seventh	Greene, Jersey, Macoupin, Morgan, Sangamon, and Scott
Eighth	Adams, Brown, Calhoun, Cass, Mason, Menard, Pike, and Schuyler
Ninth	Fulton, Hancock, Henderson, Knox, Mc Donough, and Warren
Tenth	Marshall, Peoria, Putnam, Stark, and Tazewell
Eleventh	Ford, Livingston, Logan, Mc Lean, and Woodford
Twelfth	Iroquois, Kankakee, and Will
Thirteenth	Bureau, Grundy, and La Salle
Fourteenth	Henry, Mercer, Rock Island, and Whiteside
Fifteenth	Carroll, Jo Daviess, Lee, Ogle, and Stephenson
Sixteenth	De Kalb, Kane, and Kendall
Seventeenth	Boone and Winnebago
Eighteenth	Du Page

Nineteenth	Lake and Mc Henry
Twentieth	Monroe, Perry, Randolph, St. Clair, and Washington

Probate Court

Decedent estates, decedent wills, minors' estates, and incompetency estates are on file with the Probate Court and are open for public inspection.

Divorce Records

Divorce records are also filed with Probate Court and are open to public inspection.

Voter's Registration

Voter's Registration information is most always obtained at the county level and may include: full name, address, occupation, birthdate (year may be deleted), birthplace, party affiliation, social security number, telephone number, and a physical description.

The City of Chicago's records, however, are separate from Cook County and are housed with the Board of Elections. The original Voters Registration application record is not available for public inspection. However, a name and address card is available by contacting:

> Board of Election Commissioners
> 121 North La Salle
> Chicago, IL 60602
> (312) 269-7900

CITY AND LOCAL SOURCES

Cemeteries and Funeral Homes

Cemetery and funeral home records are one of the
most vital keys to the completion of a search. The
records will give full and complete names, dates,
list survivors and their addresses, name the
informant, and usually have a copy of the obituary
as it appeared in the newspaper. Many times there
are family plots, and records for each member
buried there will also be available to the
researcher.

Cemeteries are listed by county on Pages 129
through 148.

Chambers of Commerce

Most cities or communities have Chambers of Commerce. It is their function to maintain records on
businesses and prominent members of the community.
Many Chambers hold their own collection of local
city directories, criss cross directories, as well
as being familiar with activities of the area.

Chambers of Commerce are listed by county on
Pages 149 through 154.

Church Records

Ceremonies are recorded in the church records for
most all denominations. Baptisms and christenings,
marriages, deaths and, in some churches, confirma-
tion records are kept. Many churches will not permit the researcher to look through the records, but
are quite willing to do it for you. Mail requests
most always seem to be handled promptly. There is

usually no fee for this service; however, a small donation is always appreciated.

City Halls

Many large cities have city halls which oftentimes contain records of birth, marriage, and death. This source is particularly useful when attempts to obtain records at the state or county level have been unsuccessful.

Colleges and Universities

Information pertaining to a person who attained a higher education may be obtained by contacting the Registrar of Past Student Records. This information could include name of student, dates of attendance, birthdate or age at entrance to the school, degrees earned, social security number, last school attended, address upon entrance, next of kin, and student's membership in any fraternal organizations.

Colleges and universities are listed by county on Pages 155 through 159.

Hospitals

Retention of hospital records varies dramatically from hospital to hospital. The American Hospital Association and the American Medical Record Association has a recommended retention period for hospital records; however, Illinois health care institutions retain records according to their own needs. This retention could be from 10 to 22 years for medical records. Some are retained in their original form, others are on microfilm.

Permanent retention is recommended for patient registers, delivery room registers, emergency room registers (log), birth and death registers.

Most hospitals retain their medical records permanently.

The Code of Civil Procedure, Part 20, states:

§8-2001. Examination of records. Every private and public hospital shall, upon the request of any patient who has been treated in such hospital and after his or her discharge therefrom, permit the patient, his or her physician or authorized attorney to examine the hospital records, including but not limited to the history, bedside notes, charts, pictures and plates, kept in connection with the treatment of such patient, and permit copies of such records to be made by him or her or his or her physician or authorized attorney. A request for examination of the records shall be in writing and shall be delivered to the administrator of such hospital.
P.A. 82-280, § 8-2001, effective July 1, 1982.

When searching for birth and delivery records, remember that records are independent for mother and child. For the child, there may be a birth ledger or an obstetrician logbook. If the birth index card is located, there usually is a number on it that will correspond to the mother's records.

Hospitals are listed by county on Pages 160 through 168.

Libraries

Libraries are the most valuable source of information. City directories, telephone directories, criss cross directories, genealogical materials, newspapers, etc., are available at the library or through interlibrary loan.

In addition to the county libraries, state libraries, and archive libraries, the Church of Jesus Christ of Latter Day Saints is a willing helper in family searches. Requests should be directed to:

LDS Church Historical Library
50 East North Temple
Salt Lake City, Utah   84150

Libraries are listed by county on Pages 169 through 183.

Newspapers

Obituary notices have proven to be a valuable source of information. They could include date and place of birth, occupation and place of employment, names of parents and other members of the immediate family, many times including current city and state of residence, name of funeral home and cemetery, and their church and local organization affiliations. The society page lists engagements, weddings, and 25th and 50th wedding anniversaries. Many local newspapers list birth announcements.

Newspapers are listed by county on Pages 184 through 198.

SECTION II

COUNTY INFORMATION

ADAMS
Pop. 71,622

County Seat	Quincy	62301
Assessor	521 Vermont St. Quincy	62301
County Clerk & Recorder	521 Vermont St. Quincy	62301
Courts Circuit	521 Vermont St. Quincy	62301
Voters Registration	County Clerk 521 Vermont St. Quincy	62301

ALEXANDER
Pop. 12,264

County Seat	Cairo	62914
Assessor	2000 Washington Ave. Cairo	62914
County Clerk & Recorder	2000 Washington Ave. Cairo	62914
Courts Circuit	2000 Washington Ave. Cairo	62914
Voters Registration	County Clerk 2000 Washington Ave. Cairo	62914

BOND Pop. 16,224

County Seat	Greenville	62246
Assessor	200 W. College Greenville	62246
County Clerk & Recorder	200 W. College Greenville	62246
Courts Circuit	200 W. College Greenville	62246
Voters Registration	County Clerk 200 W. College Greenville	62246

BOONE Pop. 28,630

County Seat	Belvidere	61008
Assessor	613 N. Main Belvidere	61008
County Clerk & Recorder	521 N. Main Belvidere	61008
Courts Circuit	521 N. Main Belvidere	61008
Voters Registration	County Clerk 521 N. Main Belvidere	61008

BROWN

Pop. 5,411

County Seat	Mt. Sterling	62353
Assessor	County Courthouse Mt. Sterling	62353
County Clerk & Recorder	County Courthouse Mt. Sterling	62353
Courts Circuit	County Courthouse Mt. Sterling	62353
Voters Registration	County Clerk County Courthouse Mt. Sterling	62353

BUREAU

Pop. 39,114

County Seat	Princeton	61356
Assessor	County Courthouse Princeton	61356
County Clerk & Recorder	County Courthouse Princeton	61356
Courts Circuit	County Courthouse Princeton	61356
Voters Registration	County Clerk County Courthouse Princeton	61356

CALHOUN

Pop. 5,867

County Seat	Hardin	62047
Assessor	County Courthouse Hardin	62047
County Clerk & Recorder	County Courthouse Hardin	62047
Courts Circuit	County Courthouse Hardin	62047
Voters Registration	County Clerk County Courthouse Hardin	62047

CARROLL

Pop. 18,779

County Seat	Mount Carroll	61053
Assessor	County Courthouse Mount Carroll	61053
County Clerk & Recorder	County Courthouse Mount Carroll	61053
Courts Circuit	County Courthouse Mount Carroll	61053
Voters Registration	County Clerk County Courthouse Mount Carroll	61053

CASS   Pop. 15,084

<u>County Seat</u>	Virginia	62691
<u>Assessor</u>	County Courthouse Virginia	62691
<u>County Clerk & Recorder</u>	County Courthouse Virginia	62691
<u>Courts</u> <u>Circuit</u>	County Courthouse Virginia	62691
<u>Voters Registration</u>	County Clerk County Courthouse Virginia	62691

CHAMPAIGN   Pop. 168,392

<u>County Seat</u>	Urbana	61801
<u>Assessor</u>	201 E. Main Urbana	61801
<u>County Clerk & Recorder</u>	201 E. Main Urbana	61801
<u>Courts</u> <u>Circuit</u>	County Courthouse 204 E. Elm Urbana	61801
<u>Voters Registration</u>	County Clerk 201 E. Main Urbana	61801

CHRISTIAN <u>Pop.</u> 36,446

<u>County Seat</u>	Taylorville	62568
<u>Assessor</u>	County Courthouse Taylorville	62568
<u>County Clerk & Recorder</u>	County Courthouse Taylorville	62568
<u>Courts</u> <u>Circuit</u>	County Courthouse Taylorville	62568
<u>Voters Registration</u>	County Clerk County Courthouse Taylorville	62568

CLARK <u>Pop.</u> 16,913

<u>County Seat</u>	Marshall	62441
<u>Assessor</u>	County Courthouse Marshall	62441
<u>County Clerk & Recorder</u>	County Courthouse Marshall	62441
<u>Courts</u> <u>Circuit</u>	County Courthouse Marshall	62441
<u>Voters Registration</u>	County Clerk County Courthouse Marshall	62441

CLAY
Pop. 15,283

County Seat	Louisville	62858
Assessor	County Courthouse Louisville	62858
County Clerk & Recorder	County Courthouse Louisville	62858
Courts Circuit	County Courthouse Louisville	62858
Voters Registration	County Clerk County Courthouse Louisville	62858

CLINTON
Pop. 32,617

County Seat	Carlyle	62231
Assessor	County Courthouse Carlyle	62231
County Clerk & Recorder	County Courthouse Carlyle	62231
Courts Circuit	County Courthouse Carlyle	62231
Voters Registration	County Clerk County Courthouse Carlyle	62231

COLES   Pop. 52,260

County Seat	Charleston	61920
Assessor	County Courthouse Charleston	61920
County Clerk & Recorder	County Courthouse Charleston	61920
Courts Circuit	County Courthouse Charleston	61920
Voters Registration	County Clerk County Courthouse Charleston	61920

COOK   Pop. 5,253,655

County Seat	Chicago	60607
Assessor	118 N. Clark Chicago	60602
County Clerk	118 N. Clark Chicago	60602
Courts	Richard J. Daley Center Chicago	60602
Recorder & Registrar of Titles	118 N. Clark Chicago	60602
Vital Statistics	130 N. Wells Chicago	60606
Voters Registration	100 N. La Salle Chicago	60602

CRAWFORD

Pop. 20,818

<u>County Seat</u>	Robinson	62454
<u>Assessor</u>	County Courthouse Robinson	62454
<u>County Clerk & Recorder</u>	County Courthouse Robinson	62454
<u>Courts</u> <u>Circuit</u>	County Courthouse Robinson	62454
<u>Voters Registration</u>	County Clerk County Courthouse Robinson	62454

CUMBERLAND

Pop. 11,062

<u>County Seat</u>	Toledo	62468
<u>Assessor</u>	County Courthouse Toledo	62468
<u>County Clerk & Recorder</u>	County Courthouse Toledo	62468
<u>Courts</u> <u>Circuit</u>	County Courthouse Toledo	62468
<u>Voters Registration</u>	County Clerk County Courthouse Toledo	62468

De KALB   Pop. 74,624

   <u>County Seat</u>   Sycamore   60178

   <u>Assessor</u>   County Courthouse
                      Sycamore   60178

   <u>County Clerk &</u> County Courthouse
   <u>Recorder</u>   Sycamore   60178

   <u>Courts</u>
     <u>Circuit</u>   County Courthouse
                      Sycamore   60178

   <u>Voters</u>
   <u>Registration</u>   County Clerk
                      County Courthouse
                      Sycamore   60178

De WITT   Pop. 18,108

   <u>County Seat</u>   Clinton   61727

   <u>Assessor</u>   County Courthouse
                      Clinton   61727

   <u>County Clerk &</u> County Courthouse
   <u>Recorder</u>   Clinton   61727

   <u>Courts</u>
     <u>Circuit</u>   County Courthouse
                      Clinton   61727

   <u>Voters</u>
   <u>Registration</u>   County Clerk
                      County Courthouse
                      Clinton   61727

DOUGLAS   Pop. 19,774

   <u>County Seat</u>   Tuscola   61953

   <u>Assessor</u>   County Courthouse
                    Tuscola   61953

   <u>County Clerk &</u> County Courthouse
   <u>Recorder</u>   Tuscola   61953

   <u>Courts</u>
     <u>Circuit</u>   County Courthouse
                    Tuscola   61953

   <u>Voters</u>
   <u>Registration</u>   County Clerk
                    County Courthouse
                    Tuscola   61953

Du PAGE   Pop. 658,835

   <u>County Seat</u>   Wheaton   60187

   <u>Assessor</u>   421 N. County Farm Rd.
                    Wheaton   60187

   <u>County Clerk &</u> 421 N. County Farm Rd.
   <u>Recorder</u>   Wheaton   60187

   <u>Courts</u>
     <u>Circuit</u>   421 N. County Farm Rd.
                    Wheaton   60187

   <u>Voters</u>
   <u>Registration</u>   County Clerk
                    421 N. County Farm Rd.
                    Wheaton   60187

EDGAR   Pop. 21,725

County Seat   Paris   61944

Assessor   County Courthouse
                     Paris   61944

County Clerk &   County Courthouse
Recorder   Paris   61944

Courts
  Circuit   County Courthouse
                     Paris   61944

Voters   County Clerk
Registration   County Courthouse
                     Paris   61944

EDWARDS   Pop. 7,961

County Seat   Albion   62806

Assessor   County Courthouse
                     Albion   62806

County Clerk &   County Courthouse
Recorder   Albion   62806

Courts
  Circuit   County Courthouse
                     Albion   62806

Voters   County Clerk
Registration   County Courthouse
                     Albion   62806

EFFINGHAM   Pop. 30,944

  <u>County Seat</u>   Effingham   62401

  <u>Assessor</u>   County Courthouse
                    Effingham   62401

  <u>County Clerk &</u>   County Courthouse
  <u>Recorder</u>   Effingham   62401

  <u>Courts</u>
    <u>Circuit</u>   County Courthouse
                    Effingham   62401

  <u>Voters</u>   County Clerk
  <u>Registration</u>   County Courthouse
                    Effingham   62401

FAYETTE   Pop. 22,167

  <u>County Seat</u>   Vandalia   62471

  <u>Assessor</u>   County Courthouse
                    Vandalia   62471

  <u>County Clerk &</u>   County Courthouse
  <u>Recorder</u>   Vandalia   62471

  <u>Courts</u>
    <u>Circuit</u>   County Courthouse
                    Vandalia   62471

  <u>Voters</u>   County Clerk
  <u>Registration</u>   County Courthouse
                    Vandalia   62471

FORD Pop. 15,265

County Seat	Paxton	60957
Assessor	County Courthouse Paxton	60957
County Clerk & Recorder	County Courthouse Paxton	60957
Courts Circuit	County Courthouse Paxton	60957
Voters Registration	County Clerk County Courthouse Paxton	60957

FRANKLIN Pop. 43,201

County Seat	Benton	62812
Assessor	County Courthouse Benton	62812
County Clerk & Recorder	County Courthouse Benton	62812
Courts Circuit	County Courthouse Benton	62812
Voters Registration	County Clerk County Courthouse Benton	62812

FULTON

Pop. 43,687

County Seat	Lewistown	61542
Assessor	County Courthouse Lewistown	61542
County Clerk & Recorder	County Courthouse Lewistown	61542
Courts Circuit	County Courthouse Lewistown	61542
Voters Registration	County Clerk County Courthouse Lewistown	61542

GALLATIN

Pop. 7,590

County Seat	Shawneetown	62984
Assessor	County Courthouse Shawneetown	62984
County Clerk & Recorder	County Courthouse Shawneetown	62984
Courts Circuit	County Courthouse Shawneetown	62984
Voters Registration	County Clerk County Courthouse Shawneetown	62984

GREENE

Pop. 16,661

County Seat	Carrollton	62016
Assessor	County Courthouse Carrollton	62016
County Clerk & Recorder	County Courthouse Carrollton	62016
Courts Circuit	County Courthouse Carrollton	62016
Voters Registration	County Clerk County Courthouse Carrollton	62016

GRUNDY

Pop. 30,592

County Seat	Morris	60450
Assessor	County Courthouse Morris	60450
County Clerk & Recorder	County Courthouse Morris	60450
Courts Circuit	County Courthouse Morris	60450
Voters Registration	County Clerk County Courthouse Morris	60450

HAMILTON

Pop. 9,172

County Seat	Mc Leansboro	62859
Assessor	County Courthouse Mc Leansboro	62859
County Clerk & Recorder	County Courthouse Mc Leansboro	62859
Courts Circuit	County Courthouse Mc Leansboro	62859
Voters Registration	County Clerk County Courthouse Mc Leansboro	62859

HANCOCK

Pop. 23,876

County Seat	Carthage	62321
Assessor	County Courthouse Carthage	62321
County Clerk & Recorder	County Courthouse Carthage	62321
Courts Circuit	County Courthouse Carthage	62321
Voters Registration	County Clerk County Courthouse Carthage	62321

HARDIN

Pop. 5,383

County Seat	Elizabethtown	62931
Assessor	County Courthouse Elizabethtown	62931
County Clerk & Recorder	County Courthouse Elizabethtown	62931
Courts Circuit	County Courthouse Elizabethtown	62931
Voters Registration	County Clerk County Courthouse Elizabethtown	62931

HENDERSON

Pop. 9,114

County Seat	Oquawka	61469
Assessor	County Courthouse Oquawka	61469
County Clerk & Recorder	County Courthouse Oquawka	61469
Courts Circuit	County Courthouse Oquawka	61469
Voters Registration	County Clerk County Courthouse Oquawka	61469

HENRY Pop. 57,968

County Seat	Cambridge	61238
Assessor	County Courthouse Cambridge	61238
County Clerk & Recorder	County Courthouse Cambridge	61238
Courts Circuit	County Courthouse Cambridge	61238
Voters Registration	County Clerk County Courthouse Cambridge	61238

IROQUOIS Pop. 32,976

County Seat	Watseka	60970
Assessor	County Courthouse Watseka	60970
County Clerk & Recorder	County Courthouse Watseka	60970
Courts Circuit	County Courthouse Watseka	60970
Voters Registration	County Clerk County Courthouse Watseka	60970

JACKSON   <u>Pop.</u>   61,522

<u>County Seat</u>   Murphysboro   62966

<u>Assessor</u>   County Courthouse
                        Murphysboro   62966

<u>County Clerk &</u>   County Courthouse
<u>Recorder</u>   Murphysboro   62966

<u>Courts</u>
  <u>Circuit</u>   County Courthouse
                        Murphysboro   62966

<u>Voters</u>   County Clerk
<u>Registration</u>   County Courthouse
                        Murphysboro   62966

JASPER   <u>Pop.</u>   11,318

<u>County Seat</u>   Newton   62448

<u>Assessor</u>   County Courthouse
                        Newton   62448

<u>County Clerk &</u>   County Courthouse
<u>Recorder</u>   Newton   62448

<u>Courts</u>
  <u>Circuit</u>   County Courthouse
                        Newton   62448

<u>Voters</u>   County Clerk
<u>Registration</u>   County Courthouse
                        Newton   62448

JEFFERSON

Pop. 36,354

County Seat	Mt. Vernon	62864
Assessor	County Courthouse Mt. Vernon	62864
County Clerk & Recorder	County Courthouse Mt. Vernon	62864
Courts Circuit	County Courthouse Mt. Vernon	62864
Voters Registration	County Clerk County Courthouse Mt. Vernon	62864

JERSEY

Pop. 20,538

County Seat	Jerseyville	62052
Assessor	County Courthouse Jerseyville	62052
County Clerk & Recorder	County Courthouse Jerseyville	62052
Courts Circuit	County Courthouse Jerseyville	62052
Voters Registration	County Clerk County Courthouse Jerseyville	62052

JO DAVIESS

Pop. 23,520

County Seat	Galena	61036
Assessor	County Courthouse Galena	61036
County Clerk & Recorder	County Courthouse Galena	61036
Courts Circuit	County Courthouse Galena	61036
Voters Registration	County Clerk County Courthouse Galena	61036

JOHNSON

Pop. 9,624

County Seat	Vienna	62995
Assessor	County Courthouse Vienna	62995
County Clerk & Recorder	County Courthouse Vienna	62995
Courts Circuit	County Courthouse Vienna	62995
Voters Registration	County Clerk County Courthouse Vienna	62995

KANE   Pop. 278,405

County Seat	Geneva	60134

Assessor	County Courthouse Geneva	60134

County Clerk & Recorder	County Courthouse Geneva	60134

Courts Circuit	County Courthouse Geneva	60134

Voters Registration	County Clerk County Courthouse Geneva	60134

KANKAKEE   Pop. 102,926

County Seat	Kankakee	60901

Assessor	County Courthouse Kankakee	60901

County Clerk & Recorder	County Courthouse Kankakee	60901

Courts Circuit	County Courthouse Kankakee	60901

Voters Registration	County Clerk County Courthouse Kankakee	60901

KENDALL   Pop. 37,202

County Seat	Yorkville	60560
Assessor	County Courthouse Yorkville	60560
County Clerk & Recorder	County Courthouse Yorkville	60560
Courts Circuit	County Courthouse Yorkville	60560
Voters Registration	County Clerk County Courthouse Yorkville	60560

KNOX   Pop. 61,607

County Seat	Galesburg	61401
Assessor	County Courthouse Galesburg	61401
County Clerk & Recorder	County Courthouse Galesburg	61401
Courts Circuit	County Courthouse Galesburg	61401
Voters Registration	County Clerk County Courthouse Galesburg	61401

LAKE

County Seat	Waukegan	60085
Assessor	County Courthouse 18 North County St. Waukegan	60085
County Clerk & Recorder	County Courthouse 18 North County St. Waukegan	60085
Courts Circuit	County Courthouse 18 North County St. Waukegan	60085
Voters Registration	County Clerk 18 North County St. Waukegan	60085

La SALLE

Pop. 112,033

County Seat	Ottawa	61350
Assessor	County Courthouse Ottawa	61350
County Clerk & Recorder	County Courthouse Ottawa	61350
Courts Circuit	County Courthouse Ottawa	61350
Voters Registration	County Clerk County Courthouse Ottawa	61350

LAWRENCE   Pop.   17,807

    County Seat   Lawrenceville   62439

    Assessor   County Courthouse
                    Lawrenceville   62439

    County Clerk &   County Courthouse
    Recorder   Lawrenceville   62439

    Courts
      Circuit   County Courthouse
                    Lawrenceville   62439

    Voters   County Clerk
    Registration   County Courthouse
                    Lawrenceville   62439

LEE   Pop.   36,328

    County Seat   Dixon   61021

    Assessor   County Courthouse
                    Dixon   61021

    County Clerk &   County Courthouse
    Recorder   Dixon   61021

    Courts
      Circuit   County Courthouse
                    Dixon   61021

    Voters   County Clerk
    Registration   County Courthouse
                    Dixon   61021

LIVINGSTON

Pop. 41,381

County Seat	Pontiac	61764
Assessor	County Courthouse Pontiac	61764
County Clerk & Recorder	County Courthouse Pontiac	61764
Courts Circuit	County Courthouse Pontiac	61764
Voters Registration	County Clerk County Courthouse Pontiac	61764

LOGAN

Pop. 31,802

County Seat	Lincoln	62656
Assessor	County Courthouse Lincoln	62656
County Clerk & Recorder	County Courthouse Lincoln	62656
Courts Circuit	County Courthouse Lincoln	62656
Voters Registration	County Clerk County Courthouse Lincoln	62656

MC DONOUGH

Pop. 37,467

<u>County Seat</u>	Macomb	61455
<u>Assessor</u>	County Courthouse Macomb	61455
<u>County Clerk & Recorder</u>	County Courthouse Macomb	61455
<u>Courts</u> Circuit	County Courthouse Macomb	61455
<u>Voters Registration</u>	County Clerk County Courthouse Macomb	61455

MC HENRY

Pop. 147,897

<u>County Seat</u>	Woodstock	60098
<u>Assessor</u>	County Courthouse Woodstock	60098
<u>County Clerk & Recorder</u>	County Courthouse Woodstock	60098
<u>Courts</u> Circuit	County Courthouse Woodstock	60098
<u>Voters Registration</u>	County Clerk County Courthouse Woodstock	60098

MC LEAN   Pop. 119,149

    <u>County Seat</u>   Bloomington   61701

    <u>Assessor</u>   County Courthouse
                      Bloomington   61701

    <u>County Clerk &</u>
    <u>Recorder</u>   County Courthouse
                      Bloomington   61701

    <u>Courts</u>
        Circuit   County Courthouse
                      Bloomington   61701

    <u>Voters</u>
    <u>Registration</u>   County Clerk
                      County Courthouse
                      Bloomington   61701

MACON   Pop. 131,375

    <u>County Seat</u>   Decatur   62521

    <u>Assessor</u>   County Courthouse
                      Decatur   62521

    <u>County Clerk &</u>
    <u>Recorder</u>   County Courthouse
                      Decatur   62521

    <u>Courts</u>
        Circuit   County Courthouse
                      Decatur   62521

    <u>Voters</u>
    <u>Registration</u>   County Clerk
                      County Courthouse
                      Decatur   62521

MACOUPIN   Pop. 49,384

County Seat   Carlinville   62626

Assessor   County Courthouse
                     Carlinville   62626

County Clerk &   County Courthouse
Recorder   Carlinville   62626

Courts
  Circuit   County Courthouse
                     Carlinville   62626

Voters   County Clerk
Registration   County Courthouse
                     Carlinville   62626

MADISON   Pop. 247,691

County Seat   Edwardsville   62025

Assessor   County Courthouse
                     Edwardsville   62025

County Clerk &   County Courthouse
Recorder   Edwardsville   62025

Courts
  Circuit   County Courthouse
                     Edwardsville   62025

Voters   County Clerk
Registration   County Courthouse
                     Edwardsville   62025

MARION

MARION   Pop. 43,523

County Seat	Salem	62881
Assessor	County Courthouse Salem	62881
County Clerk & Recorder	County Courthouse Salem	62881
Courts Circuit	County Courthouse Salem	62881
Voters Registration	County Clerk County Courthouse Salem	62881

MARSHALL   Pop. 14,479

County Seat	Lacon	61540
Assessor	County Courthouse Lacon	61540
County Clerk & Recorder	County Courthouse Lacon	61540
Courts Circuit	County Courthouse Lacon	61540
Voters Registration	County Clerk County Courthouse Lacon	61540

MASON   Pop. 19,492

   | County Seat | Havana | 62644 |

   | Assessor | County Courthouse
Havana | 62644 |

   | County Clerk &
Recorder | County Courthouse
Havana | 62644 |

   | Courts
  Circuit | County Courthouse
Havana | 62644 |

   | Voters
Registration | County Clerk
County Courthouse
Havana | 62644 |

MASSAC   Pop. 14,990

   | County Seat | Metropolis | 62960 |

   | Assessor | County Courthouse
Metropolis | 62960 |

   | County Clerk &
Recorder | County Courthouse
Metropolis | 62960 |

   | Courts
  Circuit | County Courthouse
Metropolis | 62960 |

   | Voters
Registration | County Clerk
County Courthouse
Metropolis | 62960 |

MENARD

Pop. 11,700

County Seat	Petersburg	62675
Assessor	County Courthouse Petersburg	62675
County Clerk & Recorder	County Courthouse Petersburg	62675
Courts Circuit	County Courthouse Petersburg	62675
Voters Registration	County Clerk County Courthouse Petersburg	62675

MERCER

Pop. 19,286

County Seat	Aledo	61231
Assessor	County Courthouse Aledo	61231
County Clerk & Recorder	County Courthouse Aledo	61231
Courts Circuit	County Courthouse Aledo	61231
Voters Registration	County Clerk County Courthouse Aledo	61231

MONROE

County Seat	Waterloo	62298
Assessor	County Courthouse Waterloo	62298
County Clerk & Recorder	County Courthouse Waterloo	62298
Courts Circuit	County Courthouse Waterloo	62298
Voters Registration	County Clerk County Courthouse Waterloo	62298

MONTGOMERY

Pop. 31,780

County Seat	Hillsboro	62049
Assessor	County Courthouse Hillsboro	62049
County Clerk & Recorder	County Courthouse Hillsboro	62049
Courts Circuit	County Courthouse Hillsboro	62049
Voters Registration	County Clerk County Courthouse Hillsboro	62049

MORGAN Pop. 37,502

   County Seat   Jacksonville   62650

   Assessor   County Courthouse
                Jacksonville   62650

   County Clerk &   County Courthouse
   Recorder   Jacksonville   62650

   Courts
     Circuit   County Courthouse
                Jacksonville   62650

   Voters   County Clerk
   Registration   County Courthouse
                Jacksonville   62650

MOULTRIE Pop. 14,540

   County Seat   Sullivan   61951

   Assessor   County Courthouse
                Sullivan   61951

   County Clerk &   County Courthouse
   Recorder   Sullivan   61951

   Courts
     Circuit   County Courthouse
                Sullivan   61951

   Voters   County Clerk
   Registration   County Courthouse
                Sullivan   61951

OGLE

<u>Pop.</u> 46,338

<u>County Seat</u>	Oregon	61061
<u>Assessor</u>	County Courthouse Oregon	61061
<u>County Clerk & Recorder</u>	County Courthouse Oregon	61061
<u>Courts</u> <u>Circuit</u>	County Courthouse Oregon	61061
<u>Voters Registration</u>	County Clerk County Courthouse Oregon	61061

PEORIA

<u>Pop.</u> 200,466

<u>County Seat</u>	Peoria	61602
<u>Assessor</u>	County Courthouse Peoria	61602
<u>County Clerk & Recorder</u>	County Courthouse Peoria	61602
<u>Courts</u> <u>Circuit</u>	County Courthouse Peoria	61602
<u>Voters Registration</u>	County Clerk County Courthouse Peoria	61602

PERRY Pop. 21,714

    County Seat   Pinckneyville   62274

    Assessor   County Courthouse
                      Pinckneyville   62274

    County Clerk &   County Courthouse
    Recorder   Pinckneyville   62274

    Courts
      Circuit   County Courthouse
                      Pinckneyville   62274

    Voters   County Clerk
    Registration   County Courthouse
                      Pinckneyville   62274

PIATT Pop. 16,581

    County Seat   Monticello   61856

    Assessor   County Courthouse
                      Monticello   61856

    County Clerk &   County Courthouse
    Recorder   Monticello   61856

    Courts
      Circuit   County Courthouse
                      Monticello   61856

    Voters   County Clerk
    Registration   County Courthouse
                      Monticello   61856

PIKE <u>Pop.</u> 18,896

    <u>County Seat</u>   Pittsfield   62363

    <u>Assessor</u>   County Courthouse
                      Pittsfield   62363

    <u>County Clerk &</u> County Courthouse
    <u>Recorder</u>   Pittsfield   62363

    <u>Courts</u>
      <u>Circuit</u>   County Courthouse
                      Pittsfield   62363

    <u>Voters</u>   County Clerk
    <u>Registration</u>   County Courthouse
                      Pittsfield   62363

POPE <u>Pop.</u> 4,404

    <u>County Seat</u>   Golconda   62938

    <u>Assessor</u>   County Courthouse
                      Golconda   62938

    <u>County Clerk &</u> County Courthouse
    <u>Recorder</u>   Golconda   62938

    <u>Courts</u>
      <u>Circuit</u>   County Courthouse
                      Golconda   62938

    <u>Voters</u>   County Clerk
    <u>Registration</u>   County Courthouse
                      Golconda   62938

PULASKI
Pop. 8,840

County Seat	Mound City	62963
Assessor	County Courthouse Mound City	62963
County Clerk & Recorder	County Courthouse Mound City	62963
Courts Circuit	County Courthouse Mound City	62963
Voters Registration	County Clerk County Courthouse Mound City	62963

PUTNAM
Pop. 6,085

County Seat	Hennepin	61327
Assessor	County Courthouse Hennepin	61327
County Clerk & Recorder	County Courthouse Hennepin	61327
Courts Circuit	County Courthouse Hennepin	61327
Voters Registration	County Clerk County Courthouse Hennepin	61327

RANDOLPH

Pop. 35,652

<u>County Seat</u>	Chester	62233
<u>Assessor</u>	County Courthouse Chester	62233
<u>County Clerk & Recorder</u>	County Courthouse Chester	62233
<u>Courts</u> Circuit	County Courthouse Chester	62233
<u>Voters Registration</u>	County Clerk County Courthouse Chester	62233

RICHLAND

Pop. 17,587

<u>County Seat</u>	Olney	62450
<u>Assessor</u>	Route 1 Noble	62868
<u>County Clerk & Recorder</u>	County Courthouse Olney	62450
<u>Courts</u> Circuit	County Courthouse Olney	62450
<u>Voters Registration</u>	County Clerk County Courthouse Olney	62450

ROCK ISLAND   Pop. 165,968

County Seat	Rock Island	61201
Assessor	County Courthouse Rock Island	61201
County Clerk & Recorder	County Courthouse Rock Island	61201
Courts 　Circuit	County Courthouse Rock Island	61201
Voters Registration	County Clerk County Courthouse Rock Island	61201

ST. CLAIR   Pop. 267,531

County Seat	Belleville	62220
Assessor	10 Public Square Belleville	62220
County Clerk & Recorder	County Courthouse Belleville	62220
Courts 　Circuit	County Courthouse Belleville	62220
Voters Registration	County Clerk 10 Public Square Belleville	62220

SALINE Pop. 28,448

<u>County Seat</u>	Harrisburg	62946
<u>Assessor</u>	County Courthouse Harrisburg	62946
<u>County Clerk &</u> <u>Recorder</u>	County Courthouse Harrisburg	62946
<u>Courts</u> <u>Circuit</u>	County Courthouse Harrisburg	62946
<u>Voters</u> <u>Registration</u>	County Clerk County Courthouse Harrisburg	62946

SANGAMON Pop. 176,089

<u>County Seat</u>	Springfield	62701
<u>Assessor</u>	County Courthouse Springfield	62701
<u>County Clerk &</u> <u>Recorder</u>	County Courthouse Springfield	62701
<u>Courts</u> <u>Circuit</u>	County Courthouse Springfield	62701
<u>Voters</u> <u>Registration</u>	County Clerk County Courthouse Springfield	62701

SCHUYLER

Pop. 8,135

County Seat	Rushville	62681
Assessor	County Courthouse Rushville	62681
County Clerk & Recorder	County Courthouse Rushville	62681
Courts Circuit	County Courthouse Rushville	62681
Voters Registration	County Clerk County Courthouse Rushville	62681

SCOTT

Pop. 6,142

County Seat	Winchester	62694
Assessor	County Courthouse Winchester	62694
County Clerk & Recorder	County Courthouse Winchester	62694
Courts Circuit	County Courthouse Winchester	62694
Voters Registration	County Clerk County Courthouse Winchester	62694

SHELBY Pop. 23,923

<u>County Seat</u>	Shelbyville	62565
<u>Assessor</u>	County Courthouse Shelbyville	62565
<u>County Clerk & Recorder</u>	County Courthouse Shelbyville	62565
<u>Courts</u> 　Circuit	County Courthouse Shelbyville	62565
<u>Voters Registration</u>	County Clerk County Courthouse Shelbyville	62565

STARK Pop. 7,389

<u>County Seat</u>	Toulon	61483
<u>Assessor</u>	County Courthouse Toulon	61483
<u>County Clerk & Recorder</u>	County Courthouse Toulon	61483
<u>Courts</u> 　Circuit	County Courthouse Toulon	61483
<u>Voters Registration</u>	County Clerk County Courthouse Toulon	61483

STEPHENSON

Pop. 49,536

County Seat	Freeport	61032
Assessor	County Courthouse Freeport	61032
County Clerk & Recorder	County Courthouse Freeport	61032
Courts Circuit	County Courthouse Freeport	61032
Voters Registration	County Clerk County Courthouse Freeport	61032

TAZEWELL

Pop. 132,078

County Seat	Pekin	61554
Assessor	County Courthouse Pekin	61554
County Clerk & Recorder	County Courthouse Pekin	61554
Courts Circuit	County Courthouse Pekin	61554
Voters Registration	County Clerk County Courthouse Pekin	61554

UNION   Pop. 17,765

    <u>County Seat</u>   Jonesboro   62952

    <u>Assessor</u>   County Courthouse
                    Jonesboro   62952

    <u>County Clerk &</u> County Courthouse
    <u>Recorder</u>   Jonesboro   62952

    Courts
      <u>Circuit</u>   County Courthouse
                    Jonesboro   62952

    <u>Voters</u>   County Clerk
    <u>Registration</u>   County Courthouse
                    Jonesboro   62952

VERMILION   Pop. 95,222

    <u>County Seat</u>   Danville   61834

    <u>Assessor</u>   County Courthouse
                    Danville   61834

    <u>County Clerk &</u> County Courthouse
    <u>Recorder</u>   Danville   61834

    Courts
      <u>Circuit</u>   County Courthouse
                    Danville   61834

    <u>Voters</u>   County Clerk
    <u>Registration</u>   County Courthouse
                    Danville   61834

WABASH Pop. 13,713

County Seat	Mt. Carmel	62863
Assessor	County Courthouse Mt. Carmel	62863
County Clerk & Recorder	County Courthouse Mt. Carmel	62863
Courts Circuit	County Courthouse Mt. Carmel	62863
Voters Registration	County Clerk County Courthouse Mt. Carmel	62863

WARREN Pop. 21,943

County Seat	Monmouth	61462
Assessor	County Courthouse Monmouth	61462
County Clerk & Recorder	County Courthouse Monmouth	61462
Courts Circuit	County Courthouse Monmouth	61462
Voters Registration	County Clerk County Courthouse Monmouth	61462

WASHINGTON   Pop. 15,472

<u>County Seat</u>	Nashville	62263
<u>Assessor</u>	County Courthouse Nashville	62263
<u>County Clerk & Recorder</u>	County Courthouse Nashville	62263
<u>Courts</u> <u>Circuit</u>	County Courthouse Nashville	62263
<u>Voters Registration</u>	County Clerk County Courthouse Nashville	62263

WAYNE   Pop. 18,059

<u>County Seat</u>	Fairfield	62937
<u>Assessor</u>	County Courthouse Fairfield	62937
<u>County Clerk & Recorder</u>	County Courthouse Fairfield	62937
<u>Courts</u> <u>Circuit</u>	County Courthouse Fairfield	62937
<u>Voters Registration</u>	County Clerk County Courthouse Fairfield	62937

WHITE   Pop. 17,864

| County Seat | Carmi | 62821 |

| Assessor | County Courthouse
Carmi | 62821 |

| County Clerk &
Recorder | County Courthouse
Carmi | 62821 |

Courts
    Circuit   County Courthouse
                           Carmi   62821

| Voters
Registration | County Clerk
County Courthouse
Carmi | 62821 |

WHITESIDE   Pop. 65,970

| County Seat | Morrison | 61270 |

| Assessor | County Courthouse
Morrison | 61270 |

| County Clerk &
Recorder | County Courthouse
Morrison | 61270 |

Courts
    Circuit   County Courthouse
                           Morrison   61270

| Voters
Registration | County Clerk
County Courthouse
Morrison | 61270 |

WILL   Pop. 324,460

County Seat	Joliet	60431
Assessor	County Courthouse Joliet	60431
County Clerk & Recorder	County Courthouse Joliet	60431
Courts Circuit	County Courthouse Joliet	60431
Voters Registration	County Clerk County Courthouse Joliet	60431

WILLIAMSON   Pop. 56,538

County Seat	Marion	62959
Assessor	County Courthouse Marion	62959
County Clerk & Recorder	County Courthouse Marion	62959
Courts Circuit	County Courthouse Marion	62959
Voters Registration	County Clerk County Courthouse Marion	62959

WINNEBAGO

Pop. 250,884

County Seat	Rockford	61101
Assessor	County Courthouse 400 W. State Rockford	61101
County Clerk & Recorder	County Courthouse 400 W. State Rockford	61101
Courts Circuit	County Courthouse 400 W. State Rockford	61101
Voters Registration	County Clerk County Courthouse 400 W. State Rockford	61101

WOODFORD

Pop. 33,320

County Seat	Eureka	61530
Assessor	County Courthouse Eureka	61530
County Clerk & Recorder	County Courthouse Eureka	61530
Courts Circuit	County Courthouse Eureka	61530
Voters Registration	County Clerk County Courthouse Eureka	61530

CEMETERIES

Adams

Name	Address	City	ZIP
Beverly	R. R. 1	Barry	62312
Clayton Mausoleum	R. R. 1	Camp Point	62320
Columbus		Clayton	62324
Evergreen		Fowler	62338
G. Stewart		Hull	62343
Greenmount	S. 12th St.	Quincy	62301
Hebron	331 N. Maine St.	Camp Point	62320
Independence	518 Vermont	Quincy	62301
Keith		Loraine	62349
Kingston Park	R. R. 1, Box 99	Liberty	62347
Liberty	R. R. 1	Liberty	62347
Mount Horeb		La Prairie	62346
Nations		Liberty	62347
New Providence		Ursa	62376
Paloma		Coatsburg	62325
Payson		Payson	62360
Pleasant View		Camp Point	62320
Quincy Graceland	1441 Hampshire St.	Quincy	62301
Quincy Memorial Park	1800 Maine St.	Quincy	62301
Quincy National	36th & Maine St.	Quincy	62382
St. Boniface	2001 State	Quincy	62301
St. Peters	3300 Broadway	Quincy	62301
South Side		Clayton	62324
Walker		La Prairie	62346
Wolf Ridge		Clayton	62324
Woodland	1020 S. 5th	Quincy	62301

Alexander

Greenlawn Memorial Gardens	3615 Sycamore St.	Cairo	62914
Olive Branch	Box 163	Olive Branch	62969

Bond

Bethel	R. R. 1	Donnellson	62019
Brown	R. R. 2	Pocahontas	62275
Greene	R. R. 3	Greenville	62246
Hazel Dell	501 Alice Ave.	Greenville	62246
Mc Kendree Chapel	R. R. 4, Box 160C	Greenville	62246
Mount Auburn	R. R. 2	Mulberry Grove	62262
Old Camp Ground	R. R. 4	Greenville	62246
Wisetown	R. R. 1	Carlyle	62231

Boone

Name	Address	City	ZIP
Blaine		Poplar Grove	61065
Belvidere	N. Main	Belvidere	61008
Bloods Point	915 E. Lincoln Ave.	Belvidere	61008
Capron	9900 Edson Rd.	Capron	61012
County Line	9239 N. Boone School Rd.	Capron	61012
Flora	1157 Irene Rd.	Cherry Valley	61016
Gardens Prairie	Box 5	Garden Prairie	61038
Highland Garden of Memories	9800 Route 76	Belvidere	61008
Poplar Grove	201 S. State St.	Poplar Grove	61065

Brown

Bell Keith	R. R. 1	Mt. Sterling	62353
Hebron	508 S. Capitol	Mt. Sterling	62353
Hersman	R. R. 3, Box 217	Mt. Sterling	62353
Howes		Timewell	62375
Mound		Timewell	62375

Bureau

Bunker Hill		Buda	61314
Cross	427 E. Griswold St.	Princeton	61356
Elm Lawn Memorial	503 N. Knox	Princeton	61356
Greenfield	R. R. 1	Ohio	61349
Greenville Chapel		New Bedford	61346
Greenville Fairfield Union		New Bedford	61346
Hopeland		Buda	61314
Ladd	211 N. Bureau Ave.	Ladd	61329
Malden	215 S. Vernon	Princeton	61356
Manlius		Wyanet	61379
Milo Mound	R. R. 2, Box 77	Bradford	61421
Mt. Pleasant	417 High St.	Buda	61314
Neponset Floral Hill	Box 243	Neponset	61345
Prairie Repose	Box 48	Dover	61323
Princeton Elm Lawn Memorial	503 N. Knox St.	Princeton	61356
St. Joseph's	R. 6	Spring Valley	61362
Union		Ohio	61349
Valley Memorial Park	R. R. 1	Spring Valley	61362
Van Orin Repose	R. R. 1	Ohio	61349
Yorktown	R. R. 1, Box 112	Tampico	61283

Calhoun

Indian Creek	Box 276	Kampsville	62053

Carroll

Arnold Grove	R. R. 2	Mt. Carroll	61053
Brookville	R. R. 2	Forreston	61030
Daggert	R. R. 1	Milledgeville	61051
Oakville	512 S. College St.	Mt. Carroll	61053
Schriner	R. R. 2	Polo	61064
Zions Grove	8155 E. Goodmiller Rd.	Elizabeth	61028

Cass

Beardstown Oak Grove	917 E. 7th St.	Beardstown	62618
Jokisch	R. R. 1, Box 174	Arenzville	62611

Champaign

Bailey Memorial		Tolono	61880
Davis Memorial		Pesotum	61863
East Lawn Burial Park	1101 N. Eastern Ave.	Urbana	61801
Locust Grove	Box 247	Philo	61864
Maplewood	356 Illinois Dr.	Rantoul	61866
Mt. Hope	611 E. Pennsylvania	Champaign	61820
Mt. Hope	Box 87	Sidney	61877
Mt. Olive	R. R. 2	Urbana	61801
Patterson	505 E. Lincoln St.	St. Joseph	61873
Prairie View	910 Lincolnshire Dr. 302	Champaign	61820
Roselawn	1710 Northfield Sq.	Northfield	60093
Willowbrook		Fisher	61843
Woodlawn	Box 2156	Champaign	61820

Christian

Bethany	R. R. 2, Box 29	Edinburgh	62531
Buckeye Prairie	R. R. 1	Owaneco	61555
Fraley	R. R. 1, Box 191	Taylorville	62568
Glenhaven Memory Garden	Box 358	Palmer	62556
Greenwood Fairview	R. R. 1	Nokomis	62075
Mound Chapel	R. R. 1	Owaneco	62555
Old Stonington		Stonington	62567
Pana	302 Cedar St.	Pana	62557
Pana Mound	514 S. Walnut	Pana	62557
Rosamond Grove	R. R. 4, Box 94	Pana	62083
Union	204 W. Market	Taylorville	62568

Clark

Maple Hill		Westfield	62474
Paris Memorial Garden	W. Steidl Rd.	Paris	61944

Clay

Iola	R. R. 4	Louisville	62858
Newton Chapel	R. R. 4	Louisville	62858

Clinton

Yingst	1191 15th St.	Carlyle	62231

Coles

Charleston	W. Route 316	Charleston	61920
Gordon Graveyard		Janesville	62435
Mound	2004 11th St.	Charleston	61920
Resthaven Memorial Gardens	1221 Charleston	Mattoon	61938

Cook

Acadia Park	7800 Irving Park Rd.	Chicago	60634
All Saints	700 N. River Rd.	Des Plaines	60016
All Saints Polish National	Higgins Rd. & River Rd.	Park Ridge	60068
Archer Woods Memorial Park	Keane Ave. & 83rd St.	Willow Springs	60480
Arlington Heights	E. Euclid Ave.	Arlington Heights	60004
Assumption	19500 Cottage Grove Ave.	Glenwood	60425
Bartlett	North Ave.	Bartlett	60103
Berger	1485 Sibley Blvd.	Dolton	60419
Bethania	7701 Archer Ave.	Justice	60459
Bethany Lutheran	123rd St.	Lemont	60439
Bethel	5800 N. Pulaski Rd.	Chicago	60646
Beverly	120th & Kedzie	Chicago	60658
Bloom Evangelical Lutheran	Vollmer Rd.	Chicago Heights	60411
Bluff City	Wright Ave. & Bluff City	Elgin	61020
Bohemian National	5155 N. Pulaski Rd.	Chicago	60630
Burr Oaks	44th Ave. & 127th St.	Alsip	60658
Cady	Ela Rd.	Palatine	60067
Calvary	301 Chicago Ave.	Evanston	60202
Calvary	Steger Rd.	Steger	60475
Cedar Park	12540 S. Halsted St.	Chicago	60643
Chapel Hill Gardens	5501 W. 111th St.	Worth	60482
Chiago Burr Oaks	471 E. 31st St.	Chicago	60616
Christ Lutheran	82nd Ave. & 147th St.	Orland Park	60462
Concordia	7900 W. Madison St.	Forest Park	60130
Congregation A.D. Beth Hamedrash Hagadol	71st & Ellis Ave.	Chicago	60619
Congregation Anshe Sholan	71st & Ingleside Ave.	Chicago	60619
Cooper's Grove	183rd St.	Tinley Park	60477

Name	Address	City	Zip
Danish	127th St.	Lemont	60439
Deer Grove	Dundee & Ela Rds.	Palatine	60067
Dutton	Euclid Rd.	Arlington Heights	60004
Ebenezer	162nd & Cicero Ave.	Oak Forest	60452
Eden Memorial Park	9851 W. Irving Park Rd.	Schiller Park	60176
Evangelical Lutheran	1850 W. Lake Ave.	Glenview	60025
Evergreen	W. 87th & S. Kedzie Ave.	Chicago	60642
Evergreen	520 Shorely Dr.	Barrington	60010
Fairmount Hills	7234 W. North Ave.	Elmwood Park	60635
Fairmount Memorial Park	9100 Archer Rd.	Willow Springs	60480
Fairview Memorial Park	900 W. Wolf Rd.	Northlake	60164
First Evangelical Lutheran	4135 W. 127th St.	Alsip	60658
First Reform	Ridge Rd. & Burnham Ave.	Lansing	60130
Forest Home	863 S. Des Plaines Ave.	Forest Park	60130
Glen Oak	Roosevelt & Mannheim Rds.	Hillside	60162
Glen View	Lake Ave.	Glenview	60025
Graceland	4001 N. Clark St.	Chicago	60613
Hazel Green	115th St. & 52nd Ave.	Oak Lawn	60453
Hazelwood	Ridge Rd. & Halsted St.	Homewood	60430
Hillside	Smith St. & Cornell Ave.	Palatine	60067
Holy Cross	Michigan City Rd.	Calumet City	60409
Holy Sepulchre	6001 W. 111th St.	Worth	60482
Homewood Memorial Gardens	600 Ridge Rd.	Homewood	60430
Immanuel Evangelical	Sauk Trail & Cicero Ave.	Richton Park	60471
Immanuel Lutheran	Roselle & Schaumburg Rds.	Schaumburg	60194
Immanuel Lutheran	Rand Rd. & Golf Rd.	Des Plaines	60016
Irving Park	7777 Irving Park Rd.	Chicago	60634
Jewish Graceland	3919 N. Clark St.	Chicago	60613
Jewish Waldheim	1800 S. Harlem	Forest Park	60130
La Grange	Fifth Ave. & 27th St.	La Grange Park	60525
Lake St. Memorial Park	U.S. 30	Elgin	60120
Lincoln	123rd & Kedzie Ave.	Blue Island	60406
Lithuanian National	82nd & Kean Ave.	Willow Springs	60480
Lyonsville	5931 Wolf Rd.	Western Springs	60525
Maryhill	8600 Milwaukee Ave.	Niles	60648
Matteson	Lincoln Hwy.	Matteson	60443
Memorah Gardens	2630 S. 17th Ave.	Broadview	60153
Memorial Park	9900 Gross Pt. Rd.	Skokie	60077
Memory Gardens	2501 Euclid	Arlington	60004
Montrose	5400 N. Pulaski	Chicago	60630
Mt. Auburn Memorial Park	4101 S. Oak Park	Stickney	60402
Mt. B'nai B'rith	6600 W. Addison St.	Chicago	60634
Mt. Carmel	14003 Wolf Rd.	Hillside	60162
Mt. Glenwood	111st & S. California	Chicago	60655
Mt. Glenwood Memory Gardens	8301 Kean Ave.	Willow Springs	60480
Mt. Glenwood Park	18301 Glenwood Thornton	Glenwood	60425
Mt. Hope	Algonquin & Roselle Rds.	Palatine	60067
Mt. Hope	11500 S. Fairfield Ave.	Chicago	60655
Mt. Isaiah Israel	6600 W. Addison	Chicago	60634
Mt. Mayriv	3800 N. Narragansett Ave.	Chicago	60634
Mt. Olive	3800 N. Narragansett Ave.	Chicago	60634
Mount Olivet	2755 W. 111th St.	Chicago	60655
Mt. Prospect		Mt. Prospect	60056
Northfield Oakwood	1010 Gladison Ln.	Glenview	60025
North Northfield	1532 Chapel St.	Northbrook	60062
Oak Forest	159th & Cicero Ave.	Oak Forest	60452
Oakglen	Ridge Rd.	Lansing	60438
Oak Hill	Kedzie Ave. & 119th St.	Chicago	60655
Oakland Memory	15200 Lincoln Ave.	Dolton	60419
Oaklawn	Ridge Rd. & Halstad	Homewood	60430
Oak Ridge		South Holland	60473
Oakridge	Roosevelt & Oakridge	Hillside	60162
Oakwoods	Milwaukee Ave.	Northfield	60093
Oak Woods	1035 E. 67th St.	Chicago	60637
Order of Knight of Joseph	17th & Des Plaines	Forest Park	60130
Organd German	84th Ave. & 171 St.	Tinley Park	60477

132

Orland Memorial Park	West Ave.	Orland Park	60462
Orland Tinley Park	157 S. Harlem Ave.	Tinley Park	60477
Our Lady of Sorrows	Rosevelt Rd.	Hillside	60162
Palatine Hillside	921 Stark Dr.	Palatine	60067
Palos Oak Hills	131st St.	Palos Park	60464
Parkholm	657 Lake Rd.	Glen Ellyn	60127
Proviso Lutheran	Wolf Rd. & 22nd St.	La Grange	60525
Presbyterian	Chicago Rd.	Chicago Heights	60411
Queen of Heaven	1400 S. Wolf Rd.	Hillside	60162
Resurrection	7200 Archer Ave.	Justice	60459
Restvale	111th St. & Laramie Ave.	Worth	60482
Ridgelawn	5736 N. Pulaski Rd.	Chicago	60646
Ridgewood	9900 N. Milwaukee Ave.	Des Plaines	60616
Rosehill	5800 Ravenswood Ave.	Chicago	60660
Rosemont Park	6758 W. Addison	Chicago	60634
Sacred Heart	Lee Rd.	Northbrook	60062
St. Adalbert	6800 N. Milwaukee Ave.	Niles	60648
St. Alphonsus	State St.	Lemont	60439
St. Anne	Sauk Trail & Westwood	Park Forest	60466
St. Bede	Wilson Rd. & Grand Ave.	Ingleside	60041
St. Boniface	4901 N. Clark St.	Chicago	60640
St. Casimir	4401 W. 111th St.	Chicago	60655
Sts. Cyril & Methodius	Keepataw Dr.	Lemont	60439
St. Gabriel	Cicero Ave.	Oak Forest	60452
St. Henry	1920 W. Devon Ave.	Chicago	60660
St. James	Sauk Trail	Sauk Village	60411
St. John's Evangelical	Algonquin & Roselle Rds.	Palatine	60067
St. John's Evangelical	Euclid Rd.	Arlington Heights	60004
St. John's Evangelical		Schaumberg	60194
St. Joseph	W. Belmont & Cumberland	River Grove	60171
St. Joseph	Lake Ave. & Ridge Rd.	Wilmette	60091
St. Lucas	5330 N. Pulaski Rd.	Chicago	60646
St. Mary	W. 87th St. & Hamlin Ave.	Evergreen Park	60642
St. Mary's	Old Buffalot Grove Rd.	Arlington Heights	60004
St. Matthew's Evangelical	129th St.	Lemont	60439
St. Michael	159th St.	Orland Park	60462
St. Michael the Archangel	Algonquin & Roselle Rds.	Palatine	60067
St. Nicholas Ukrainian	Higgins & River Rds.	Park Ridge	60068
St. Patrick	Bluff Rd.	Lemont	60439
St. Paul's Evangelical	Harms Rd.	Niles	60648
St. Paul's Evangelical	Russell & Henry St.	Arlington Heights	60004
St. Peter	8115 Niles Center Rd.	Skokie	60077
St. Peter's Catholic	School St. & Niles Ctr.	Skokie	60077
St. Peter's Evangelical	Harris Rd.	Niles Center	60648
Schaumburg Lutheran	Schaumburg Rd.	Schaumburg	60194
Schwarzback Sons Jewish	1700 S. Des Plaines	Forest Park	60130
Shalom Memorial Park	Wilke & Rand Rds.	Palatine	60067
Silverman & Weiss	1303 S. Des Plaines	Forest Park	60130
South Chapel Hill Gardens	Roosevelt Rd.	Elmhurst	60126
Sunset Memorial Gardens	3100 Sherman Rd.	Northbrook	60062
Tinley Park Memorial	84th Ave. & 171 St.	Tinley Park	60477
Trinity Lutheran	83rd St.	Willow Springs	60480
Union Ridge	6700 Higgins Ave.	Chicago	60656
Waldheim	863 S. Des Plaines	Forest Park	60130
Washington Memory Gardens	701 Ridge Rd.	Homewood	60430
Westlawn	7801 W. Montrose	Chicago	60634
Willow Hills Memorial Park	9100 Archer Ave.	Willow Springs	60480

Crawford

Palestine	R. R. 1	Palestine	62451

De Kalb

Afton	2116 S. 1st St.	De Kalb	60115
East Pierce	Pritchard Rd.	Maple Park	60151
Elmwood	Box 96	Sycamore	60178
Fairview Park	Barber Greene Rd.	De Kalb	60115
Greenview		Esmond	60129
Malta		Malta	60150
Millers Hinckley	Box 171	Hinckley	60520
Mound Rest	921 State St.	De Kalb	60115
Oakridge Union		Sandwich	60548
Ohio Grove	230 W. State St.	Sycamore	60178
Somonauk	R. R. 1	Sandwich	60548
South Grove	R. R. 1	Kirkland	60146
Union	363 E. Lincoln Hwy.	De Kalb	60115
Victor	R. R. 1	Leland	60531

De Witt

Maple Grove	506 N. Main	Farmer City	61842

Douglas

Albin		Newman	61942
Hugo	R. R. 2	Tuscola	61953
Newman		Newman	61942
Pleasant Grove		Oakland	61943
Vanvoorhis	R. R. 1	Hindsboro	61930

Du Page

Arlington	1102 Midwest Club	Oak Brook	60521
Bronswood	3805 S. Madison	Oak Brook	60521
Chapel Hills Garden	Roosevelt Rd., Rt. 83	Elmhurst	61026
Clarendon Hills	6900 S. Cass Rd.	Westmont	60559
Forest Hill	111 Sunset Ave.	Glen Ellyn	60137
Fullerburg	5612 County Line Rd.	Hinsdale	60521
Hinsdale Burial	1000 Oak Brook Rd.	Oak Brook	60521
Lombard	534 E. Washington	Villa Park	60181
Naperville	136 S. Washington	Naperville	60566
Oak Hill	1923 Elmore Rd.	Downers Grove	60515
Warrenville	2 S. 335 Williams Rd.	Warrenville	60555
Wheaton	480 St. Moritz Ct.	Glen Ellyn	60137

Edgar

Edgar		Paris	61944
Light Carmel	R. R. 2	Chrisman	61924
New Goshen	R. R. 5	Paris	61944
New Grandview	R. R. 5	Paris	61944
Paris Memorial Gardens	122 E. Madison	Paris	61944
Reed Sugar Grove	R. R. 3	Chrisman	61924

Edwards

Bone Gap		Bone Gap	62815
Graceland	31 S. 4th	Albion	62806
Oak Grove		Grayville	62844

Effingham

Arborcrest Memorial Park	2108 S. Willow	Effingham	62401
Edgewood		Edgewood	62426
Effingham - Woodlawn	114 N. 5th	Effingham	62401
Pleasant Grove	R. R. 2, Box 340	Beecher City	62414

Fayette

Liberty Burying Ground	R. R. 1, Box 236	Ramsey	62080
Little Hickory		Fillmore	62032
Loogootee		Loogootee	62857
Pleasant Grove	R. R. 2, Box 154	Loogootee	62857

Ford

Glenn	602 E. Summer	Paxton	60957
Kempton Hill Burial Park		Kempton	60946

Fulton

Avon		Avon	61415
Babbitt		St. Augustine	61474
Foster	R. R. 4	Canton	61520
Ipava		Ipava	61441
Virgil	R. R. 1	Avon	61415

Gallatin

Bethlehem		Omaha	62871

Greene

Eastern United	R. R. 2	Roodhouse	62082
Eldred		Eldred	62027
Eldred Memory Garden		Eldred	62027
Fernwood	W. Clay St.	Roodhouse	62082
Providence	R. R. 1	Carrollton	62016
White Hall	450 Centennial	White Hall	62092
William Edwards	R. R. 3	Roodhouse	62082

Grundy

Aux. Sable	R. R. 4	Morris	60450
Braceville & Gardner		Braceville	60407
Good Farm	R. R. 1	Dwight	60420
Mazon Brookside	Box 185	Mazon	60444
Morris	707 Wauponsee St.	Morris	60450
Sample		Morris	60450
Ward		Mazon	60444
Wheeler	R. R. 1	Mazon	60444

Hamilton

Glenview Development	R. R. 1	Mc Leansboro	62859

Hancock

Augusta Woodlawn		Augusta	62311
Bowen Abbey		Bowen	62316
Byler	R. R. 2	Dallas City	62330
Chili		Bowen	62316
Durham		Dallas City	62330
Oakland	330 Main St.	Warsaw	62379
St. Marys	R. R. 2	Plymouth	62367
Thornber	R. R. 2	Burnside	62321

Henderson

Old South Henderson	Box 182	Biggsville	61418
Rariton		Rariton	61471
Shady Rest	519 N. "A" St.	Monmouth	61462

Henry

Alpha	Box 46	Alpha	61413
Atkinson Cornwall		Atkinson	61235
Clover Chapel	Box 486	Woodhull	61490
Henry County Liberty		Atkinson	61235
Hooppole		Hooppole	61258
Red Oak	205 S. West St.	Cambridge	61238
Saxon Community	423 E. Division St.	Kewanee	61443
Woodhull		Woodhull	61490

Iroquois

Beaver		Donovan	60931
Beaver Creek	R. R. 1	Chebanse	60922
Chebanse Evergreen		Chebanse	60922
Cissna Park	435 N. 2nd St.	Cissna Park	60924
Clifton		Clifton	60927
Gilman		Gilman	60938
Morris Chapel		Iroquois	60945
Papineau	R. R. 5	St. Anne	60964
Prairie Dell	R. R. 4	Watseka	60970
Wenger Green Ridge		Gilman	60938

Jackson

Ava Evergreen		Ava	62907
Campbell Hill		Campbell Hill	62916
Murdale Gardens of Memory	R. R. 2	Murphysboro	62966
Pleasant Grove Memorial	2020 Illinois Ave.	Murphysboro	62966
Rowan	R. R. 1, Box 32	Makanda	62958

Jasper

Westlawn Memorial Park	217 W. Washington	Newton	62448

Jefferson

Anderson Smith	Box 185	Opdyke	62872
Belle Rive	Box 122	Belle Rive	62810
Bethel Memorial	R. R. 1	Mt. Vernon	62864
Hams Grove		Ewing	62836
Moores Prairie Sugar Camp	R. R. 1	Belle Rive	62810
Mt. Vernon Memorial Gardens	R. R. 1, Box 62	Waltonville	62894
Mt. Vernon Oakwood	1018 Jordan St.	Mt. Vernon	62864
Old Union	2 Indian Trail	Mt. Vernon	62864
Opdyke		Opdyke	62872
Sunset Memorial	800 N. Market St.	Marion	62959
Woodlawn Odd Fellow	R. R. 1	Woodlawn	62898

Jersey

Lamb Memorial	Box 254	Dow	62022
Medora		Medora	62063

Jo Daviess

Chelsea	14568 E. Chelsea Rd.	Lena	61048
Elmwood	415 Stauer	Warren	61087
Greenwood	217 S. High	Galena	61036

Johnson

New Burnside		New Burnside	62967

Kane

Aurora	745 S. Lincoln	Aurora	60505
Blackberry	125 Capes Dr.	Elburn	60118
Campton	727 S. Calhoun Ave.	Aurora	60505
Fowler Grove	207 Bevier Pl.	Aurora	60505
Gardner	R. R. 2	Maple Park	60151
Jericho	2272 Fitchome St.	Aurora	60538
Kaneville		Maple Park	60151
Lily Lake	5N030 Hanson Rd.	St. Charles	60174
River Hills Memorial Park	1650 S. River St.	Batavia	60510
Riverside	480 Eagle Dr.	Elk Grove Village	60007
River Valley Mem. Gardens	R. R. 1 Canterfield Farm	Dundee	60118
Sugar Grove	Box 465	Sugar Grove	60554
Udina	61 S. Melrose Ave.	Elgin	60120
Welsh	R. R. 1, Box 414B	Sugar Grove	60554
West Aurora	34 S. Broadway	Aurora	60507
West Big Rock	R. R. 1	Hinckley	60520

Kankakee

Blooms Grove	R. R. 1	Manteno	60950
Coleman	R. R. 1	Herscher	60941
Elmwood	21 N. Main St.	Manteno	60950
Guilding Star Memorial	R. R. 1, Box 81	St. Anne	60964
Momence	617 N. Locust	Momence	60954
Mound Grove Garden	1000 N. Greenwood Ave.	Kankakee	60901
Mount Airy	303 N. Dixie Hwy.	Momence	60954
Union Corners	107 S. Meadows St.	Grant Park	60940

Kendall

Lincoln Memorial Park	R. R. 2, Box 142	Aurora	60504
Lisbon	R. R. 2, Box 177	Newark	60541
Millington-Newark	Box 367	Newark	60541
Na Au Say	R. R. 2, Box 79	Oswego	60543
Oak Grove	R. R. 1	Bristol	60512
Pearce	495 N. Lake St.	Aurora	60506
Plattville	R. R. 2, Box 279	Yorkville	60560
Seward Mound	Box 147	Minooka	60447

Knox

Dunndale	1801 W. Main St.	Galesburg	61401
Gilson		Gilson	61436
Henderson	Box 91	Henderson	61439
Hope	1801 W. Main St.	Galesburg	61401
Oneida		Oneida	61467
Ontario		Altona	61414
Rio		Rio	61472

Lake

Antioch Hillside	440 Lake St.	Antioch	60002
Angola	68 Cedar Ave.	Lake Villa	60046
Ascension	1920 Buckley Rd.	Libertyville	60048
Avon Centre	1910 N. Wabash	Round Lake	60073
Deerfield	72 Westgate	Deerfield	60015
Fairfield	28 Caroline Ct.	Lake Zurich	60047
Fox Lake	2116 N. Arcade Dr.	Lake Villa	60046
Grant	26557 W. Nippersink	Ingleside	60041
Home Oaks	R. R. 4, Box 336	Antioch	60002
Ivanhoe	276 N. Seymour Ave.	Mundelein	60060
Lake Mound	2116 Elizabeth	Zion	60099
Lakeside	1131 Pine Tree Ln.	Libertyville	60048
Lake Zurich	964 Wilmette Terr.	Lake Zurich	60047

Millburn	38811 N. Highway 45	Lake Villa	60046
Modern	18th & Greenbay Rd.	North Chicago	60064
Mount Olivet Memorial Park	3028 Sheridan Rd.	Zion	60099
Oakdale	609 Barron Blvd.	Grayslake	60030
Pine View	Box 236	Barrington	60064
St. Joseph	114 N. Lincoln	Round Lake	60073
St. Mary	Sheridan at Spruce	Lake Forest	60045
St. Mary	Ridge Rd.	Highland Park	60035
St. Mary	Sheridan & 8th Sts.	Waukegan	60085
Transfiguration	Route 176	Wauconda	60084
Union of Waukegan	2309 Seminole	Waukegan	60085
Warren	Box 63	Gurnee	60031
Wauconda	235 N. Main St.	Wauconda	60084
Willow Lawn Memorial	R. R. 1, Box 207	Mundelein	60060

La Salle

Baker	R. R. 1	Leland	60531
Dana		Dana	61321
Deer Park	R. R. 1, Box 2288	Oglesby	61348
Elerding	P. O. Box 116	Serena	60549
Forest Lawn Memory Gardens	R. R. 1	La Salle	61301
Freedom Lutheran	R. R. 2	Earlville	61518
Grand Ridge	245 E. Liberty	Grand Ridge	61325
Grand Rapids	R. R. 1	Grand Rapids	61325
Harding	Box 769	Ottawa	61350
Hill		Grand Ridge	61325
Hope Town		Lostant	61334
Leland	Sunset Knoll	Leland	60531
Little Indian Creek	R. R. 1	Somonauk	60552
Mendota	1416 Lakewood Dr.	Mendota	61342
Mount Hope	234 E. Scott	Seneca	61360
Nichol	905 Pearl St.	Marsaille	61341
Northville	Box 444	Sheridan	60551
Norway	R. R. 2	Sheridan	60551
Oakwood		La Salle	61301
Ottawa Ave.	850 Westwood	Ottawa	61350
Parklawn	R. R. 1	Ottawa	61350
Prairie Center	R. R. 2	Ottawa	61350
Riverview	308 S. Illinois St.	Streator	61364
South Emery Green	R. R. 1	Streator	61364
Streator Memorial Park	1422 E. Broadway	Streator	61364
Summitview	806 Hitt St.	Ottawa	61350
Tonica	Box 123	Tonica	61370
Troy Grove	R. R. 2	Mendota	61342
Utica Oak Hill		Utica	61373
Waltham	R. R. 1	Utica	61373
Wenona		Wenona	61377
West Sergna	145 Riverview Dr.	Ottawa	61350
Wisner	R. R. 3	Mendota	61342
Wolfe Creek	301 E. 4th St.	Streator	61364

Lee

Brooklyn Union	R. R. 1	Compton	61318
Chapel Hill Memorial Park	1121 N. Galena Ave.	Dixon	61021
City of Dixon	416 Dement Ave.	Dixon	61021
De Wolf	R. R. 4	Dixon	61021
Ellsworth	Box 97	Paw Paw	61353
Franklin Grove	Box 243	Franklin Grove	61031
Harmon	R. R. 1, Box 181	Harmon	61042
Palmyra	R. R. 1	Dixon	61021
Pine Grove	R. R. 2	Dixon	61021
Prairie Repose	R. R. 1, Box 17	Amboy	61310
Prairieville	R. R. 1	Rock Falls	61081

Sublette Evergreen	R. R. 2	Amboy	61310
Temperance Hill	218 W. Provost	Amboy	61310
Twin Grove	R. R. 1	Steward	60553
Union		Steward	60553
West Brooklyn Union		West Brooklyn	61378

Livingston

Ancona		Ancona	61311
Blackstone		Blackstone	61313
Central IL Memorial Park	119 E. Lee St.	Pontiac	61764
Defenbaugh	R. R. 1	Ancona	61311
Dwight	317 E. Seminole	Dwight	60420
Graceland	301 W. Chestnut	Fairbury	61739
Lawrenceville	7615 Bonus Hall Rd.	Garden Prairie	61038
McDowell	308 E. Delaware	Dwight	60420
Moons Point	R. R. 5	Streator	61364
Phillips	R. R. 1, Box 55	Ancona	61311
Sunbury	409 S. Main	Pontiac	61764
Union		Emington	60934
Union		Odell	60460
West Lawn	112 E. Washington	Pontiac	61764

Logan

Blue Grass		Atlanta	61723
Elkhart	511 E. Harry St.	Mt. Pulaski	62548
Harmony	508 Broadway	Lincoln	62656
Hartsburg Union		Hartsburg	62643
Ladies		Atlanta	61723
Laenna		Chestnut	62518
Lincoln Zion	R. R. 2	Lincoln	62656
Mount Joy		Atlanta	61723
Mount Pulaski		Mt. Pulaski	62548
Patterson	Box 211	Emden	62635
Pleasant Valley	Box 212	Middletown	62666
Union	333 Park Pl.	Lincoln	62656

Macon

Fairlawn	2101 N. Oakland Ave.	Decatur	62526
Graceland	2101 N. Oakland Ave.	Decatur	62526
Macon Co. Memorial Park	540 Millikin Ct.	Decatur	62523

Macoupin

Benld	210 S. Main	Benld	62009
Bethel Ridge	R. R. 3	Carlinville	62626
Brighton	Box 66	Brighton	62012
Bunker Hill	Box 65	Bunker Hill	62014
Chapmans Point Oak Grove		Modesto	62667
Chesterfield Gelder	R. R. 1	Chesterfield	62630
Land	R. R. 2	Greenfield	62044
Memorial Park	108 W. Henry	Staunton	62088
Moore	R. R. 2	Carlinville	62626
Mount Olive	R. R. 1, Box 196	Mount Olive	62069
Pleasant Hill	R. R. 1, Box 68	Virden	62690
Pulliam	Box 98	Modesto	62667
Rural	Box 495	Carlinville	62626
Scottville West		Scottville	62683
Shiloh Baptist	Box 141	Chesterfield	62630
Sulpher Springs	317 S. 8th	Girard	62640
Summerville	R. R. 1	Medora	62063
Union Chapel	R. R. 1	Girard	62640
Virden	115 E. Jackson St.	Virden	62690
Woodburn	R. R. 2	Bunker Hill	62014

Madison

Name	Address	City	ZIP
Alton	111 E. Broadway	Alton	62002
Buck Road	424 Randle	Edwardsville	62025
Fosterburg	R. R. 1, Box 539	Alton	62002
Godfrey	2216 Virginia Ave.	Alton	62002
Harris	R. R. 2	Edwardsville	62025
Hoxley	725 Taylor	Edwardsville	62025
Keystone		St. Jacob	62001
Liberty Prairie	524 Olive St.	Edwardsville	62025
New Douglas		New Douglas	62074
New Spangel	R. R. 2	Staunton	62088
Oaklawn	R. R. 2, Box 216	Highland	62249
Olive	R. R. 3, Box 310	Edwardsville	62085
Prairietown	R. R. 1, Box 31	Dorsey	62021
Rose Lawn Memorial Garden	201 Main St.	Moro	62067
St. Pauls	R. R. 6, Box 246	Edwardsville	62025
Short	Box 218 Culp Lane R. 2	Bethalto	62010
Sunset Hill	1909 Edison Ave.	Granite City	62040
Valley View Gardens	R. R. 7, Box 8	Edwardsville	62025
Valhalla Memorial Park	2306 W. Delmar	Godfrey	62035
Wanda	616 Hawthorne	Wood River	62095
Woodland Hill	370 6th St.	East Alton	62024
Woodlawn	715 Sherman Ave.	Edwardsville	62025

Marion

Hillcrest Memorial Park	16 S. Edgewood Ln.	Centralia	62801
Old Covenanter	Carter Rd.	Kell	62853
Salem Paradise	P. O. Box 156	Sandoval	62882
Summitt Prairie	R. R. 3	Salem	62881

Marshall

Bell	824 Luke St.	Ottawa	61350
Belle Plain		Toluca	61369
Evans Township Cumberland		Wenona	61377
Henry	105 Hickory	Henry	61537
Lacon	504 James St.	Lacon	61540
La Prairie Methodist	204 N. Broad St.	Sparland	61565
La Prairie U P		Sparland	61565
Rutland		Wenona	61377

Mason

Name	Address	City	ZIP
Meadow Lawn		Manito	61547
Pleasant Hill		Forest City	61532

Massac

Metropolis Memorial Gardens	R. R. 2, Box 226	Metropolis	62960

Mc Donough

Archer Bethal		Colchester	62326
Bushnell Mausoleum	22 Hillcrest	Bushnell	61422
Colchester		Colchester	62326
Doddsville	R. R. 1	Littleton	61452
Gibson		Colchester	62326
Harris		Table Grove	61482
Hickory Grove	R. R. 2	Good Hope	61438
Hill Grove		Tennessee	62374
Hutchinson		Tennessee	62374
Spring Creek		Sciota	61475
Vance	Box 114	Industry	61440

Mc Henry

Alden	9907 Knickerbocker Rd.	Harvard	60033
Big Foot	Box 220	Harvard	60033
Coral	650 E. Grant Hwy.	Marengo	60152
Crystal Lake Union	Box 464	Crystal Lake	60014
Dunham-Chemung		Harvard	60033
Franklinville	16018 R. R. 176	Union	60180
Greenwood	226 Mc Henry Ave.	Woodstock	60098
Harmony	17602 Harmony Rd.	Marengo	60152
Harvard	1107 Grant St.	Harvard	60033
Hebron	12004 4th St.	Hebron	60034
Highland Memorial Park	Box 209	Algonquin	60102
Jerome	1007 N. Jefferson St.	Harvard	60033
Linn Hebron	12201 Bigelow Ave.	Hebron	60034
Mc Henry Memorial Park	Box 4	Woodstock	60098
Ostend	1118 Zimmerman Rd.	Woodstock	60098
Riley	920 E. Grant Hwy.	Marengo	60152
Ringwood	5117 Barnard Mill Rd.	Ringwood	60072
St. Johns	142 Franke Ave.	Cary	60013
South Hebron	10418 Vander Karr Rd.	Hebron	60034
Union	6402 Elm	Union	60180
Windridge Memorial Gardens	7014 S. Radson Bridge Rd.	Cary	60013
Woodland	508 S. Rt. 31	Mc Henry	60050
Woodstock	315 S. Jefferson St.	Woodstock	60098

Mc Lean

Blooming Grove	R. R. 1	Heyworth	61743
Blue Mound		Cooksville	61730
Dawson		Lexington	61753
Denman	R. R. 1	Carlock	61725
East Lawn Memorial Garden	1002 Airport Rd.	Bloomington	61701
Friends	R. R. 1	Arrowsmith	61722
Funks Grove	1400 Mark Ln.	Normal	61761
Hinthorn	722 Normal Ave.	Normal	61761
Imhoff		Congerville	61729
Kampf	Box C	Stanford	61774
Mc Lean		Mc Lean	61754
New East Twin Grove	R. R. 1	Mc Lean	61754
Oak Grove	R. R. 2	Leroy	61752
Park Hill	Box 246	Bloomington	61701
Park Lawn	402 N. Sherman	Danvers	61732
Pennell	R. R. 1	Towanda	61776
Pleasant Hill	713 N. Main	Bloomington	61701
Rosewood	R. R. 4	Bloomington	61701
Scogin Hill		Mc Lean	61754
Smiths Grove	R. R. 1, Box 136	Towanda	61776
Stouts Grove	R. R. 2	Danvers	61732
White Oak	R. R. 3, Box 243	Eureka	61530
Wiley		Colfax	61728

Menard

Concord	Chapin State Bank	Chapin	62631
Indian Point		Athens	62613
Joel Hall	206 N. Main	Athens	62613
Menard Rock Creek	R. R. 1	Petersburg	62675
Petersburg Oakland	Box 439	Petersburg	62675
Rose Hill	Box 299	Petersburg	62675
Sugar Grove	R. R. 1	Greenview	62642
Walnut Ridge	R. R. 1	Greenview	62642

Mercer

Alexis	Box 505	Alexis	61412
Eliza Creek	28215 190th Ave. W.	Illinois City	61272
Hamlet	R. R. 3	Aledo	61231
Hopewell	Box 110	New Windsor	61465
Leech	Box 295	Joy	61260
Mannon	R. R. 1	New Boston	61272
Millersburg	307 S. East 8th Ave.	Aledo	61231
Mt. Vernon		North Henderson	61466
Mt. Vernon Lutheran		North Henderson	61466
New Windsor	Box 193	New Windsor	61465
Norwood	R. R. 1, Box 84	Aledo	61412
Peniel		New Boston	61272
Preemption	916 127th Ave. W.	Preemption	61276
Sugar Grove	R. R. 1	Reynolds	61279

Montgomery

Cedar Ridge	R. R. 1	Litchfield	62056
Crabtree	802 S. Jackson St.	Litchfield	62056
Cress Hill	309 Hunt Ave.	Hillsboro	62049
Donnellson	Box 37	Donnellson	62019
Edgewood		Litchfield	62056
Elm Lawn Memorial Park	Box 130	Taylorville	62568
Elmwood	401 N. Madison	Litchfield	62056
Fillmore Glendale		Fillmore	62032
Irving	Box 185	Irvine	52051
Kirkland		Sorento	62086
Macoupin Creek		Waggoner	62572
Montgomery		Butler	62015
Mount Moriah	R. R. 2	Greenville	62246
Nokomis		Nokomis	62075
Oak Grove	718 S. Main St.	Hillsboro	62049
Olive Hill	406 Grand	Coffeen	62017
Raymond	R. R. 2	Raymond	62560
Rovey		Girard	62640
Trinity Lutheran	R. R. 3	Litchfield	62056
Wares Grove	R. R. 3	Litchfield	62056
Woodside	R. R. 1	Fillmore	62032

Morgan

Antioch	R. R. 3	Jacksonville	62650
Arcadia	R. R. 1	Jacksonville	62650
Asbury	R. R. 5	Jacksonville	62650
Berea		Ashland	62612
Diamond Grove Memorial	73 Central Park Plaza	Jacksonville	62650
East	343 W. Temple	Waverly	62692
Ebenezer	R. R. 1	Jacksonville	62650
Franklin	R. R. 2	Franklin	62638
Grace	R. R. 1	Meredosia	62665
Jacksonville Memorial Lawn	4 Dunlap Ct.	Jacksonville	62650
Morgan Co. Concord	716 Cooper St.	Chapin	62631
Sheppard	R. R. 5	Jacksonville	62650
West Liberty	R. R. 2	Franklin	62638
Yatesville	R. R. 1	Ashland	62612

Moultrie

Graham Chapel	R. R. 1	Sullivan	61951
Waggoner	Box 4	Gays	61928

Ogle

Adeline	R. R. 1	Mt. Morris	61039
Byron	427 W. 3	Byron	61010
Chapel Hill		Chana	61015
Daysville	402 N. 6th St.	Oregon	61061
Fairmount	R. R. 2	Polo	61064
Flagg Center	R. R. 1	Chana	61015
Grand Detour	R. R. 3	Dixon	61021
Haldane	R. R. 2	Forreston	61030
Lighthouse	R. R. 1	Oregon	61061
Lightsville		Leaf River	61047
Lindenwood	Box 54	Lindenwood	61049
Monroe Center	901 Carlisle Dr.	Rochelle	61068
Mount Pleasant		Stillman Valley	61084
North Grove		Egan	61026
Oakwood	405 E. Hitt	Mount Morris	61054
Pine Creek	R. R. 2	Polo	61064
Plainview	208 E. Brayton Rd.	Mount Morris	61054
Riverside	R. R. 2 Bottom Rd.	Freeport	61032
River View	200 S. 7	Oregon	61061
Roseland	R. R. 1	Kirkland	60146
Silver Creek	405 W. Front	Mount Morris	61054
Stillman		Stillman Valley	61084
Stinsonian	803 Webster	Oregon	61061
Trinity Memory Gardens	308-1/2 Lincoln Hwy.	Rochelle	61068
Washington Grove	' 508 10th Ave.	Rochelle	61068
West Grove	604 3rd Ave.	Forreston	61030
White Oak		Forreston	61030
White Rock		Kings	61045
Woodlawn	R. R. 1	Esmond	60129

Peoria

American Mausoleum	1400 S. 2nd St.	Morton	61550
Blue Ridge	R. R. 1	Edelstein	61526
Catholic	2105 W. Heading	Peoria	61603
Dickison	R. R. 2, Box 159	Princeville	61559
French Grove	R. R. 3	Elmwood	61529
Glendale		Laura	61451
Hillcrest Memorial Gardens	4601 Rt. 150	Peoria	61603
Lancaster		Glasford	61533
Lutheran	914 S. Pleasant	Peoria	61603
Maple Ridge	Box 171	Glasford	61533
Memorial Consultants	1916 N. Knoxville Ave.	Peoria	61603
Mount Hawley	Martin Rd.	Edelstein	61526
Parkview Memorial Park	Box 702	Peoria	61533
Springdale Memorial	3014 N. Prospect	Peoria	61603

Perry

Sunset Memorial Park	403 N. Hickory	Du Quoin	62832

Pike

Barry		Barry	62312
Baylis		Baylis	62314
Bethel	R. R. 1	Griggsville	62340
Blue River	R. R. 1, Box 236	Pittsfield	62363
Brown		Chambersburg	62323
Brown Simpkins	Box 414	Griggsville	62340
Burbridge	408 Commerce	Pleasant Hill	62366
Crescent Heights		Pleasant Hill	62366
Douglas	R. R. 1	Pearl	62361
French	R. R. 1	Pearl	61261

Gray		New Salem	62357
Green Pond	R. R. 1	Pittsfield	62363
Griggsville		Griggsville	62340
Hinman	R. R. 1	Griggsville	62340
Kinderhook		Kinderhook	62345
Maysville		Griggsville	62340
Milton Smith		Milton	62352
Mound City National	P. O. Box 128	Mound City	62963
Nebo	R. R. 1	Nebo	62355
New Canton	R. R. 2	Barry	62312
New Pleasant Grove	R. R. 3	Pittsfield	62363
Oakwood	Box 498	Perry	62362
Park Lawn		Barry	62312
Perry Wells	117 S. Monroe	Pittsfield	62363
Pittsfield West	Box 371	Pittsfield	62363
Prairie Mound	R. R. 2, Box 138	Pittsfield	62363
Samuel Taylor		Rockport	62370
Summer Hill	R. R. 1	Summer Hill	62372
Swiggett		New Salem	62357
Taylor Martin	R. R. 1	Pleasant Hill	62366
Time		Pittsfield	62363
Woodland	R. R. 1	Baylis	62314

Pope

Independence	R. R. 2	Golconda	62938

Pulaski

Beech Grove	Box 56	Mound City	62963
Cairo		Villa Ridge	62996
Spencer Heights Memorial	R. R. 1, Box 50	Mounds	62964
Ullin		Ullin	62992

Putnam

Granville		Granville	61326
Granville Mausoleum	R. R. 1, Box 53F	Granville	61326
Henepin Riverside		Hennepin	61327

Randolph

Coulterville	Box 155	Coulterville	62237
New Palestine		Ellis Grove	62241
Randolph Methodist		Walsh	62297
Union	R. R. 1	Sparta	62286

Richland

Crest Haven Memorial Park	R. R. 1, Hwy. 50	Claremont	62421
Parkersburg Oak Hill		Parkersburg	62452

Rock Island

Buffalo Prairie	Box 2	Buffalo Prairie	61237
Chippiannock	2901 12th St.	Rock Island	61201
Edgington	14321 134th Ave. W.	Taylor Ridge	61284
Fairfield	23725 115th Ave. N.	Port Byron	61275
Memorial Park	3217 15th St.	Moline	61265
Pleasant Point	25802 94th Ave.	Port Byron	61275
Reynolds		Reynolds	61279
Rock Island National	Park Island Arsenal	Rock Island	61299

St. Clair

Freedom Hecker	705 S. Jackson	Belleville	62221
Green Mount	17 N. 3rd	Belleville	62221
Lake View Memorial Gardens	1 Alhambra Ct.	Belleville	62221
Shiloh	R. R. 1	O'Fallon	62269
Sunset Gardens of Memory	2114 Missouri Ave.	E. St. Louis	62205

Saline

Durham	R. R. 2	Galatia	62935

Sangamon

Auburn	302 S. 6th St.	Auburn	62615
Brunk	R. R. 1	Pawnee	62558
Brush Creek		Divernon	62530
Campbell	R. R. 1	Loami	62661
Camp Butler National	R. F. D. 1	Springfield	62707
Cumberland Sugar Creek	R. R. 2	Auburn	62615
Fancy Creek	One Old Capitol Plaza N.	Springfield	62701
Mechanicsburg	Box 346	Buffalo	62515
Mottarville	209 E. Mill St.	Rochester	62563
Oak Hill	R. R. 1	Springfield	62707
Philemon Stout	R. R. 1	Chatham	62629
Roselawn Memorial Park	437 S. Grand W.	Springfield	62705
South Fork	R. R. 1	Rochester	62563
Taylor	R. R. 1	Riverton	62561
West	2129 S. Walnut	Springfield	62704
Woodreath	R. R. 2	New Berlin	62670

Schuyler

Bethany	474 W. Madison	Rushville	62681
Round Prairie		Plymouth	62367

Scott

Benjamin Green		Bluffs	62621
Bowers	R. R. 1	Roodhouse	62082
Exeter	14 E. Jefferson St.	Winchester	62694
Fairview		Bluffs	62621
Glasgow	R. R. 1	Winchester	62694
Hillcrest		Bluffs	62621
Manchester		Manchester	62663
Naples		Bluffs	62621
Winchester Public		Winchester	62694

Shelby

Oconee Mound	R. R. 1	Oconee	62553
Tower Hill	Box 5	Tower Hill	62571

Stark

Osceola Grove		Bradford	61421
Stringtown		Tonlon	61483
Wyoming	409 N. 7th	Wyoming	61491

Stephenson

Name	Address	City	ZIP
Afolkey	R. R. 1	Dakota	61018
Basswood		Winslow	61089
Belleview	1436 S. Oak	Freeport	61032
Cedarville		Cedarville	61013
Chapel Hill Memorial Park	2514 Illinois	Freeport	61032
Christian Hollow	R. R. 1	Winslow	61089
City	902-959 W. Lincoln Blvd.	Freeport	61032
Cranes Grove	701 Alamo Dr.	Freeport	61032
Ellis	5988 Loran Rd.	Freeport	61032
Eleroy	1656 S. Highland Ave.	Freeport	61032
Frankenbergen	R. R. 1	Rock City	61070
Freeport Memorial Garden	1330 Monticello	Freeport	61032
Grandview	2438 Hwy. 26 N.	Freeport	61032
Greenwood	R. R. 2	Lena	61048
Gund	710 John St.	Pecatonica	61063
Lane		Shannon	61078
Louisa		Lena	61048
Manny	Box 593	Lena	61048
Mount Pleasant	110 S. East St.	Orangeville	61060
New Dakota		Dakota	61018
Oakland	1449 Bolkinwood Dr.	Freeport	61032
Oneco	Box 213	Orangeville	61060
Orangeville	Box 127	Orangeville	61060
Richland Center	216 Valley View Dr.	Orangeville	61060
Rock City		Rock City	61070
Rock Grove Union		Rock City	61070
Rock Lily	234 Carver	Winslow	61089
Rock Run Pioneer	R. R. 1, Box 124	Dakota	61018
St. James Union		Orangeville	61060
Schudt, J. G.	14507 W. Coomber Rd.	Lena	61043
Silent Hill	Box 37	Mc Connell	61050
Silver Springs	3749 S. Walnut Rd.	Freeport	61032
State Road	11763 Goddard Rd.	Lena	61048
Yellow Creek Union	R. R. 1	Pearl City	61062

Tazewell

Name	Address	City	ZIP
Antioch	R. R. 2	Tremont	61568
Delavan	701 Oak St.	Delavan	61734
Dillon	1716 Deppert Dr.	Pekin	61554
Glenwood	Box 403	Mackinaw	61755
Green Valley		Green Valley	61534
Hirstein	339 N. Nebraska	Morton	61550
Hollands Grove	127 Hollands Grove Rd.	Washington	61571
Ladies Mount Hope	Box 231	Tremont	61568
Lakeside & Lakeview	1800 N. 8th St.	Pekin	61555
Little Mackinaw	311 N. Main Ave.	Minier	61759
Minier		Minier	61759
Orendorff		Hopedale	61747
Sand Prairie		Green Valley	61534
Shiloh		Hopedale	61747
Union	R. R. 1	Washington	61571
Woodrow	1224 Prince St.	Pekin	61554

Vermilion

Atherton	10 E. Williams	Danville	61832
Danville	1900 E. Main St.	Danville	61832
Davis		Fairmount	61841
Dougherty	R. R. 1, Box 235	Fairmount	61841
Embery		Collison	61831
Farmers Chapel	R. R. 3	Danville	61832
Fithian & Muncie Stearns	Box 128	Fithian	61844

146

Forest Park	320 Vermilion	Georgetown	61846
Gordon	1800 Perrysville Rd. #8	Danville	61832
Greenview	103 S. Park St.	Fairmount	61841
Greenwood	R. R. 1, Box 11	Danville	61832
Partlow		Armstrong	61812
Pleasant Grove	R. R. 1	Oakwood	61858
Spring Hill	15 W. Main	Danville	61832
Sunset Memorial Park	R. R. 3, Box 11	Danville	61832
Walnut Corner	R. R. 1	Bismarck	61814
Woodlawn		Indianola	61850

Wabash

Adams Corner	R. R. 1	Allendale	624,10
Allendale		Allendale	62410
Armstrong	R. R. 1	Allendale	62410
Highland Memorial	527 Mulberry St.	Mount Carmel	62863

Warren

Gerlaw	Box 44	Gerlaw	61435
Little York		Little York	61453
Monmouth	720 N. 6th St.	Monmouth	61462
Mosher	R. R. 1	Monmouth	61462
Ogden	R. R. 2, Box 158A	Galesburg	61401
Point Pleasant	R. R. 1	Roseville	61473
Roseville Memorial Park		Roseville	61473
Silent Home	Box 202	Cameron	61423
Sugar Tree Grove	R. R. 3	Monmouth	61462
Warren County Memorial	R. R. 2	Monmouth	61462

Washington

Beaucoup	R. R. 2	Ashley	62808
Greenwood	411 W. Lebanon	Nashville	62263

Wayne

Fransworth		Wayne City	62895
Maple Hill	E. Highway	Fairfield	62837
Willow Branch	R. R. 1	Rinard	62878

White

Union Ridge	R. R. 1	Norris City	62869

Whiteside

Cottonwood Community	R. R. 1	Morrison	61270
East Jordan	R. R. 2	Chadwick	61014
Heaton	22434 Lyndon Rd.	Morrison	61270
Lyndon	107 4th St. E.	Lyndon	61261
North Clyde	21272 Lyndon Rd.	Morrison	61270
Oakknoll	704 W. 11th St.	Sterling	61081
Oakknoll Memorial Park	R. R. 2	Sterling	61081
Riverside	113 High St.	Prophetstown	61277
Rock Creek	507 Market St.	Prophetstown	61277
Tampico Memorial	Box 398	Tampico	61283

Will

Adams	1087 Douglas Ln.	Crete	60417
Barnett	R. R. 1, Box 370	Lockport	60441
Braidwood Oakwood	114 S. Center	Braidwood	60408
Brooks	Box 255	Lockport	60441
Brown Church	R. R. 1, Box 143	Elwood	60421

Crete	732 Jefferson St.	Crete	60417
Evergreen Hill	P. O. Box 283	Steger	60475
Elmhurst	1212 E. Washington St.	Joliet	60433
Frankfort	112 Luther Ln.	Frankfort	60423
Green Garden Green View	R. R. 2	Manhattan	60442
Hillcrest	540 S. Webster	Naperville	60540
Lockport	538 Madison St.	Lockport	60441
Lutheran Memorial	23060 W. Jefferson	Joliet	60435
Manhattan	130 Eastern Ave.	Manhattan	60442
Maple Hill	R. R. 1 Box 176	Elmwood	60421
North Providence Ridge	R. R. 1, Box 147	Manhattan	60442
Oakwood		Joliet	60431
Oakwood	453 Fulton St.	Willmington	60481
Rosehill	R. R. 1, Box 259	Frankfort	60423
Peotone	Box 488	Peotone	60468
Pleasant Hill	136 Nebraska St.	Frankfort	60423
Skyline Memorial Park	R. R. 50	Monee	60449
Twining	637 Locust St.	Frankfort	60423
Wesley	R. R. 1, Box 34	Willmington	60481
Willard Grove	R. R. 2	Minooka	60447
Woodlawn Memorial Park	Troy Rd.	Joliet	60435

Winnebago

Arlington Memorial	1015 20th St.	Rockford	61110
Cedar Bluff	301 Main St.	Genoa	60135
Cherry Valley	4633 River Rd.	Cherry Valley	61016
Durand	520 Medina St.	Durand	61024
Durand Crane	R. R. 1	Durand	61024
Floral Lawns	835 Dearborn	S. Beloit	61080
Guilford	125 S. Highland Ave.	Rockford	61108
Guilford Union	7141 Guilford Rd.	Rockford	61107
Harlem	5424 Mc Farland Rd.	Rockford	61111
Howard	9256 N. Pecatonica Rd.	Pecatonica	61063
Hulse	15983 Trask Bridge Rd.	Pecatonica	61063
Middle Creek	12439 Montague Rd.	Winnebago	61082
New Milford	2161 New Milford School	Rockford	61109
Oakland Burial Grounds	R. R. 1	Durand	61024
Pecatonica	405 W. Fourth St.	Pecatonica	61063
Rockford	N. Main & Auburn Sts.	Rockford	61103
Scandinavian	1700 Rural St.	Rockford	61110
Scottish - Willow Creek		Caledonia	61011
Twelve Mile Grove		Pecatonica	61063
Willwood Burial Park	7111 W. State St.	Rockford	61102
Winnebago		Winnebago	61088

Woodford

Baptist	101 N. Main St.	Washburn	61570
Deer Creek Mount Zion		Deer Creek	61733
East White Oak		Carlock	61725
Linn Mount Vernon	101 S. Jefferson	Washburn	61570
Oakwood	117 E. Partridge	Metamora	61548
Spring Bay	R. R. 1	East Peoria	61611
Stewart Harmony	417 W. Monroe	Metamora	61548

CHAMBERS OF COMMERCE

Adams	314 Maine	Quincy	62301
Alexander	222 8th St.	Cairo	62914
Bond	P. O. Box 283	Greenville	62246
Boone	402 S. State St.	Belvidere	61008
Brown	None		
Bureau	435 S. Main St.	Princeton	61356
		Walnut	61376
	P. O. Box 321	Wyanet	61379
Calhoun	None		
Carroll	423 Main St.	Savanna	61074
Cass	307 State	Beardstown	62618
Champaign	109 W. University Ave.	Champaign	61820
	117 N. Garrard	Rantoul	61866
	P. O. Box 459	Urbana	61801
Christian	Third & Poplar Sts.	Pana	62557
	200 W. Market St.	Taylorville	62568
Clark	P. O. Box 343	Casey	62420
	P. O. Box 263	Marshall	62441
	P. O. Box 429	Martinsville	62442
Clay	127 W. North Ave.	Flora	62839
Clinton	None		
Coles	501 Jackson	Charleston	61920
	1701 Wabash Ave.	Mattoon	61938
Cook	12159 S. Pulaski Rd.	Alsip	60658
	215 N. Arlington Hts. Rd.	Arlington Heights	60006
	335 S. Main	Bartlett	60103
	324 N. Hough St.	Barrington	60010
	P. O. Box 86	Bellwood	60104
	13122 S. Western Ave.	Blue Island	60406
	8929 S. Harlem Ave.	Bridgeview	60455
	P. O. Box 1192	Calumet City	60409
	4363 S. Archer Ave.	Chicago	60632
	130 S. Michigan Ave.	Chicago	60603
	3258 W. 64th Pl.	Chicago	60629
	1402 W. 103rd St.	Chicago	60643
	One N. La Salle St.	Chicago	60602
	7022 S. Shore Dr.	Chicago	60649
	5415 W. Devon	Chicago	60646
	36 S. State St.	Chicago	60603
	4651 N. Milwaukee Ave.	Chicago	60630
	11 W. Illinois St.	Chicago	60610
	310 S. Michigan Blvd.	Chicago	60604
	2449 N. Harlem Ave.	Chicago	60635
	4920 W. Irving Park Rd.	Chicago	60641
	7001 N. Clark St.	Chicago	60626
	500 N. Michigan Ave.	Chicago	60611
	135 S. La Salle	Chicago	60603
	J. Reardon, Britannica Ctr.	Chicago	60604

	4753 N. Broadway	Chicago	60640
	1630 Chicago Rd.	Chicago Heights	60411
	P. O. Box 75	Chicago Ridge	60415
	5341 W. Cermak Rd.	Cicero	60650
	800 S. Lee St.	Des Plaines	60016
	14020 Park Ave.	Dolton	60419
	20 Lively Blvd.	Elk Grove Village	60007
	807 Davis St.	Evanston	60201
	2805 W. 95th St.	Evergreen Park	60642
	7451 Madison St.	Forest Park	60130
	9606 Franklin Ave.	Franklin Park	60131
	710 Glencoe Rd.	Glencoe	60022
	2320 Glenview Rd.	Glenview	60025
	340 Illinois Ave.	Glenwood	60425
	154th & Broadway	Harvey	60426
	7800 W. 95th St.	Hickory Hills	60457
	2020 Chestnur Rd.	Homewood	60430
	P. O. Box 387	La Grange	60525
	6618 Osceola Trail	La Grange	60525
	21 W. Hillgrove	La Grange	60525
	18225 Burnham	Lansing	60438
	111 Illinois St.	Lemont	60439
	4433 W. Touhy	Lincolnwood	60646
	7710 W. Ogden Ave.	Lyons	60534
	411 W. Madison	Maywood	60153
	1816 Lake St.	Melrose Park	60160
	6101 Capulina Ave.	Morton Grove	60053
	100 S. Emerson	Mount Prospect	60056
	328 Golf Mill Prof. Bldg.	Niles	60648
	1435 Shermer Rd.	Northbrook	60062
	140 E. North Ave.	Northlake	60164
	15440 S. Central Ave.	Oak Forest	60452
	9526 S. Cook Ave.	Oak Lawn	60453
	P. O. Box 14	Oak Lawn	60454
	948 Lake St.	Oak Park	60301
	500 Ravinia Pl.	Orland Park	60462
	101 S. Northwest Hwy.	Palatine	60067
	P. O. Box 1949	Park Forest	60466
	800 Busse Hwy.	Park Ridge	60068
	208 W. 144th St.	Riverdale	60627
	P. O. Box 7	Riverside	60546
	3240 Kirchoff Rd.	Rolling Meadows	60008
	2600 Sauk Trail	Sauk Village	60411
	1900 E. Golf Rd.	Schaumburg	60195
	P. O. Box 53	Skokie	60077
	7655 W. 63rd St.	Summit	60501
	17032 Oak Park Ave.	Tinley Park	60477
	255 W. Dundee	Wheeling	60090
	1150 Wilmette Ave.	Wilmette	60091
	841 Spruce St.	Winnetka	60093
	P. O. Box 217	Worth	60482
Crawford	220 S. Main	Palestine	62451
	1-1/2 W. Walnut	Robinson	62454
Cumberland	P. O. Box 487	Neoga	62447
De Kalb	363-1/2 E. Lincoln Hwy.	De Kalb	60115
	425 W. Main St.	Genoa	60135
	8 E. Railroad St.	Sandwich	60548
	303 Navaho	Shabbona	60550
	206 W. State St.	Sycamore	60178
De Witt	100 S. Center St.	Clinton	61727

County	Address	City	ZIP
Douglas	P. O. Box 337	Tuscola	61953
Du Page	131 W. Lake St.	Addison	60101
	3724 Grand Blvd.	Brookfield	60513
	1037 Curtiss St.	Downers Grove	60515
	5202 Washington	Downers Grove	60515
	122 N. York St.	Elmhurst	60126
	526 Crescent Blvd.	Glen Ellyn	60137
	22 E. First St.	Hinsdale	60521
	1040 Burlington	Lisle	60532
	901 S. Main	Lombard	60148
	P. O. Box 832	Naperville	60566
	616 Enterprise Dr.	Oak Brook	60521
	31 S. Prospect	Roselle	60172
	53 E. St. Charles Rd.	Villa Park	60181
	P. O. Box 432	Warrenville	60555
	306 Main St.	West Chicago	60185
	117 S. Linden Ave.	Westmont	60559
	211 W. Wesley St.	Wheaton	60187
Edgar	156 E. Wood St.	Paris	61944
Edwards	404 S. 2nd St.	Albion	62806
Effingham	201 S. St. Clair St.	Altamont	62411
	307 N. Third St.	Effingham	62401
Fayette	P. O. Box 238	Vandalia	62471
Ford	126 N. Sangamon Ave.	Gibson City	60936
	518 E. Orleans	Paxton	60957
Franklin	500 W. Main St.	Benton	62812
	P. O. Box 367	Sesser	62884
	610 W. Main St.	West Frankfort	62896
Fulton	49 S. Main	Canton	61520
	501 E. Euclid Ave.	Lewistown	61542
Greene	P. O. Box 257	White Hall	62092
Grundy	112 E. Washington	Morris	60450
Hamilton	402 S. Jackson St.	Mc Leansboro	62859
Hancock	523 Main St.	Carthage	62321
	C of C Tourist Center	Nauvoo	62354
Henderson	208 E. Broadway	Monmouth	61462
Henry	300 Main St.	Galva	61434
	200 N. State	Geneseo	61254
	113 E. Second	Kewanee	61443
Iroquois	P. O. Box 127	Cissna Park	60924
	108 N. Central	Gilman	60938
	P. O. Box 283	Milford	60953
	109 W. Seminary Ave.	Onarga	60955
	119 W. Walnut St.	Watseka	60970
Jackson	105 S. University Ave.	Carbondale	62901
	19 N. 11th St.	Murphysboro	62966
Jefferson	P. O. Box 1047	Mr. Vernon	62864
Jersey	120 W. Pearl	Jerseyville	62052

Jo Daviess	101 Bouthillier	Galena	61036
Kane	40 W. Downer Pl.	Aurora	60507
	327 W. Wilson St.	Batavia	60510
	1200 L. W. Besinger Dr.	Carpentersville	60110
	28 N. Grove Ave.	Elgin	60120
	5 N. Third	Geneva	60134
	201 S. State	Hampshire	60140
	4 E. Main St.	St. Charles	60174
Kankakee	409 S. Main	Bourbonnais	60914
	P. O. Box 437	Herscher	60941
	388 E. Court St.	Kankakee	60901
	P. O. Box 574	Manteno	60950
	111 N. Dixie Hwy.	Momence	60954
Kendall	101 W. Main St.	Plano	60545
	1304 Sunset Ave.	Yorkville	60560
Knox	P. O. Box 21	Abingdon	61410
	154 E. Simmons St.	Galesburg	61401
Lake	880 Main St.	Antioch	60002
	730 Waukegan Rd.	Deerfield	60015
	P. O. Box 66	Fox Lake	60020
	202 Center St.	Grayslake	60030
	1811 St. John Ave.	Highland Park	60035
	272 Market Square	Lake Forest	60045
	522 W. Main St.	Lake Zurich	60047
	430 E. Hawley	Mundelein	60060
	Goodnow/Avilon Blvds.	Round Lake	60073
	368 E. Liberty St.	Wauconda	60084
	414 N. Sheridan Rd.	Waukegan	60085
	2820 Sheridan Rd.	Zion	60099
La Salle	535 Third St.	La Salle	61301
	469 Main St.	Marseilles	61341
	728 Main St.	Mendota	61342
	100 W. Lafayette St.	Ottawa	61350
	124 N. Bloomington St.	Streator	61364
Lawrence	1104 Jefferson St.	Lawrenceville	62439
Lee	74 S. Galena	Dixon	61021
	13 E. 4th St.	Sterling	61081
Livingston	120 S. Franklin St.	Dwight	60420
	P. O. Box 178	Fairbury	61739
	223 N. Mill	Pontiac	61764
Logan	419 Pulaski	Lincoln	62656
Mc Donough	P. O. Box 111	Bushnell	61422
	301 W. Calhoun St.	Macomb	61455
Mc Henry	179 S. Northwest Hwy.	Cary	60013
	427 Virginia St.	Crystal Lake	60014
	P. O. Box 51	Fox River Grove	60021
	79 N. Ayer St.	Harvard	60033
	108 W. Prairie	Marengo	60152
	1257 N. Green St.	Mc Henry	60050
	105 E. Judd St.	Woodstock	60098
Mc Lean	210 S. East St.	Bloomington	61701
Macon	250 N. Water	Decatur	62525

County	Address	City	ZIP
Macoupin	801 Warren St.	Bunker Hill	62014
	126 S. Broad	Carlinville	62626
	P. O. Box 199	Mount Olive	62069
	213 W. Main St.	Staunton	62088
Madison	200 Piasa St.	Alton	62002
	211 W. Main St.	Collinsville	62234
	N. 20 Terminal Dr.	East Alton	62024
	118 Hillsboro	Edwardsville	62025
	1831 Delmar Ave.	Granite City	62040
	109 E. 1st St.	Hartford	62048
	429 Walnut	Highland	62249
	437 Dulany Ave.	Wood River	62095
Marion	213 S. Locust St.	Centralia	62801
	101 S. Broadway	Salem	62881
Marshall	429 Edward St.	Henry	61537
Mason	P. O. Box 109	Havana	62644
Massac	610 Market St.	Metropolis	62960
Menard	117 N. 6th St.	Petersburg	62675
Mercer	P. O. Box 168	Aledo	61231
	P. O. Box 345	Viola	61486
Monroe	120 N. Main St.	Waterloo	62298
Montgomery	114-1/2 E. Wood St.	Hillsboro	62049
	115 E. Ryder St.	Litchfield	62056
Morgan	220 E. Morgan	Jacksonville	62650
Moultrie	P. O. Box 221	Arthur	61911
	200 W. Harrison	Sullivan	61951
Ogle	P. O. Box 364	Oregon	61061
	116 S. Franklin	Polo	61064
	501 N. Sixth St.	Rochelle	61068
Peoria	1007 N. Second	Chillicothe	61523
	116 S. Capitol St.	Pekin	61554
	230 S. W. Adams	Peoria	61602
Perry	412 S. Main St.	Pinckneyville	62274
Piatt	102 E. Livingston	Monticello	61856
Pike	P. O. Box 283	Pittsfield	62363
Randolph	R.R. 2, Box 177a	Chester	62233
	P. O. Box 93	Sparta	62286
	P. O. Box 177	Steeleville	62288
Richland	110 E. York St.	Olney	62450
Rock Island	622 19th St.	Moline	61265
	329 18th St.	Rock Island	61201
St. Clair	334 W. Main St.	Belleville	62222
	905 Falling Springs Rd.	Cahokia	62206
	327 Missouri Ave.	E. St. Louis	62201
	10850 Lincoln Trail	Fairview Heights	62208
	301 N. Main St.	Freeburg	62243
	126 W. Main St.	Lebanon	62254

	P. O. Box 175	Mascoutah	62258
	P. O. Box A	New Athens	62264
	P. O. Box 722	New Baden	62265
	111 W. State	Ofallon	62269
Saline	Harrisburg Nation Bank	Harrisburg	62946
Sangamon	3 W. Old State Capitol Plz.	Springfield	62701
	215 E. Adams St.	Springfield	62701
Schuyler	645 W. Lafayette	Rushville	62681
Shelby	246 E. Main St.	Shelbyville	62565
Stark	105 N. Seventh	Wyoming	61491
Stephenson	10 N. Galena Ave.	Freeport	61032
Tazewell	113 E. Washington St.	East Peoria	61611
	134 W. Adams St.	Morton	61550
	100 Washington Savings Ct.	Washington	61571
Union	125 W. Davie St.	Anna	62906
Vermilion	211 N. Walnut	Danville	61832
	P. O. Box 346	Hoopeston	60942
Wabash	123 W. 4th St.	Mt. Carmel	62863
Warren	Route 1	Roseville	61473
Washington	P. O. Box 128	Okawville	62271
Wayne	P. O. Box 528	Cisne	62823
	107 N. E. Second St.	Fairfield	62837
White	225 E. Main	Carmi	62821
Whiteside	P. O. Box 253	Fulton	61252
	129-1/2 E. Main St.	Morrison	61270
	601 W. 10th St.	Rock Falls	61071
Will	536 Maxwell St.	Beecher	60401
	498 W. Boughton Rd.	Bolington	60439
	P. O. Box 431	Channahon	60410
	1395 C. Main	Crete	60417
	9 W. Nebraska	Frankfort	60423
	906 S. State St.	Lockport	60441
	P. O. Box 555	Manhattan	60442
	P. O. Box 67	Mokena	60448
	P. O. Box 183	Monee	60449
	P. O. Box 18	New Lenox	60451
	204 S. West St.	Peotone	60468
	626 Town Hall Dr.	Romeoville	60441
	201 Winchester Ct.	Wilmington	60481
Williamson	1 S. Park Ave.	Herrin	62948
	1007-1/2 W. Main	Marion	62959
Winnebago	P. O. Box 2203	Loves Park	61131
	815 E. State St.	Rockford	61110
	P. O. Box 316	Rockton	61072
Woodford	52 N. Elm	El Paso	61738

COLLEGES AND UNIVERSITIES

Adams

John Wood Community	48th & Main	Quincy	62301
Quincy	1831 College	Quincy	62301

Bond

Greenville	315 E. College	Greenville	62246

Champaign

Parkland	2400 W. Bradley Ave.	Champaign	61820
University of IL - Urbana		Urbana	61801

Coles

Eastern IL		Charleston	61920
Lakeland	South Rt. 45	Mattoon	61938

Cook

Aero-Space Institute	160 E. Grand	Chicago	60610
Alfred Adler Institute	159 N. Dearborn	Chicago	60601
American Academy of Art	220 S. State St.	Chicago	60604
American Con. of Music	116 S. Michigan Ave.	Chicago	60603
Catholic Theological Union	5401 S. Cornell Ave.	Chicago	60615
Central YMCA Community	211 W. Wacker Dr.	Chicago	60606
Chicago Academy of Music	300 N. State St.	Chicago	60610
Chicago City-Wide	209 N. Michigan Ave.	Chicago	60601
Chicago College of Comm.	36 S. Wabash Ave.	Chicago	60603
Chicago College of Osteo-pathic Medicine	1122 E. 53rd St.	Chicago	60615
Chicago Conservatory	410 S. Michigan Ave.	Chicago	60605
Chicago-Kent College of Law	77 S. Wacker Dr.	Chicago	60606
Chicago Medical School	2020 W. Ogden	Chicago	60612
Chicago State University	95th & M. L. King Dr.	Chicago	60628
Chicago Technical	2000 S. Michigan Ave.	Chicago	60616
Chicago Theological Seminary	5757 S. University	Chicago	60637
Columbia	600 S. Michigan Ave.	Chicago	60605
Concordia Teachers	7400 Augusta St.	Oak Park	60305
Coyne American Institute	1235 W. Fullerton Ave.	Chicago	60614
Daniel Hale Williams	5247 W. Madison St.	Chicago	60644
De Lourdes	353 N. River Rd.	Des Plaines	60016
De Paul	25 E. Jackson St.	Chicago	60604
De Vry Inst. of Technology	3300 N. Campbell	Chicago	60618
Emmaus Bible School	156 N. Oak Park Ave.	Oak Park	60301
Felician	3800 W. Peterson Ave.	Chicago	60659
Garrett Theological Seminary	2121 Sheridan Rd.	Evanston	60201
Harrington Institute of Interior Design	410 S. Michigan Ave.	Chicago	60605
Hebrew Theological	7135 Carpenter Rd.	Skokie	60077
IL College of Optometry	3241 S. Michigan Ave.	Chicago	60616
IL Institute of Technology	3300 S. Federal	Chicago	60616
IL College of Podiatric Med.	1001 N. Dearborn St.	Chicago	60610
Industrial Engineering	205 W. Wacker Dr.	Chicago	60605
Jesuit School of Theology	5430 S. University Ave.	Chicago	60615
John Marshall Law	315 S. Plymouth Ct.	Chicago	60604
Keller Graduate School of Management	10 S. Riverside Plaza	Chicago	60606
Kendall	2408 Orrington Ave.	Evanston	60201
Kennedy-King	6800 S. Wentworth Ave.	Chicago	60621

Loop	64 E. Lake St.	Chicago	60601
Loyola Univ. of Chicago	6525 N. Sheridan	Chicago	60611
Lutheran School of Theology	1100 E. 55th St.	Chicago	60615
MacCormac Junior	327 S. La Salle St.	Chicago	60604
Malcolm X	1900 W. Van Buren	Chicago	60612
Mallinckrodt	1041 Ridge	Wilmette	60091
Mc Cormick Theological Seminary	5555 S. Woodlawn	Chicago	60637
Meadville Lombard Theological	5701 S. Woodlawn	Chicago	60637
Metro. School of Business	5840 N. Lincoln	Chicago	60659
Midwest Montessori Teacher Training Center	1010 W. Chicago	Chicago	60622
Moody Bible Institute	820 N. La Salle St.	Chicago	60610
Moraine Valley Community	10900 88th Ave.	Palos Hills	60465
Morris Robert	180 N. La Salle St.	Chicago	60601
Morton	3801 S. Central Ave.	Cicero	60650
Mundelein	6363 N. Sheridan	Chicago	60660
Nat'l College of Education	2840 Sheridan Rd.	Evanston	60201
Nat'l College of Education	18 S. Michigan Ave.	Chicago	60603
Native American Educational Services	4550 N. Hermitage St.	Chicago	60640
North Park	5125 N. Spaulding Ave.	Chicago	60625
North Park Theological Seminary	5125 N. Spaulding Ave.	Chicago	60625
Northeastern Illinois	5500 N. St. Louis	Chicago	60625
Northwestern Business	4959 W. Belmont Ave.	Chicago	60641
Northwestern-Chicago Campus	339 E. Chicago	Chicago	60611
Northwestern	633 Clark St.	Evanston	60201
Northwestern - Law School	820 N. Michigan	Chicago	60611
Oakton Community	7900 Nagle Ave.	Des Plaines	60016
Olive-Harvey	10001 S. Woodlawn Ave.	Chicago	60628
Prairie State	197th & Halsted	Chicago Hgts.	60411
Richard Daley	7500 S. Pulaski Rd.	Chicago	60652
Roosevelt	430 S. Michigan	Chicago	60605
Rosary	7900 Division St.	River Forest	60305
Rush Medical	1725 W. Harrison	Chicago	60612
Rush	1753 W. Congress Pkwy.	Chicago	60612
St. Xavier	3700 W. 103rd St.	Chicago	60655
School of the Art Institute of Chicago	Columbus Dr. & Jackson Blvd.	Chicago	60603
Seabury-Western Theological Seminary	2122 Sheridan Rd.	Evanston	60201
Sherwood Music	1014 S. Michigan Ave.	Chicago	60605
Spertus College of Judaica	618 S. Michigan Ave.	Chicago	60605
Telshe-Yeshiva Chicago	3535 W. Foster Ave.	Chicago	60625
Thornton Community	15800 S. State	South Holland	60473
Trinity Christian	6601 College Dr.	Palos Heights	60463
Triton	2000 5th Ave.	River Grove	60171
Truman	1145 W. Wilson	Chicago	60640
University of Chicago	5801 S. Ellis	Chicago	60637
University of Health Sciences Chicago Medical School	233 S. Wacker Dr.	Chicago	60612
U of IL, Chgo Circle Campus	601 S. Morgan	Chicago	60607
U of IL, Med. Center Campus	1737 W. Polk	Chicago	60612
Vandercook College of Music	3209 S. Michigan Ave.	Chicago	60616
William Rainey Harper	N. Algonquin Rd. & S. Roselle Rd.	Palatine	60067
Worsham College of Mortuary Science	3701 Davis	Skokie	60076
Wright	3400 N. Austin	Chicago	60634

De Kalb

Kishwaukee	Hwy. 38 W. & Malta Blacktop	Malta	60150
Northern Illinois		De Kalb	60115

Du Page

Bethany Theological Seminary	Butterfield & Myers Rd.	Oak Brook	60521
College of Du Page	425 22nd	Glen Ellyn	60137
Elmhurst	190 Prospect Ave.	Elmhurst	60126
George Williams	555 31st	Downers Grove	60515
IL Benedictine	5700 College Rd.	Lisle	60532
Midwest College of Engr.	420 S. Finley	Lombard	60148
National College of Chiropractic	200 E. Roosevelt	Lombard	60148
North Central	30 N. Brainard	Naperville	60566
Northern Baptist Theological Seminary	660 E. Butterfield Rd.	Lombard	60148
Wheaton	501 E. Seminary	Wheaton	60187

Fulton

Spoon River	Route 1	Canton	61520

Henderson

Monmouth	700 E. Broadway	Monmouth	61462

Henry

Black Hawk - East Campus	Route 78	Kewanee	61443

Jackson

Southern Illinois		Carbondale	62901

Jefferson

Rend Lake	R. R. I	Ina	62846

Jersey

Principia		Elsah	62028

Kane

Aurora	347 S. Gladstone Ave.	Aurora	60507
Elgin Community	1700 Sparton Dr.	Elgin	60120
Judson	1151 N. State	Elgin	60120
Waubonsee Community	Route 47	Sugar Grove	60554

Kankakee

Kankakee Community	River Rd.	Kankakee	60901
Olivet Nazarene	240 Marsile-Bourbonnais	Kankakee	60901

Knox

Carl Sandburg	2232 S. Lake Story Rd.	Galesburg	61401
Knox		Galesburg	61401

Lake

Barat	700 E. Westleigh Rd.	Lake Forest	60045
College of Lake County	19361 W. Washington	Grayslake	60030
Lake Forest	Sheridan Rd.	Lake Forest	60045
Trinity	2065 W. Half Day Rd.	Deerfield	60015
Trinity Evangelical Divinity	2065 W. Half Day Rd.	Deerfield	60015

La Salle

IL Valley Community	Route 1	Oglesby	61348

Lee

| Sauk Valley | Route 5 | Dixon | 61021 |

Logan

| Lincoln Christian | N. Limit | Lincoln | 62656 |
| Lincoln | 300 Keokuk | Lincoln | 62656 |

Macon

| Milliken | 1184 W. Main St. | Decatur | 62522 |
| Richland Community | 2425 Federal Dr. | Decatur | 62526 |

Macoupin

| Blackburn | 700 College Ave. | Carlinville | 62626 |

Madison

| Lewis & Clark Community | | Godfrey | 62035 |
| Southern Illinois | Edwardsville Rd. | Edwardsville | 62026 |

Marion

| Kaskaskia | Shattuc Rd. | Centralia | 62801 |

Mc Donough

| Western Illinois | | Macomb | 61455 |

Mc Henry

| Mc Henry County | Route 14 & Lucas Rd. | Crystal Lake | 60014 |

Mc Lean

| Illinois State | | Normal | 61761 |
| Illinois Wesleyan | | Bloomington | 61701 |

Morgan

| Illinois | 1101 W. College | Jacksonville | 62650 |
| MacMurray | 447 E. College | Jacksonville | 62650 |

Ogle

| Oregon Bible | 110 N. 7th | Oregon | 61061 |

Peoria

| Bradley | 1502 Bradley | Peoria | 61625 |
| Midstate | 244 S. W. Jefferson Ave. | Peoria | 61602 |

Pulaski

| Shawnee | Shawnee Rd. | Ullin | 62992 |

Richland

| Olney Central | Route 3 | Olney | 62450 |

Rock Island

| Augustana | | Rock Island | 61201 |
| Black Hawk - Main Campus | 6600 34th Ave. | Moline | 61265 |

St. Clair

Belleville Area	2500 Carlyle Ave.	Belleville	62221
Mc Kendree	701 College	Lebanon	62254
Park College of Aero-Tech.	Falling Springs Rd.	E. St. Louis	62201
Parks of St. Louis Univ.		Cahokia	62206

Saline

Southeastern Illinois	Route 4	Harrisburg	62946

Sangamon

Lincoln Land Community	Shepherd Rd.	Springfield	62708
Sangamon State	Shepherd Rd.	Springfield	62708
Springfield College in IL	1500 N. 5th	Springfield	62702

Stephenson

Highland Community	2998 W. Pearl City Rd.	Freeport	61032

Tazewell

Illinois Central		East Peoria	61635

Vermilion

Danville Junior	2000 E. Main	Danville	61832

Wabash

Wabash Valley	2200 College	Mt. Carmel	62863

Whiteside

Morrison Institute of Tech.	R. R. 78	Morrison	61270

Will

Governors State	Governors Hwy. & Stunkel Rd.	Park Forest So.	60466
Joliet Junior	1216 Houbolt Rd.	Joliet	60436
Lewis	Route 53	Lockport	60441
Saint Francis	500 Wilcox St.	Joliet	60435

Williamson

John A. Logan	Route 2	Carterville	62918

Winnebago

Rockford Business	319 W. Jefferson	Rockford	61101
Rockford	5050 E. State St.	Rockford	61101
Rockford School of Medicine	1601 Parkview Ave.	Rockford	61101
Rock Valley	3301 N. Mulford Rd.	Rockford	61101

Woodford

Eureka	300 E. College	Eureka	61530

HOSPITALS

Adams

Blessing	1005 Broadway St.	Quincy	62301
St. Mary's	1415 Vermont St.	Quincy	62301

Alexander

Southern Medical Center	2020 Cedar St.	Cairo	62914

Bond

Edward A. Utlaut Mem.	Hillview Rd. & N. Grigg	Greenville	62246

Boone

Highland	1625 S. State St.	Belvidere	61008
St. Joseph's	1005 Julien St.	Belvidere	61008

Bureau

Perry Memorial	530 Park Ave. E.	Princeton	61356
St. Margaret's	600 E. First St.	Spring Valley	61362

Carroll

Savanna City	1125 N. Fifth St.	Savanna	61074

Cass

Beardstown	Boulevard Rd.	Beardstown	62618

Champaign

Burnham	407 S. Fourth St.	Champaign	61820
Carle Foundation	611 W. Park St.	Urbana	61801
Cole	809 W. Church St.	Champaign	61820
Herman M. Adler	2204 Griffith Dr.	Champaign	61820
Mc Kinley Memorial	1109 S. Lincoln Ave.	Urbana	61801
Mercy	1400 W. Park Ave.	Urbana	61801
U.S. Air Force	Chanute Air Force Base	Chanute AFB	61868

Christian

Pana Community	S. Locust St.	Pana	62557
St. Vincent Memorial	201 E. Pleasant St.	Taylorville	62568

Clay

Clay County	700 N. Mill St.	Flora	62839

Clinton

St. Joseph's/Clinton Co.	Jamestown Rd.	Breese	62230

Coles

Sarah Bush Lincoln Ctr.	Rt. 16, Box 372	Mattoon	61938

Cook

Alexian Brothers	800 W. Biesterfield Rd.	Elk Grove Village	60007
American	850 W. Irving Park Rd.	Chicago	60613
Augustana	411 W. Dickens Ave.	Chicago	60614
Barclay	4700 N. Clarendon Ave.	Chicago	60640
Belmont Community	4058 W. Melrose St.	Chicago	60641
Bethany	3821 W. Washington Blvd.	Chicago	60624
Bethany Methodist	5025 N. Paulina St.	Chicago	60640
Bethesda	2451 W. Howard St.	Chicago	60645
Billings	950 E. 59th St.	Chicago	60637
Bob Roberts Memorial	950 E. 59th St.	Chicago	60637
Booth Memorial	5040 N. Pulaski Rd.	Chicago	60630
Cabrini	2520 N. Lakeview	Chicago	60614
Central Community	5701 S. Wood	Chicago	60636
Cermak Memorial	2800 S. California	Chicago	60608
Chicago Eye/Ear/Throat	231 W. Washington	Chicago	60606
Chicago Center	426 W. Wisconsin	Chicago	60614
Chicago Lakeshore	4840 N. Marine Dr.	Chicago	60640
Chicago Lying-In	5841 S. Maryland	Chicago	60637
Chicago Osteopathic	5200 S. Ellis Ave.	Chicago	60615
Chicago-Read Mental	4200 N. Oak Park	Chicago	60634
Chicago Wesley Memorial	see Northwestern Mem.		
Children's Memorial	2300 Childrens Plaza	Chicago	60614
Christ	4440 W. 95th St.	Oak Lawn	60453
Clarissa C. Peck	See Univ. of Chicago		
Columbus-Cuneo-Carbini	2520 N. Lakeview	Chicago	60614
Community Memorial	5101 Willow Springs Rd.	La Grange	60525
Contagious Disease	3026 S. California Ave.	Chicago	60608
Cook County Hospital	1825 W. Harrison	Chicago	60612
Covenant	5145 N. California	Chicago	60625
Doctors General	6970 N. Clark	Chicago	60626
Dunning	6500 W. Irving Park Rd.	Chicago	60634
Edgewater	5700 N. Ashland	Chicago	60660
Englewood, Hospital of	6001 S. Green	Chicago	60621
Evanston	2650 Ridge Ave.	Evanston	60201
Forest Hills	555 Wilson Lane	Des Plaines	60016
Forkosh Memorial	2544 W. Montrose Ave.	Chicago	60618
Foster G. McGraw	2160 S. First Ave.	Maywood	60153
Frank Cuneo Memorial	750 N. Winchester	Chicago	60622
Franklin Blvd. Community	3240 W. Franklin	Chicago	60624
Garfield Park	3821 W. Washington Rd.	Chicago	60624
Glenbrook	2100 Pfingsten Rd.	Glenview	60025
Glendale Hgts. Community	1505 Jill Court	Glendale Heights	60137
Gottlieb Memorial	8700b W. North Ave.	Melrose Park	60160
Grant	550 W. Webster Ave.	Chicago	60614
Henrotin	111 W. Oak St.	Chicago	60610
Henry Horner Children	4200 N. Oak Park	Chicago	60634
Hinsdale Santarium	120 N. Oak St.	Hinsdale	60521
Holy Cross	2701 W. 68th St.	Chicago	60629
Holy Family	100 N. River Rd.	Des Plaines	60016
Ida Mae Scott	5027 S. Priarie	Chicago	60615
IL Central Comm.	5800 Stony Island Ave.	Chicago	60637
IL Masonic	836 W. Wellington Ave.	Chicago	60657
Ingalls Memorial	One Ingalls Dr.	Harvey	60426
Institute of Psychiatry	320 E. Huron	Chicago	60610
Jackson Park	7531 S. Stony Island	Chicago	60649
John L. Madden	1200 S. First Ave.	Hines	60141
La Rabida Children's	E 65th St.	Chicago	60649
Little Company of Mary	2800 W. 95th St.	Evergreen Park	60642
Loretto	645 S. Central Ave.	Chicago	60644
Louis A. Weiss	4646 N. Marine Dr.	Chicago	60640
Louise Burg	255 W. Cermak Rd.	Chicago	60616
Loyola Univ. Medical	2160 S. First	Maywood	60153
Luthern General	1775 Dempster St.	Park Ridge	60068
Macneal Memorial	3249 S. Oak Park Ave.	Berwyn	60402
Martha Washington	4055 N. Western Ave.	Chicago	60618
Mary Thompson	140 N. Ashland	Chicago	60607

161

Mc Elwee Nancy Adele Mem.	950 E. 59th	Chicago	60637
Mercy	Stevenson Expressway	Chicago	60616
Michael Reese	2929 S. Ellis Ave.	Chicago	60616
Misercordia	2916 W. 47th St.	Chicago	60632
Mt. Sinai	California at 15th	Chicago	60608
Nathan Goldblatt Mem.	950 E. 59th	Chicago	60637
Nicholas J. Pritzker Children's	800 E. 55th	Chicago	60615
North Avenue	1625 W. North St.	Chicago	60622
Northlake Community	365 E. North Ave.	Northlake	60164
Northwest Community	800 W. Central Rd.	Arlington Heights	60005
Northwest	5645 W. Addison St.	Chicago	60634
Northwestern Memorial	Superior & Fairbanks	Chicago	60611
Norwegian-American	1044 N. Francisco Ave.	Chicago	60622
Oak Forest	15900 S. Cicero Ave.	Oak Park	60452
Olympia Fields Ost.	20201 Crawford	Olympia Fields	60461
Palos Community	12251 S. 80th St.	Palos Heights	60463
Passavant Memorial	303 E. Superior St.	Chicago	60611
Prentice Women's	333 E. Superior	Chicago	60611
Provident	426 E. 51st	Chicago	60615
Ravenswood	4550 N. Winchester	Chicago	60640
Rehabilitation Inst.	345 E. Superior	Chicago	60611
Resurrection	7435 W. Talcott Ave.	Chicago	60631
Ridgeway	520 N. Ridgeway Ave.	Chicago	60624
Riveredge	8311 W. Roosevelt Rd.	Forest Park	60130
Riverside	8311 W. Roosevelt Rd.	Forest Park	60130
Roosevelt Memorial	426 W. Wisconsin	Chicago	60614
Roseland Community	45 W. 111th St.	Chicago	60628
Rush Presbyterian	1753 W. Congress Parkway	Chicago	60612
St. Anne's	4950 W. Thomas St.	Chicago	60651
St. Anthony De Padua	2875 W. 19th St.	Chicago	60623
St. Bernards	326 W. 64th St.	Chicago	60621
St. Elizabeth's	1431 N. Claremont Ave.	Chicago	60622
St. Francis	12935 S. Gregory	Blue Island	60406
St. Francis	355 Ridge Ave.	Evanston	60202
St. Francis Xav. Cabrini	811 S. Lytle St.	Chicago	60607
St. James	1423 Chicago Rd.	Chicago Heights	60411
St. Josephs	2900 N. Lake Shore Dr.	Chicago	60657
St. Luke's Medical Ctr	710 S. Paulina	Chicago	60612
St. Mary's of Nazareth	2233 W. Division St.	Chicago	60622
Salvation Army Booth	5040 N. Polaski Rd.	Chicago	60630
Schwab Rehab	1401 S. California Blvd.	Chicago	60608
Sheridan Road	6130 N. Sheridan	Chicago	60626
Shriners	2211 N. Oak Park Ave.	Chicago	60635
Skokie Valley Community	9600 Gross Point Rd.	Skokie	60076
So. Chicago Comm.	2320 E. 93rd St.	Chicago	60617
South Shore	8015 S. Luella Ave.	Chicago	60617
South Suburban	178th St. & Kedzie	Hazel Crest	60429
Suburban	55th & County Line Rd.	Hinsdale	60521
Suburban Medical	1555 N. Barrington Rd.	Hoffman Estates	60194
Swedish Convenant	5145 N. California	Chicago	60625
Tabernacle	5421 S. Morgan	Chicago	60609
Tinley Pk Mental Health	7400 W. 183rd St.	Tinley Park	60477
Thorek	850 W. Irving Park Rd.	Chicago	60613
Univ. of Chicago	950 E. 59th St.	Chicago	60637
Univ. of Illinois	840 S. Wood	Chicago	60612
Veterans Admin.	Fifth Ave. & Roosevelt	Chicago	60611
VA West Side	820 S. Damen Ave.	Chicago	60612
Walther Memorial	1116 N. Kedzie Ave.	Chicago	60651
Westlake Community	1225 Superior St.	Chicago	60160
West Suburban	518 N. Austin Blvd.		
Woodlawn	6060 S. Drexel Ave.	Chicago	60637
Wyler Silvain & Arma	950 E. 59th	Chicago	60637
Zion Benton	Shiloh Pl.	Zion	60099

Crawford

Crawford Memorial	1000 N. Allen	Robinson	62454

De Kalb

Kishwaukee Community	Bethany Rd.	De Kalb	60115
Sandwich Community	11 E. Pleasant Ave.	Sandwich	60548
Sycamore Municipal	225 Edward St.	Sycamore	60178

De Witt

Dr. John Warner	422 W. White St.	Clinton	61727

Douglas

Jarman Memorial	704 N. Main St.	Tuscola	61953

Du Page

Central DuPage	0 N. 025 Winfield	Winfield	60190
Edward	S. Washignton	Naperville	60566
Good Samaritan	3815 Highland	Downers Grove	60515
Marion Joy Rehabilitation	26 W. 171 Roosevelt Rd.	Wheaton	60187
Memorial of DuPage Co.	200 Berteau Ave.	Elmhurst	60126

Edgar

Paris Community	E. Court St.	Paris	61944

Effingham

St. Anthony's Memorial	503 N. Maple St.	Effingham	62401

Fayette

Fayette County	Seventh & Taylor Sts.	Vandalia	62471

Ford

Gibson Community	1120 N. Melvin St.	Gibson City	60936
Paxton Community	651 E. Pellis St.	Paxton	60957

Franklin

Franklin	201 Bailey Lane	Benton	62812
West Frankfort	507 W. St. Louis St.	West Frankfort	62896

Fulton

Graham	210 W. Walnut St.	Canton	61520

Greene

Thomas H. Boyd Mem.	800 School St.	Carrollton	62016
White Hall	407 N. Main St.	White Hall	62092

Grundy

Morris	150 W. High St.	Morris	60450

Hamilton

Hamilton Memorial	611 S. Marshall Ave.	Mc Leansboro	62859

Hancock

La Harpe	B St. & Archer Ave.	La Harpe	61450
Memorial	S. Adams St.	Carthage	62321

Hardin

Hardin County General	Ferrell Rd.	Rosiclare	62982

163

Henry

Good Samaritan Home	704 S. Illinois St.	Geneseo	61254
Hammond-Henry Dist.	210 W. Elk St.	Geneseo	61254
Kewanee Public	719 Elliott St.	Kewanee	61443

Iroquois

Central Community	Fifth Ave.	Clifton	60927
Iroquois Memorial	200 Fairman St.	Watseka	60970

Jackson

Memorial	404 W. Main St.	Carbondale	62901
St. Joseph Memorial	800 N. Second St.	Murphysboro	62966

Jefferson

Good Samaritan	605 N. 12th St.	Mt. Vernon	62864

Jersey

Jersey Community	400 Maple Summit Rd.	Jerseyville	62032

Jo Daviess

Galena-Stauss	215 Summit St.	Galena	61036

Kane

Community	416 S. Second St.	Geneva	60134
Copley Memorial	Lincoln & Weston	Aurora	60507
Delnor	975 N. Fifth Ave.	St. Charles	60174
Elgin Mental Health	750 S. State St.	Elgin	60120
Mercy Ctr for Health Care	1325 N. Highland Ave.	Aurora	60506
St. Joseph	77 N. Airlite St.	Elgin	60120
Sherman	934 Center St.	Elgin	60120

Kankakee

Hillman Memorial	411 W. Division St.	Manteno	60950
Manteno Mental Health	100 Barnard	Manteno	60950
Riverside Medical	350 N. Wall St.	Kandakee	60901
St. Mary's	500 W. Court St.	Kankakee	60901

Knox

Galesburg Cottage	695 N. Kellogg St.	Galesburg	61401
Galesburg Mental Health	1801 N. Seminary St.	Galesburg	61401
St. Mary's	3333 N. Seminary St.	Galesburg	61401

Lake

American International	Emmaus & Shiloh	Zion	60099
Condell Memorial	900 Garfield	Libertyville	60048
Good Shepherd	450 W. Hwy. 22	Barrington	60010
Highland Park	718 Glenview Ave.	Highland Park	60035
Lake Forest	660 N. Westmoreland Rd.	Lake Forest	60045
Naval Regional Medical		Great Lakes	60088
St. Therese	2615 W. Washington St.	Waukegan	60085
Veterans Admin. Center		North Chicago	60064
Victory Memorial	1324 N. Sheridan Rd.	Waukegan	60085

La Salle

Comm. Hosp. of Ottawa	1100 E. Norris Dr.	Ottawa	61350
Illinios Valley Comm.	925 West St.	Peru	61354
Mendota Community	Memorial Dr.	Mendota	61342
Ottawa General	900 E. Center St.	Ottawa	61350
People's	925 W. St.	Peru	61354
St. Mary's	111 E. Spring St.	Streator	61364

Lawrence

Lawrence County	W. State St.	Lawrenceville	62439

Lee

Dixon Devel. Center	2600 N. Brinton	Dixon	61021
Katherine Shaw Bethea	403 E. First St.	Dixon	61021

Livingston

Fairbury	519 S. Fifth St.	Fairbury	61739
St. James	610 E. Water St.	Pontiac	61764

Logan

Abraham Lincoln Mem.	315 Eighth St.	Lincoln	62656
Lincoln Development Ctr.	861 S. State St.	Lincoln	62656

Macon

Adolf Meyer Center	E Mound Rd.	Decatur	62526
Decatur Memorial	2300 N. Edwards St.	Decatur	62526
St. Mary's	1800 E. Lake Shore Dr.	Decatur	62525

Macoupin

Carlinville Area	Morgan St.	Carlinville	62626
Community Memorial	216 W. Pennsylvania	Staunton	62088

Madison

Alton Memorial	Memorial Dr.	Alton	62002
Alton Mental Health Ctr.	4500 College Ave.	Alton	62002
Oliver C. Anderson	Rt. 162	Maryville	62062
St. Anthony's	St. Anthony's Way	Alton	62002
St. Elizabeth	2100 Madison Ave.	Granite City	62040
St. Joseph	915 E. Fifth St.	Alton	62002
St. Joseph's	1515 Main St.	Highland	62249
Wood River Township	Edwardsville Rd.	Wood River	62095

Marion

Public /Salem	Bryan Memorial Park	Salem	62881
St. Mary's	400 N. Pleasant	Centralia	62801
Warren G. Murray Development Center	1717 W. Broadway	Centralia	62801

Mason

Mason District	520 E. Franklin St.	Havana	62644

Massac

Massac Memorial	Memorial Heights	Metropolis	62960

Mc Donough

Mc Donough County	525 E. Grant St.	Macomb	61455

Mc Henry

Harvard Community	Grant & Mc Kinley Sts.	Harvard	60033
Mc Henry	3516 W. Waukegan Rd.	Mc Henry	60050
Memorial	527 W. South St.	Woodstock	60098

Mc Lean

Brokaw	Virginia & Franklin	Normal	61761
Mennonite	807 N. Main St.	Bloomington	61701
St. Joseph's	2200 E. Washington St.	Bloomington	61701

Mercer

Mercer County	308 N.W. Fourth St.	Aledo	61231

Montgomery

Hillsboro	1200 E. Tremont St.	Hillsboro	62049
St. Francis	1215 E. Union Ave.	Litchfield	62056

Morgan

Jacksonville Mental Hlt.	1201 S. Main St.	Jacksonville	62650
Passavant Memorial	1600 W. Walnut St.	Jacksonville	62650

Ogle

Rochelle Community	900 N. Second St.	Rochelle	61068

Peoria

G.A. Zeller Mental Hlt.	5407 N. University St.	Peoria	61614
Methodist Medical	221 N E. Glen Oaks Ave.	Peoria	61636
Proctor Community	5409 N. Knoxville Ave.	Peoria	61614
St. Francis	530 N.E. Glen Oak Ave.	Peoria	61637

Perry

Marshall Browning	900 N. Washington St.	DuQuoin	62832
Pinckneyville Community	101 N. Walnut St.	Pinckneyville	62274

Piatt

John & Mary Kirby	1111 N. State St.	Monticello	61856

Pike

Illini Community	640 W. Washington	Pittsfield	62363

Randolph

Chester Mental Health	Box 31	Chester	62233
Memorial	1900 State St.	Chester	62233
St. Clement	325 Spring St.	Red Bud	62278
Sparta Community	818 E. Broadway St.	Sparta	62286

Richland

Richland Memorial	800 E. Locust St.	Olney	62450

Rock Island

Illini	801 13th Ave.	Silvis	61282
Lutheran	501 Tenth Ave.	Moline	61265
Moline Public	635 Tenth Ave.	Moline	61265
Rock Island Franciscan	2701 17th St.	Rock Island	61201

St. Clair

Centreville Township	5900 Bond Avenue	Centreville	62207
Community	1509 Martin Luther King	East St. Louis	62201
Memorial	4501 N. Park Dr.	Belleville	62223
St. Elizabth's	211 S. Third St.	Belleville	62223
St. Mary's	129 N. Eighth St.	East St. Louis	62201
U.S. Air Force	Medical Center	Scott AFB	62225

Saline

A. L. Bowen Dev. Ctr.	Box 281	Harrisburg	62946
Ferrell	1201 Pine St.	Eldorado	62930
Harrisburg Medical	17 Country Club Ct.	Harrisburg	62946
Pearce	1901 Organ St.	Eldorado	62930

Sangamon

A. McFarland Mental Health Center	901 Southwind Rd.	Springfield	62703
Memorial Medical	800 N. Rutledge St.	Springfield	62781
St. John's	800 E. Carpenter St.	Springfield	62769
Springfield Community	5230 S. Sixth St.	Springfield	62703

Schuyler

Sarah D. Culbertson	238 S. Congress St.	Rushville	62681

Shelby

Shelby Memorial	S. First & Cedar Sts.	Shelbyville	62565

Stephenson

Freeport Memorial	1045 W. Stephenson	Freeport	61032

Tazewell

Hopedale		Hopedale	61747
Pekin Memorial	Court & 14th Sts.	Pekin	61554

Union

Ann Mental Health Ctr.	1000 N. Main St.	Anna	62906
Union County	517 N. Main St.	Anna	62906

Vermilion

Hoopeston Community	701 E. Orange St.	Hoopeston	60942
Lakeview Medical	812 N. Logan Ave.	Danville	61832
St. Elizabeth	600 Sager Ave.	Danville	61832
Veterans Admin. Medical	1900 E. Main St.	Danville	61832

Wabash

Wabash General	1418 College Dr.	Mount Carmel	62863

Warren

Community Memorial	1000 W. Harlem Ave.	Monmouth	61462
Saunders	Box 250	Avon	61415

Washington

Washington County	603 S. Grand St.	Nashville	62263

Wayne

Fairfield Memorial	N.W. 11th St.	Fairfield	62837

White

Carmi Township	Plum & Webb Sts.	Carmi	62821

Whiteside

Community General	1601 First Ave.	Sterling	61081
Morrison Community	303 N. Jackson	Morrison	61270

Will

St. Joseph	333 N. Madison	Joliet	60435
Silver Cross	1200 Maple Rd.	Joliet	60432
Stateville Correctional	Box 112	Joliet	60434

Williamson

Herrin	201 S. 14th St.	Herrin	62948
Marion Memorial	917 W. Main St.	Marion	62959
Veterans Admin. Medical	W. Main St.	Marion	62959
U.S. Penitentiary		Marion	62959

Winnebago

H. Douglas Singer Mental Health	4402 N. Main St.	Rockford	61103
Rockford Memorial	2400 N. Rockton Ave.	Rockford	61101
St. Anthony	5666 E. State St.	Rockford	61101
Swedish-American	1400 Charles St.	Rockford	61101

Woodford

Eureka	101 S. Major St.	Eureka	61530

LIBRARIES

Adams

Camp Point	206 E. State St.	Camp Point	62320
Clayton Township	102 Washington St.	Clayton	62324
Great River	515 York St.	Quincy	62301
Quincy	526 Jersey St.	Quincy	62301

Alexander

Cairo	1609 Washington Ave.	Cairo	62914

Bond

Greenville	414 W. Main	Greenville	62246

Boone

Ida	320 N. State St.	Belvidere	61008

Brown

Mount Sterling	143 W. Main St.	Mount Sterling	62353

Bureau

Bureau County	109 Park Ave. W.	Princeton	61356
De Pue	211 W. Fourth St.	De Pue	61322
La Moille Clarion	Box 260	La Moille	61330
Ladd	Main St.	Ladd	61329
Leepertown Township	Box 1091	Bureau	61315
Mason Memorial	Main St.	Buda	61314
Matson	15 W. Park Ave. W.	Princeton	61356
Mineral-Gold	Main St.	Mineral	61344
Neponset	201 W. Commercial St.	Neponset	61345
Ohio Township	112 N. Main St.	Ohio	61349
Raymond A. Sapp	103 E. Main St.	Wyanet	61379
Sheffield	136 E. Cook St.	Sheffield	61361
Tiskilwa Township	119 Main St.	Tiskilwa	61368
Walnut Township	Heaton & Main	Walnut	61376

Calhoun

South County	Box 93	Brussels	62013

Carroll

Lanark	110 W. Carroll St.	Lanark	61046
Mount Carroll Township	208 N. Main	Mount Carroll	61053
Savanna Township	326 Third St.	Savanna	61074
Wysox Township	Fifth St.	Milledgeville	61501
York Township	W. Main St.	Thomson	61285

Cass

Beardstown	105 W. Third St.	Beardstown	62618
John Cheetham Memorial	116 Hardin St.	Ashland	62612
Virginia Memorial	200 N. Main	Virginia	62691

Champaign

Champaign	505 S. Randolph	Champaign	61820
Douglass	310 E. Bradley	Champaign	61820
Homer Community	101 N. Main St.	Homer	61849
IL State Geo. Survey	469 Nat. Resourses Bldg.	Urbana	61801
Lincoln Trail	1704 W. Interstate Dr.	Champaign	61820
Mahomet Township	403 E. Main St.	Mahomet	61853
Ogden Rose	Main St.	Ogden	61859
Philo Township	Washington St.	Philo	61864
Rantoul	225 S. Century Blvd.	Rantoul	61866
Saint Joseph Township	201 N. Third	Saint Joseph	61873
Sidney Community	205 S. David	Sidney	61877
Tolono Township	Main St.	Tolono	61880
University of IL	104 Law Building	Champaign	61820
Urbana	201 S. Race St.	Urbana	61801

Christian

Assumption	202 E. First St.	Assumption	62510
Blue Mound Memorial	224 Railroad Ave.	Blue Mound	62513
Carnegie-Schuyler	303 E. Second St.	Pana	62557
Kitchell Memorial	Carlin St.	Morrisonville	62546
Stonington Township		Stonington	62567
Taylorville	222 W. Market St.	Taylorville	62568

Clark

Casey Township	307 E. Main St.	Casey	62420
Marshall	612 Archer Ave.	Marshall	62441
Martinsville Township	126 W. Cumberland	Martinsville	62442

Clay

Cumberland Trail	12th & McCawley	Flora	62839
Flora Carnegie	216 N. Main St.	Flora	62839

Clinton

Breese	530 N. Third	Breese	62230
Case-Halstead	571 Franklin St.	Carlyle	62231
Trenton	25 W. Indiana St.	Trenton	62293

Coles

Ashmore Area		Ashmore	61912
Carnegie	712 Sixth St.	Charleston	61920
Mattoon	1600 Charleston Ave.	Mattoon	61938

Cook

Acorn Public	15624 S. Central Ave.	Oak Forest	60452
Alsip-Merrionette Park	11951 S. Pulaski	Alsip	60658
Arlington Hghts Memorial	500 N. Dunton Ave.	Arlington Heights	60004
Barrington	505 N. Northwest Hwy.	Barrington	60010
Bartlett	301 Railroad Ave.	Bartlett	60103
Bedford Park	7816 W. 65th Pl.	Argo	60501
Bellwood	600 Bohland Ave.	Bellwood	60104
Berkeley	1637 Taft Ave.	Berkeley	60163
Berwyn	3400 S. Oak Park Ave.	Berwyn	60402
Blue Island	2433 York St.	Blue Island	60406
Bridgeview	7840 W. 79th St.	Bridgeview	60455
Broadview	2226 S. 16th Ave.	Broadview	60153
Calumet City	760 Wentworth Ave.	Calumet City	60409
Calumet Park	1502 W. 127th St.	Calumet Park	60643

Chicago

Alfred Adler Institute	159 N. Dearborn St.	Chicago	60601
Adler Planetarium	1300 S. Lake Shore Dr.	Chicago	60605
American Bar Foundation	1155 E. 60th St.	Chicago	60637
American College of Surg.	55 E. Erie St.	Chicago	60611
American Conserv. of Music	116 S. Michigan	Chicago	60603
American Library Assoc.	50 E. Huron St.	Chicago	60611
Balzekas Lithuanian	4012 Archer Ave.	Chicago	60632
Canadian Consulate General	310 S. Michigan Ave.	Chicago	60604
Catholic Theological Union	5401 S. Cornell Ave.	Chicago	60615
Chicago Bar Assoc.	29 S. La Salle St.	Chicago	60603
Chicago Board of Education	228 N. La Salle St.	Chicago	60601
Chicago Historical Society	Clark St. at North Ave.	Chicago	60614
Chicago Public (Central)	425 N. Michigan Ave.	Chicago	60611

Chicago Public Library Branches:

Albany Park	5150 N. Kimball Ave.	Chicago	60625
Altgeld	941 E. 132nd St.	Chicago	60627
Archer	5148 S. Archer Ave.	Chicago	60632
Auburn	1364 W. 79th St.	Chicago	60620
Austin	5615 W. Race Ave.	Chicago	60644
Austin-Irving	6110 W. Irving Pk. Rd.	Chicago	60634
Avalon	8828 S. Stony Island	Chicago	60617
Back of the Yards	1743 W. 47th St.	Chicago	60609
Beverly	2114 W. 95 St.	Chicago	60643
Bezazian	1226 W. Ainslie St.	Chicago	60640
Blackstone	4904 S. Lake Park Ave.	Chicago	60615
Brainerd	8945 S. Loomis Blvd.	Chicago	60620
Bridgeport	824 W. 35th St.	Chicago	60609
Brighton Park	4314 S. Archer Ave.	Chicago	60632
Cabrini-Green	1157 N. Cleveland Ave.	Chicago	60610
Chicago Lawn	6120 S. Kedzie Ave.	Chicago	60629
Chicago - Handicapped	1055 W. Roosevelt Rd.	Chicago	60608
Chinatown	2314 S. Wentworth Ave.	Chicago	60616
Clearing	5643 W. 63rd St.	Chicago	60638
Damen Avenue	2056 N. Damen Ave.	Chicago	60647
Douglass	3353 W. 13th St.	Chicago	60623
East Side	10542 S. Ewing Ave.	Chicago	60617
Eckhart Park	1371 W. Chicago Ave.	Chicago	60622
Edgebrook	5426 W. Devon Ave.	Chicago	60646
Edgewater	1210 W. Elmdale Ave.	Chicago	60660
El Centro de la Causa	731 W. 17th St.	Chicago	60608
Gads Hill	1919 W. Cullerton St.	Chicago	60608
Gage Park	2825 W. 55th St.	Chicago	60632
Galewood-Mont Clare	6969 W. Grand Ave.	Chicago	60635
Garfield Ridge	6322 Archer Ave.	Chicago	60638
Hall	4801 S. Michigan Ave.	Chicago	60615
Hamilton Park	7200 S. Normal Blvd.	Chicago	60621
Hamlin Park	2205 W. Belmont Ave.	Chicago	60618
Harold Ickes	2420 S. State St.	Chicago	60616
Hegewisch	13445 S. Brandon Ave.	Chicago	60633
Hild Regional	4544 N. Lincoln Ave.	Chicago	60625
Humboldt	1626 N. California Ave.	Chicago	60647
IL Regional - Handicapped	1055 W. Roosevelt Rd.	Chicago	60608
Independence	3718 W. Irving Park Rd.	Chicago	60618
Jefferson Park	5363 W. Lawrence Ave.	Chicago	60630
Jeffery Manor	2435 E. 100th St.	Chicago	60617
Kelly	6151 S. Normal Blvd.	Chicago	60621
Lake View	644 W. Belmont Ave.	Chicago	60657
Legler	115 S. Pulaski Rd.	Chicago	60624
Lincoln Park	959 W. Fullerton Ave.	Chicago	60614
Logan Square	3255 W. Altgeld St.	Chicago	60647
Lorraine Hansberry	4314 S. Cottage Gr. Ave.	Chicago	60615
McKinley Park	2021 W. 35th St.	Chicago	60609
Marshall Square	2860 W. Cermak Rd.	Chicago	60623
Martin L. King, Jr.	3436 S. King Dr.	Chicago	60616

Mayfair	4200 W. Lawrence Ave.	Chicago	60630
Midwest	2335 W. Chicago Ave.	Chicago	60622
Mount Greenwood	10961 S. Kedzie Ave.	Chicago	60655
Near North	451 W. North Ave.	Chicago	60610
North Austin	5518 W. North Ave.	Chicago	60639
North Lake View	3754 N. Southport Ave.	Chicago	60613
Northtown	6435 N. California Ave.	Chicago	60645
Northwest	4041 W. North Ave.	Chicago	60639
Oriole Park	5201 N. Oketo Ave.	Chicago	60656
Pilsen	1842 Blue Island Ave.	Chicago	60608
Portage-Cragin	5108 W. Belmont Ave.	Chicago	60641
Pullman	11001 S. Indiana Ave.	Chicago	60628
Rockwell Gardens	2515 W. Jackson St.	Chicago	60612
Roden	6083 Northwest Hwy.	Chicago	60631
Rogers Park	6907 N. Clark St.	Chicago	60626
Roosevelt	1055 W. Roosevelt Rd.	Chicago	60608
Scottsdale	4101 W. 79th St.	Chicago	60652
Sherman Park	5440 S. Racine Ave.	Chicago	60609
South Chicago	9055 S. Houston Ave.	Chicago	60617
South Shore	2505 E. 73rd St.	Chicago	60649
Southeast	1934 E. 79th St.	Chicago	60649
Stateway Gardens	3618 S. State St.	Chicago	60609
Robert Taylor	4429 S. Federal St.	Chicago	60609
Toman	4005 W. 27th St.	Chicago	60623
Tuley Park	501 E. 90th Pl.	Chicago	60619
Walker	11071 S. Hoyne Ave.	Chicago	60643
Washington Park	448 E. 61st St.	Chicago	60637
Wendell Smith	722 E. 103rd St.	Chicago	60628
West Addison	7536 W. Addison St.	Chicago	60634
West Belmont	3104 N. Narragansett	Chicago	60634
West Lawn	4007 W. 63rd St.	Chicago	60629
West Town	1310 N. Milwaukee Ave.	Chicago	60622

Cook

Chicago Heights	15th St. & Chicago Rd.	Chicago Heights	60411
Chicago Ridge	6301 W. Birmingham	Chicago Ridge	60415
Cicero	5225 W. Cermak Rd.	Cicero	60650
Crestwood	13838 Cicero Ave.	Crestwood	60445
Des Plaines Historical	789 Pearson St.	Des Plaines	60017
Des Plaines Public	841 Graceland Ave.	Des Plaines	60016
Dolton Public	14037 Lincoln	Dolton	60419
Elk Grove Village	101 Kennedy Blvd.	Elk Grove Village	60007
Elmwood Park Public	4 Conti Pkwy.	Elmwood Park	60635
Evanston Historical	225 Greenwood St.	Evanston	60201
Evanston Public	1703 Orrington	Evanston	60201
Evergreen Park	9400 S. Troy Ave.	Evergreen Park	60642
Field Museum	Roosevelt Rd. & Lake Shore Dr.	Chicago	60605
Flossmoor Public	2801 School St.	Flossmoor	60422
Forest Park	7555 Jackson Blvd.	Forest Park	60130
Franklin Park	9618 Franklin Ave.	Franklin Park	60131
Glencoe Public	320 Park Ave.	Glencoe	60022
Glenview Public	1930 Glenview Rd.	Glenview	60025
Glenwood-Lynwood	315 Glenwood-Lansing Rd.	Glenwood	60425
Green Hills Public	8611 W. 103rd St.	Palos Hills	60465
Harvey	155th St/Turlington Ave.	Harvey	60426
Eisenhower Public	4652 N. Olcott	Harwood Heights	60656
Grande Prairie	17521 Stonebridge Sq.	Hazel Crest	60429
Hillside Public	405 N. Hillside Ave.	Hillside	60162
Hometown Public	4331 Southwest Hwy.	Hometown	60456
Homewood Public	17900 Dixie Hwy.	Homewood	60430
IL Bell Telephone Co.	225 W. Randolph St.	Chicago	60606
Italian Cultural Center	1621 N. 39th Ave.	Melrose Park	60165
Indian Trails Public	850 Jenkins Ct.	Wheeling	60090
Justice Public	7641 Oak Grove Ave.	Justice	60458
Kenilworth Historical	Box 81	Kenilworth	60043

La Grange	10 W. Cossitt	La Grange	60525
La Grange Park	928 Barnsdale Rd.	La Grange Park	60525
Lewis O. Flom-Lansing	2750 Indiana Ave.	Lansing	60438
Lemont Public	418 Main St.	Lemont	60439
Lincolnwood Public	4100 W. Pratt Ave.	Lincolnwood	60646
Lyons Public	4209 Joliet Ave.	Lyons	60534
Markham Public	16640 S. Kedzie Ave.	Markham	60426
Matteson Public	801 School Ave.	Matteson	60443
Maywood Public	121 S. Fifth Ave.	Maywood	60153
Melrose Park	801 N. Broadway	Melrose Park	60160
Midlothian Public	14609 S. Springfield	Midlothian	60445
Morton Grove Public	6140 Lincoln Ave.	Morton Grove	60053
Mount Prospect Public	10 S. Emerson St.	Mount Prospect	60056
Municipal Reference	121 N. La Salle St.	Chicago	60602
Ner Tamid Congregation	2754 Rosemont Ave.	Chicago	60659
Newberry Library	60 W. Walton St.	Chicago	60610
Niles Public	6960 Oakton St.	Niles	60648
Northbrook Public	1201 Cedar Lane	Northbrook	60062
Northlake Public	231 N. Wolf Rd.	Northlake	60164
North Suburban	200 W. Dundee	Wheeling	60090
Oak Lawn Public	9427 S. Raymond Ave.	Oak Lawn	60453
Oak Park Public	834 Lake St.	Oak Park	60301
Orland Park Public	14760 Park Lane	Orland Park	60462
Palatine Public	500 N. Benton St.	Palatine	60067
Palos Heights Public	12501 S. 71 Ave.	Palos Heights	60463
Palos Park Public	8817 W. 123rd St.	Palos Park	60464
Park Forest Public	400 Lakewood Blvd.	Park Forest	60466
Park Ridge Public	20 S. Prospect Ave.	Park Ridge	60068
Polish Museum of America	984 N. Milwaukee Ave.	Chicago	60622
Poplar Creek Public	1504 S. Park Blvd.	Streamwood	60103
Prairie Trails	State Rd. & Moody	Burbank	60459
Prospect Heights Public	12 N. Elm St.	Prospect Heights	60070
Richton Park Public	22365 Governors Hwy.	Richton Park	60471
Ridge Historical Soc.	10621 S. Seeley Ave.	Chicago	60643
River Forest Public	735 Lathrop	River Forest	60405
River Grove Public	8638 W. Grand Ave.	River Grove	60171
Riverdale Public	208 W. 144th St.	Riverdale	60627
Riverside Public	1 Burling Rd.	Riverside	60546
Robbins Public	13800 Trumbull Ave.	Robbins	60472
Rolling Meadows	3110 Martin Lane	Rolling Meadows	60008
Sauk Village Public	1909 Sauk Trail	Sauk Village	60411
Schaumburg Township	32 W. Library Lane	Schaumburg	60194
Schiller Park Public	4200 Old River Rd.	Schiller Park	60176
Skokie Public	5215 Oakton St.	Skokie	60077
South Holland Public	16250 Wausau Ave.	South Holland	60473
South Metropolitan	250 W. Sibley Blvd.	Dolton	60419
South Suburban Genea. & Hist. Soc.	320 E. 161st Pl.	South Holland	60473
Steger-South Chicago Hgts.	3326 Chicago Rd.	South Chicago Hgts.	60411
Stickney-Forest View	6800 W. 43rd St.	Stickney	60402
Summit-Argo Public	6209 S. Archer Rd.	Summit	60501
Swedish Pioneer Archives	5125 N. Spaulding	Chicago	60625
Temper Judea Mizpah	8610 Niles Center Rd.	Skokie	60076
Thomas Ford Memorial	800 Chestnut	Western Springs	60558
Thornton Public	115 Margaret St.	Thornton	60476
Tinley Park Public	17101 S. 71st Ave.	Tinley Park	60477
United States Courts	219 S. Dearborn St.	Chicago	60604
United States Railroad	844 N. Rush St.	Chicago	60611
Westchester Public	10700 Canterbury	Westchester	60153
Wilmette Public	1242 Wilmette Ave.	Wilmette	60091
Winnetka Public	768 Oak St.	Winnetka	60093
Worth Public	6917 W. 111th St.	Worth	60482

Crawford

Lamotte Township	116 S. Main St.	Palestine	62451
Robinson Township	606 N. Jefferson	Robinson	62454

Cumberland

Greenup Township Carnegie	101 N. Mill St.	Greenup	62428
Sumpter Township	Courthouse Square	Toledo	62468

De Kalb

Clinton Township	110 S. Elm St.	Waterman	60556
De Kalb Public	309 Oak St.	De Kalb	60115
Genoa Public	232 W. Main St.	Genoa	60135
Kirkland Public	513 Main St.	Kirkland	60146
Malta Township	Second & Adams Sts.	Malta	60150
Sandwich Township	107 E. Center St.	Sandwich	60548
Shabbona Public	119 W. Comanche Ave.	Shabbona	60550
Somonauk Public	131 S. Depot St.	Somonauk	60552
Squaw Grove Township	146 N. Maple St.	Hinckley	60520
Sycamore Public	State & Main Sts.	Sycamore	60178

De Witt

Farmer City Public	105 E. Green St.	Farmer City	61842
Vespasian Warner Public	120 W. Johnson St.	Clinton	61727
Waynesville Public		Waynesville	61778
Weldon Public	P. O. Box 8	Weldon	61882

Douglas

Arcola Public	407 E. Main	Arcola	61910
Camargo Township	116 N. Main St.	Villa Grove	61956
Newman Township	27 S. Broadway	Newman	61942
Tuscola Public	112 E. Sale St.	Tuscola	61953

Du Page

Addison Public	235 N. Kennedy Dr.	Addison	60101
Bensenville Community	200 S. Church Rd.	Bensenville	60106
Bloomingdale Public	101 Fairfield Way	Bloomingdale	60108
Brookfield Free Public	3609 Grand Blvd.	Brookfield	60513
Carol Stream Public	616 Hiawatha Dr.	Carol Stream	60187
Clarendon Hills Public	7 N. Prospect Ave.	Clarendon Hills	60514
Downers Grove Public	1050 Curtiss St.	Downers Grove	60515
Elmhurst Public	211 Prospect Ave.	Elmhurst	60126
Glen Ellyn Public	596 Crescent Blvd.	Glen Ellyn	60137
Glenside Public	550 North Ave.	Glendale Heights	60137
Helen M. Plum Memorial	110 W. Maple St.	Lombard	60148
Hinsdale Public	20 E. Maple St.	Hinsdale	60521
Itasca Community	500 W. Irving Park Rd.	Itasca	60143
Lisle Library District	1017 Front St.	Lisle	60532
Nichols	110 S. Washington St.	Naperville	60540
Oak Brook Free Public	1200 Oak Brook Rd.	Oak Brook	60521
Roselle Public	127 Main St.	Roselle	60172
Suburban Library System	125 Tower Dr.	Burr Ridge	60521
Villa Park Public	305 S. Ardmore	Villa Park	60181
West Chicago Public	332 E. Washington St.	West Chicago	60185
Westmont Public	37 E. Richmond	Westmont	60559
Wheaton Public	225 N. Cross St.	Wheaton	60187
Winfield Public	0S164 Winfield Rd.	Winfield	60190
Wood Dale	300 N. Edgebrook Rd.	Wood Dale	60191
Woodridge Public	2525 Center Dr.	Woodridge	60515

Edgar

Chrisman Public	112 S. Illinois	Chrisman	61924
Kansas Community Mem.	N. Front St.	Kansas	61933
Paris Carnegie Public	207 Main St.	Paris	61944

Edwards

Albion Public	6 N. Fourth St.	Albion	62806
West Salem Public	112 W. South St.	West Salem	62476

Effingham

Altamont Public	202 N. Second St.	Altamont	62411
Helen Matthes	100 E. Market Ave.	Effingham	62401

Fayette

Evans Public	215 S. Fifth St.	Vandalia	62471
Saint Elmo Public	Main St.	Saint Elmo	62458

Ford

Melvin Public	102 S. Center St.	Melvin	60952
Moyer	307 N. Sangamon	Gibson City	60936
Paxton Carnegie	254 S. Market St.	Paxton	60957
Piper City Public	12 W. Peoria	Piper City	60959

Franklin

Benton Public	502 S. Main	Benton	62812
Christopher Public	218 W. Market St.	Christopher	62822
West Frankfort Public	402 E. Poplar St.	West Frankfort	62896
Zeigler Public	111 S. Main	Zeigler	62999

Fulton

Avon Public	105 S. Main St.	Avon	61415
Farmington Public	266 E. Fort St.	Farmington	61531
Lewistown Carnegie Public	381 W. Lincoln Ave.	Lewistown	61542
Parlin Public	205 W. Chestnut St.	Lewistown	61520
Putman Township	201 S. Third St.	Cuba	61427
Vermont Public		Vermont	61484

Gallatin

Shawneetown Public	Lincoln Ave. & E. Posey	Shawneetown	62984

Greene

Carrollton Public	S. Main	Carrollton	62016
Greenfield Public	W. Chestnut	Greenfield	62044
Roodhouse Public	220 W. Franklin St.	Roodhouse	62082
White Hall Township	119 E. Sherman St.	White Hall	62092

Grundy

Coal City Public	515 S. Broadway St.	Coal City	60416
Morris Public	604 Liberty St.	Morris	60450

Hamilton

McCoy Memorial	Washington St.	Mc Leansboro	62859

Hancock

Carthage Public	538 Wabash	Carthage	62321
Chili Public	Fifth St.	Bowen	62316
Hamilton Public	861 N. Broadway St.	Hamilton	62341
La Harpe Carnegie Public	209 Main St.	La Harpe	61450
Nauvoo Public	Box 274	Nauvoo	62354
Tri-County Public	N. Center St.	Augusta	62311
Warsaw Free Public	Fourth & Clay Sts.	Warsaw	62379

Hardin

Rosiclare Memorial Public	Main St.	Rosiclare	62982

Henderson

Henderson County Dist.	E. Main Street	Biggsville	61418

Henry

Annawan-Alba Township	320 W. Front St.	Annawan	61234
Atkinson Public	119 W. Main	Atkinson	61235
Cambridge Township	212 W. Center St.	Cambridge	61238
Clover Township	139 N. Division St.	Woodhull	61490
Colona Township	R. R. 3, Box 322A	Colona	61241
Galva Public	120 NW Third Ave.	Galva	61434
Geneseo Township	218 S. State St.	Geneseo	61254
Kewanee Public	102 S. Tremont St.	Kewanee	61443
Western Township	1111 Fourth St.	Orion	61273

Iroquois

A. Herr Smith & E.E. Smith	42 E. First St.	Loda	60948
Douglas Township	117 E. Second St.	Gilman	60938
Milford Township	2 S. Grant Ave.	Milford	60953
Onarga Public	209 W. Seminary Ave.	Onarga	60955
Sheldon Township	125 N. 5th St.	Sheldon	60966
Watseka Public	201 S. Fourth St.	Watseka	60970

Jackson

Carbondale Public	304 W. Walnut	Carbondale	62901
Sallie Logan Public	1808 Walnut St.	Murphysboro	62966

Jasper

Newton Public	100 Van Buren St.	Newton	62448

Jefferson

Mitchell Museum	Richview Rd.	Mount Vernon	62864
Mount Vernon Public	101 S. Seventh St.	Mount Vernon	62864

Jersey

Jerseyville Free	104 N. Lafayette St.	Jerseyville	62052

Jo Daviess

East Dubuque Public	301 Sinsinawa Ave.	East Dubuque	61025
Elizabeth Township	Myrtle St.	Elizabeth	61028
Galena Public	S. Bench St.	Galena	61036
Hanover Township	204 Jefferson St.	Hanover	61041
Stockton Township	140 W. Benton St.	Stockton	61085
Warren Township	210 Burnett Ave.	Warren	61087

Johnson

Vienna Public	P. O. Box 616	Vienna	62995

Kane

Aurora Public	1 E. Benton St.	Aurora	60506
Batavia Public	11 N. Batavia Ave.	Batavia	60510
Dundee Township	555 Barrington Ave.	Dundee	60118
Du Page	127 S. First St.	Geneva	60134
Elburn Public	Box AJ	Elburn	60119
Ella Johnson Memorial	153 S. State St.	Hampshire	60140

Gail Borden Public	200 N. Grove Ave.	Elgin	60120
Geneva Public	27 S. Second St.	Geneva	60134
Kaneville Free Public	Main & Harter Rds.	Kaneville	60144
Maple Park Public	505 E. Main St.	Maple Park	60151
North Aurora Public	14 E. State St.	North Aurora	60542
St. Charles Public	One S. Sixth Ave.	St. Charles	60174
Sugar Grove Public	129 Main St.	Sugar Grove	60554

Kankakee

Bradley Public	422 W. Broadway	Bradley	60915
Edward Chipman Public	126 N. Locust St.	Momence	60954
Grant Park Public	106 W. Taylor St.	Grant Park	60940
Kankakee Co. Historical	Eighth & Water Sts.	Kankakee	60901
Manteno District	50 W. Division St.	Manteno	60950

Kendall

Little Rock Township	15 N. Center	Plano	60545
Oswego Public	Jefferson & Main St.	Oswego	60543
Yorkville Public	102 S. Bridge St.	Yorkville	60560

Knox

Galesburg Public	40 E. Simmons St.	Galesburg	61401
Greig Memorial	110 S. Joy St.	Oneida	61467
John Mosser Public	106 W. Meek St.	Abingdon	61410
Knoxville Public	Public Square	Knoxville	61448
Maquon Township	109 W. Third St.	Maquon	61458
Ransom Memorial Public	Main St.	Altona	61414
Salem Township Free	115 W. Main St.	Yates City	61572

Lake

Antioch Township	757 Main St.	Antioch	60002
Cook Memorial Public	413 N. Milwaukee	Libertyville	60048
Ela Area Public	13 S. Buesching Rd.	Lake Zurich	60047
Fox Lake District	255 E. Grand Ave.	Fox Lake	60020
Fremont Public	470 N. Lake St.	Mundelein	60060
Grayslake Area Public	148 Center St.	Grayslake	60030
Highland Park Public	494 Laurel Ave.	Highland Park	60035
Highwood Public	102 Highwood Ave.	Highwood	60040
Lake Bluff Public	123 Scranton Ave.	Lake Bluff	60044
Lake County Law	18 N. County St.	Waukegan	60085
Lake Forest	360 E. Deerpath	Lake Forest	60045
Lake Villa District	101 E. Grand Ave.	Lake Villa	60046
News-Sun	100 Madison St.	Waukegan	60085
North Chicago Public	1645 Lincoln Ave.	North Chicago	60064
Round Lake Area Public	442 Cedar Lake Rd.	Round Lake	60073
Vernon Area Public	23184 N. Indian Crk. Rd.	Prairie View	60069
Warren-Newport Public	224 N. O'Plaine Rd.	Gurnee	60031
Wauconda Township	212 Osage St.	Wauconda	60084
Waukegan Public	128 N. County St.	Waukegan	60085
Zion-Benton Public	2600 Emmaus Ave.	Zion	60099

La Salle

Earl Township	205 Winthrop St.	Earlville	60518
Graves Public	901 Washington St.	Mendota	61342
La Salle Public	305 Marquette St.	La Salle	61301
Lostant Community	Third St.	Lostant	61334
Marseilles Public	E. Bluff St.	Marseilles	61341
Oglesby Public	128 W. Walnut St.	Oglesby	61348
Peru Public	627 Putnam	Peru	61354
Reddick	1010 Canal St.	Ottawa	61350
Rutland Community		Rutland	61358
Seneca Public	210 N. Main St.	Seneca	61360

Starved Rock	900 Hitt St.	Ottawa	61350
Streator Public	130 S. Park St.	Streator	61364
Third Dist. Appellate Ct.	1004 Columbus St.	Ottawa	61350
Utica Public	Mill & Grove Sts.	Utica	61373

Lawrence

Lawrenceville Township	814 12th St.	Lawrenceville	62439

Lee

Dixon Public	221 Hennepin Ave.	Dixon	61021
Franklin Grove Public	Elm St.	Franklin Grove	61031
Mills-Petrie Memorial	N. Douglas at First St.	Ashton	61006
Pankhurst Memorial	3 S. Jefferson Ave.	Amboy	61310
Paw Paw Public	Box 446	Paw Paw	61353
Sterling Public	102 W. Fourth St.	Sterling	61081

Livingston

Chatsworth Township	432 Locust St.	Chatsworth	60921
Dominy Memorial	201 S. Third St.	Fairbury	61739
Dwight Public	S. Prairie Ave.	Dwight	60420
Forrest Township	202 N. Center St.	Forrest	61741
Odell Public	113 Front St.	Odell	60640
Pontiac Public	401 N. Main St.	Pontiac	61764

Logan

Atlanta Public	100 Race St.	Atlanta	61723
Lincoln Public	725 Pekin	Lincoln	62656
Mount Pulaski Township	320 N. Washington St.	Mount Pulaski	62548

Mc Donough

Blandinsville-Hire Dist.		Blandinsville	61420
Bushnell Public	455 N. Dean	Bushnell	61422
Colchester City	P. O. Box 217	Colchester	62326
Macomb City Public	235 S. Lafayette St.	Macomb	61455

Mc Henry

Algonquin Area Public	115 Eastgate Dr.	Algonquin	60102
Cary Public	225 Stonegate	Cary	60013
Crystal Lake Public	126 Paddock St.	Crystal Lake	60014
Delos F. Diggins Public	101 Church Blvd.	Harvard	60033
Fox River Grove Public	306 Lincoln Ave.	Fox River Grove	60021
Marengo Public	118 W. Washington St.	Marengo	60152
Mc Henry Public	1011 N. Green St.	Mc Henry	60050
Nippersink District	10308 Main St.	Richmond	60071
Woodstock Public	414 W. Judd	Woodstock	60098

Mc Lean

Bloomington Public	205 E. Olive St.	Bloomington	61701
Chenoa Free Public	211 S. Division	Chenoa	61726
Corn Belt System	1809 W. Hovey Ave.	Normal	61761
Danvers Township	105 S. West St.	Danvers	61732
Gridley Township	320 Center St.	Gridley	61744
J.T. & E.J. Crumbaugh	405 E. Center St.	Le Roy	61752
Lexington Public	207 S. Cedar	Lexington	61753
Mc Lean Co. Historical	201 E. Grove St.	Bloomington	61701
Martin Township	104 W. Main St.	Colfax	61728
Mount Hope Township	Box 337	Mc Lean	61754
Normal Public	206 W. College	Normal	61761
Randolph Township	Main St.	Heyworth	61745
Towanda Township	105 S. Jefferson St.	Towanda	61776

Macon

Barclay Public	Main & Warren	Warrensburg	62573
Decatur Public	247 E. North St.	Decatur	62523
Friends Creek Township	134 E. Prairie St.	Argenta	62501
Maroa Township	E. Main St.	Maroa	61756
Rolling Prairie	345 W. Eldorado St.	Decatur	62522
South Macon Township		Macon	62544
Village of Oreana		Oreana	62554

Macoupin

Bunker Hill Public	220 E. Warren St.	Bunker Hill	62014
Carlinville Public	112 E. First N. St.	Carlinville	62626
Gillespie Public	201 W. Chestnut	Gillespie	62033
Girard Township	147 S. Second St.	Girard	62640
Mount Olive Public	111 W. Main St.	Mount Olive	62069
Staunton Public	306 W. Main St.	Staunton	62088
Virden Public	118 W. Deane	Virden	62690

Madison

Bethalto Public	213 B. N. Prairie	Bethalto	62010
Collinsville Memorial	408 W. Main St.	Collinsville	62234
East Alton Public	Third & Washington Sts.	East Alton	62024
Edwardsville Public	112 S. Kansas	Edwardsville	62025
Granite City Public	2001 Delmar	Granite City	62040
Hartford Public	143 W. Hawthorne	Hartford	62048
Hayner Public	328 Belle St.	Alton	62002
Lewis & Clark	Goshen Rd.	Edwardsville	62025
Louis Latzer Memorial	Ninth & Washington	Highland	62249
Madison Public	1700 Fifth St.	Madison	62060
Roxana Public	Central & Tydeman	Roxana	62084
Venice Public	325 Broadway	Venice	62090
Wood River Public	326 Ferguson Ave.	Wood River	62095

Marion

Bryan-Bennett	402 S. Broadway	Salem	62881
Centralia Public	515 E. Broadway	Centralia	62801
Patoka Public	105 E. Fayette St.	Patoka	62875

Marshall

Bond	208 Chestnut St.	Wenona	61377
Henry Public	702 Front St.	Henry	61537
Lacon Public	402 Fifth St.	Lacon	61540
Toluca City	102 N. Main St.	Toluca	61369

Mason

Forman Public	State St.	Manito	61546
Havana Public	201 W. Adams St.	Havana	62644
Mason City Public	145 S. Main St.	Mason City	62664

Massac

Metropolis Public	317 Metropolis St.	Metropolis	62960

Menard

Petersburg Public	214 S. Sixth St.	Petersburg	62675

Mercer

Greene Township	1301 18th Ave.	Viola	61486
Mercer Township Free	200 N. College	Aledo	61231
Rivoli Township	205 Main St.	New Windsor	61465

179

Monroe

Columbia Public	106 N. Metter	Columbia	62236
Morrison-Talbott	219 Park St.	Waterloo	62298

Montgomery

Hillsboro Public	214 School St.	Hillsboro	62049
Litchfield Carnegie	400 N. State St.	Litchfield	62056
Nokomis Public	112 S. Pine St.	Nokomis	62075
Witt Memorial Public	18 N. Second St.	Witt	62094

Morgan

Jacksonville Public	201 W. College	Jacksonville	62650
M. C. River Valley Public	Box 687	Meredosia	62665
Waverly Public	N. Pearl St.	Waverly	62692

Moultrie

Arthur Public	232 S. Vine St.	Arthur	61911
Lovington Township	110 W. State St.	Lovington	61937
Marrowbone Township	216 W. Main St.	Bethany	61914
Sullivan City	114 E. Harrison St.	Sullivan	61951

Ogle

Buffalo Township Free	302 W. Mason St.	Polo	61064
Byron Public	220 W. Third.	Byron	61010
Flagg Township	619 Fourth Ave.	Rochelle	61068
Forreston Public	204 First St.	Forreston	61030
Julia E. Hull	112 Walnut St.	Stillman Valley	61084
Mount Morris Public	101 E. Front St.	Mount Morris	61054
Oregon Township	300 Jefferson St.	Oregon	61061

Peoria

Alpha Park Public	1609 W. Garfield	Bartonville	61607
Brimfield Public	111 S. Galena St.	Brimfield	61517
Chillicothe Township	822 N. Second St.	Chillicothe	61523
Creve Coeur Public	311 N. Highland Ave.	Creve Coeur	61611
Dunlap Public	P. O. Box 307	Dunlap	61525
Harry L. Spooner Mem.	942 N.E. Glen Oak Ave.	Peoria	61603
Lillie M. Evans Mem.	207 N. Walnut Ave.	Princeville	61559
Peoria Co. Law	County Courthouse	Peoria	61602
Peoria Heights Public	1327 E. Kelly	Peoria Heights	61614
Peoria Historical Society	942 N.E. Glen Oak Ave.	Peoria	61603
Peoria Public	107 N.E. Monroe St.	Peoria	61602

Perry

Du Quoin Public	6 S. Washington St.	Du Quoin	62832
Pinckneyville Public	312 S. Walnut St.	Pinckneyville	62274

Piatt

Allerton Public	201 N. State	Monticello	61856
Bement Township	201 E. Bodman	Bement	61813
Blue Ridge Township	101 W. Oliver	Mansfield	61854
Goose Creek Township	130 N. Highway Ave.	De Land	61839
Hope Welty Township	116 E. Wait	Cerro Gordo	61818
Unity Township	105 W. Central St.	Atwood	61913
Willow Branch Township	Box 38	Cisco	61830

Pike

Barry Public	Bainbridge St.	Barry	62312
Griggsville Public	119 S. Corey St.	Griggsville	62340
Pittsfield Public	205 N. Memorial	Pittsfield	62363

Pope

Golconda Public	Main St.	Golconda	62938

Pulaski

Mound City Public	307 Central	Mound City	62963
Mounds Public	103 S. Blanche Ave.	Mounds	62964

Putnam

Putnam County	P. O. Box 426	Hennepin	61327
Spring Valley Public	215 E. Cleveland	Spring Valley	61362

Randolph

Chester Public	733 State St.	Chester	62233
Coulterville Public	4th St.	Coulterville	62237
Evansville Public	Town Hall	Evansville	62242
Red Bud Public	112 Bloom St.	Red Bud	62278
Sparta Public	128 W. Main St.	Sparta	62286

Richland

Carnegie	401 E. Main St.	Olney	62450

Rock Island

Andalusia Township	503 W. Second St.	Andalusia	61232
Cordova Township	402 Main Ave.	Cordova	61242
East Moline Public	740 16th Ave.	East Moline	61244
Moline Public	504 17th St.	Moline	61265
Moore Memorial	509 Main St.	Hillsdale	61257
Port Byron Township	106 N. High St.	Port Byron	61275
River Bend	P. O. Box 125	Coal Valley	61240
Robert R. Jones Public	2210 1st St.	Coal Valley	61240
Rock Island Public	4th Ave. & 19th St.	Rock Island	61201
Silvis Public	105 Eighth St.	Silvis	61282
Village of Hampton	Box 347	Hampton	61256

St. Clair

A. C. Daugherty Mem.	240 S. Fifth St.	Dupo	62239
Belleville Public	121 E. Washington St.	Belleville	62220
Cahokia Public	1032 Camp Jackson Rd.	Cahokia	62206
Caseyville Public	10 W. Morris	Caseyville	62232
East Saint Louis Public	405 N. Ninth St.	East Saint Louis	62201
Kaskaskia	306 N. Main St.	Smithton	62285
Lebanon Public	314 W. St. Louis St.	Lebanon	62254
Mascoutah Public	3 W. Church St.	Mascoutah	62258
New Athens Township	201 N. Van Buren St.	New Athens	62264
O'Fallon Public	103 W. State St.	O'Fallon	62269

Saline

Carriers Mills Public	11 E. Walnut St.	Carriers Mills	62917
Eldorado Memorial	1312 Jackson St.	Eldorado	62930
Mitchell Carnegie	101 E. Church St.	Harrisburg	62946

Sangamon

Auburn Public	118 N. Fifth St.	Auburn	62615
Divernon Township	221 S. Second St.	Divernon	62530
Illinois State Archives	Archives Building	Springfield	62756
Illinois State Historical	Old State Capitol	Springfield	62706
Illinois State	Centennial Building	Springfield	62756
Illinois State Museum	Spring & Edwards Sts.	Springfield	62706
Illinois Supreme Court	Supreme Court Bldg.	Springfield	62706
Illiopolis Public	Sixth & Mary Sts.	Illiopolis	62539

Legislative Reference Bureau	State House	Springfield	62706
Lincoln	326 S. Seventh St.	Springfield	62701
Pawnee Public	Seventh & Carroll Sts.	Pawnee	62558
Village		Williamsville	62693

Schuyler

Rushville Public	104 N. Monroe St.	Rushville	62681

Scott

Bluffs Public	Main St.	Bluffs	62621
Winchester Public	215 N. Main St.	Winchester	62694

Shelby

Mount Zion Township	410 Main St.	Mount Zion	62549
Moweaqua Public	122 N. Main St.	Moweaqua	62550
Shelbyville Free Public	154 N. Broadway	Shelbyville	62565

Stark

Bradford Public	111 Peoria St.	Bradford	61421
Ira C. Reed Public	P. O. Box 185	Lafayette	61449
Toulon Public	306 W. Jefferson	Toulon	61483
Wyoming Public	North Seventh St.	Wyoming	61491

Stephenson

Freeport Public	314 W. Stephenson St.	Freeport	61032
Lena Community District	302 W. Mason	Lena	61048
Pearl City Memorial	221 S. Main St.	Pearl City	61062

Tazewell

Deer Creek District	First St.	Deer Creek	61733
Esther Washburn Public	213 S. Sampson	Lemont	61568
Fondulac Public	235 Everett St.	East Peoria	61611
H. A. Peine Memorial	202 North Main Ave.	Minier	61759
Illinois Valley	845 Brenkani Dr.	Pekin	61554
Mackinaw Township	Madison at Orchard	Mackinaw	61755
Marquette Heights Public	715 Lincoln Rd.	Marquette Heights	61554
Morton Public	217 S. Main St.	Morton	61550
Pekin Public	301 S. 4th St.	Pekin	61554
South Pekin Public	Main St.	South Pekin	61564
Washington Public	301 Walnut St.	Washington	61571

Union

Jonesboro Public	103 N. Main	Jonesboro	62952
Stinson Memorial	409 S. Main St.	Anna	62906

Vermilion

Catlin Public	Sandusky St.	Catlin	61817
Danville Public	307 N. Vermillion St.	Danville	61832
Elwood Township Carnegie	104 N. State St.	Ridge Farm	61870
Georgetown Public	107 East West St.	Georgetown	61846
Hoopeston Public	110 N. Fourth St.	Hoopeston	60942
Potomac Public	110 E. State St.	Potomac	61865
Sidell District	Box 67	Sidell	61876
Vance Township	107 S. Main St.	Fairmount	61841
Westville Public	149 N. State St.	Westville	61883

Wabash

Mount Carmel Public	727 Mulberry St.	Mount Carmel	62863

Warren

Warren County	60-62 West Side Square	Monmouth	61462

Washington

Ashley Public	E. Railroad St.	Ashley	62808
Marissa Public	212 N. Main	Marissa	62257
Nashville Public	203 S. Kaskaskia St.	Nashville	62263
Richview Public	P. O. Box 95	Richview	62877

Wayne

Fairfield Public	300 S. E. Second St.	Fairfield	62837
Wayne City Public	E. Mill St.	Wayne City	62895

White

Carmi Public	N. Church St.	Carmi	62821
Carnegie Public	110 W. Mill St.	Grayville	62844
Indian Creek Township	Main St.	Norris City	62869

Whiteside

Coloma Township	1007 Seventh Ave.	Rock Falls	61071
Henry C. Adams Memorial	209 W. Third St.	Prophetstown	61277
Odell Public	202 E. Lincolnway	Morrison	61270
Schmaling Memorial	501 Tenth Ave.	Fulton	61252

Will

Braidwood Public	220 E. Main St.	Braidwood	60408
Bur Oak	405 Earl Rd.	Shorewood	60436
Crete Public	534 First St.	Crete	60417
Fountaindale Public	300 W. Briarcliff Rd.	Bolingbrook	60439
Frankfort Public	Rt. 30 & Pfeiffer Rd.	Frankfort	60423
Joliet Public	150 N. Ottawa	Joliet	60431
Lockport Township	121 E. Eighth St.	Lockport	60441
McClester-Nimmons	705 Illinois St.	Plainfield	60544
Manhattan Township	240 Whitson St.	Manhattan	60442
Mokena Community Public	11327 W. 195th St.	Mokena	60448
New Lenox Township	516 S. Cedar Rd.	New Lenox	60451
Park Forest South Public	1003 Samson Dr.	Park Forest South	60466
Peotone Public	213 W. North St.	Peotone	60468
Wilmington Township	201 S. Kankakee St.	Wilmington	60481

Williamson

Carterville Public	125 W. Illinois Ave.	Carterville	62918
Herrin City	120 N. 13th St.	Herrin	62948
Johnston City Public	506 Washington Ave.	Johnston City	62951
Marion Carnegie	206 S. Market	Marion	62959
Shawnee	Greenbriar Rd.	Carterville	62918

Winnebago

Cherry Valley Village	209 E. State St.	Cherry Valley	61016
North Suburban District	6340 N. Second St.	Loves Park	61111
Pecatonica Public	503 Main St.	Pecatonica	61063
Rockford Public	215 N. Wyman St.	Rockford	61101
South Beloit Public	630 Blackhawk Blvd.	South Beloit	61080
Talcott Free Public	101 E. Main St.	Rockton	61072
Winnebago County Law	Courthouse Bldg.	Rockford	61101

Woodford

El Paso Public	149 W. First St.	El Paso	61738
Filger	261 E. Fifth St.	Minonk	61760
Illinois Prairie	208 E. Partridge	Metamora	61548

NEWSPAPERS

Adams

Enterprise	127 E. Jefferson	Camp Point	62320
Herald-Whig	130 S. 5th	Quincy	62301
New Era	127 E. Jefferson	Camp Point	62320
Labor News	900 State St.	Quincy	62301

Alexander

Cairo Evening Citizen	713 Washington Ave.	Cairo	62914

Bond

Advocate	305 S. Second St.	Greenville	62246
News	Box 38	Sorento	62086

Boone

Belvidere Daily Republican	401 Whitney Blvd.	Belvidere	61008

Brown

Democrat-Message	120 E. Main St.	Mount Sterling	62353

Bureau

Bureau County Republican	316 S. Main St.	Princeton	61356
Gazette	123 W. St. Paul St.	Spring Valley	61362
Leader	110 Jackson St.	Walnut	61376
Midland Gazette	123 W. St. Paul St.	Spring Valley	61362

Calhoun

Calhoun Herald	1 Main St.	Hardin	62047
Calhoun News	310 S. County Rd.	Hardin	62047

Carroll

Mirror-Democrat	308 N. Main St.	Mount Carroll	61053
Review	Box 369	Thomson	61285
Times-Journal	P. O. Box 218	Savanna	61074

Cass

Virginia Citizen	1210 Wall St.	Beardstown	62618

Champaign

Chanute This Week	1332 E. Harmon Dr.	Rantoul	61866
Citizen	103 S. Lincoln	Mahomet	61853
County Star	Drawer N	Tolona	61880
Illini	620 E. John St.	Champaign	61820
Law Review	504 E. Pennsylvania Ave.	Champaign	61820
News-Gazette	48-52 Main St.	Champaign	61820
Press	1332 E. Harmon Dr.	Rantoul	61866
Reporter	118 S. Third St.	Fisher	61843

Christian

Breeze-Courier	212 S. Main St.	Taylorville	62568
Golden Prairie News	301 S. Chestnut	Assumption	62510
Herald-Star	P. O. Box 218	Edinburg	62531
News-Palladium	205 S. Locust	Pana	62557
Times	511 Carlin St.	Morrisonville	62546

Clark

Herald	124 S. 5th St.	Marshall	62441
Independent	125 N. 6th St.	Marshall	62441
Planet	21 N. Washington	Martinsville	62442
Reporter	216 S. Central Ave.	Casey	62420
Review	P. O. Box B	Martinsville	62442

Clay

Advocate-Press	105 W. North Ave.	Flora	62839

Clinton

Clinton County News	P. O. Box AA	New Baden	62265
Journal	623-625 N. Second St.	Breeze	62230
Sun	6 S. Main St.	Trenton	62293
Union Banner	671 10th St.	Carlyle	62231

Coles

Journal-Gazette	100 Broadway	Mattoon	61938
Oakland Ledger-Messenger		Oakland	61938
Times-Courier	307 6th St.	Charleston	61920

Cook

Albany Park News	7519 N. Ashland Ave.	Chicago	60626
Alsip Express	3840 W. 147th St.	Midlothian	60445
American Bar Assoc.	77 S. Wacker Dr.	Chicago	60445
Arlington Heights Daily	217 W. Campbell	Arlington Heights	60006
Austinite	6004 W. Belmont Ave.	Chicago	60634
Barrister	1155 E. 60th St.	Chicago	60637
Belmont Central News	2319 N. Milwaukee Ave.	Chicago	60647
Belmont Central Leader	3148 N. Central Ave.	Chicago	60634
Belmont-Cragin Passage	6004 W. Belmont Ave.	Chicago	60634
Bel-Park Leader	3148 N. Central Ave.	Chicago	60634
Beverly News	3840 W. 147th St.	Midlothian	60445
Beverly Review	9925 Wood St.	Chicago	60643
Bridgeport News	3506 S. Halsted St.	Chicago	60609
Bridgeview Independent	3840 W. 147th St.	Midlothian	60445
Brighton Park Life	2949 W. Pope John Paul	Chicago	60632
Brookfield Sun	500 East Ave.	La Grange	60525
Bugle	8746 Shermer Rd.	Niles	60648
Burbank Stickney Independ.	3840 W. 147th St.	Midlothian	60445
Calumet City-Burnham Pointer	1025 E. 162nd St.	South Holland	60473
Calumet Day	18127 William St.	Lansing	60438
Chicago Heights Star	1526 Otto Blvd.	Chicago	60411
Chicago Ridge Citizen	3840 W. 147th St.	Midlothian	60445
Countryside Sun	500 East Ave.	La Grange	50525
Cragin Leader	3148 N. Central Ave.	Chicago	60634
Daily Chicago Southtown	1232 Central Ave.	Wilmette	60091
Daily South Suburban	5959 S. Harlem Ave.	Chicago	60638
Daily Southwest Suburban	5959 S. Harlem Ave.	Chicago	60638
Deerfield Review	1232 Central Ave.	Wilmette	60091
Des Plaines Highlander	1232 Central Ave.	Wilmette	60091
Des Plaines Valley News	6123 Archer Rd.	Argo	60501
Dolton Pointer Economist	1025 E. 162nd St.	South Holland	60473

Edgebrook-Sauganash Pass.	6004 W. Belmont Ave.	Chicago	60634
Elmwood Park Elm Leaves	1232 Central Ave.	Wilmette	60091
Elmwood Park-Galewood	6004 W. Belmont Ave.	Chicago	60634
Elmwood Park Post	2400 N. Harlem Ave.	Elmwood Park	60635
Elmwood Park Times	4242 N. Harlem Ave.	Chicago	60634
Evanston Review	1232 Central Ave.	Wilmette	60091
Evergreen Park Courier	3840 W. 147th St.	Midlothian	60445
Forest Park Forest Leaves	1232 Central Ave.	Wilmette	60091
Franklin Park Post	2400 N. Harlem Ave.	Elmwood	60635
Franklin Park Herald	1232 Central Ave.	Wilmette	60091
Franklin Park Journal	1232 Central Ave.	Wilmette	60091
Franklin Park Times	4242 N. Harlem Ave.	Norridge	60634
Free Press	P. O. Box 389	Park Forest	60466
Gladstone-Norwood News	2319 N. Milwaukee Ave.	Chicago	60647
Glencoe News	1232 Central Ave.	Wilmette	60091
Glenview Announcements	1232 Central Ave.	Wilmette	60091
Glenwood/Thornton Pointer	1025 E. 162nd St.	South Holland	60473
Harlem-Foster Times	4242 N. Harlem Ave.	Norridge	60634
Harlem Irving Leader	3148 N. Central Ave.	Chicago	60634
Harlem-Irving Times	7519 N. Ashland Ave.	Chicago	60626
Harvey Star Tribune	154th St. & Broadway	Harvey	60426
Harwood Heights	6004 W. Belmont Ave.	Chicago	60634
Harwood/Norridge Park	1232 Central Ave.	Wilmette	60091
Hazel Crest-Country Club		Hazel Crest	60429
Hegewisch News	3150 E. 133rd St.	Chicago	60633
Herald	5240 S. Harper	Chicago	60615
Herald	112 Main St.	Park Ridge	60068
Hickory Hills Citizen	3840 W. 147th St.	Midlothian	60445
Highland Park News	1232 Central Ave.	Wilmette	60091
Homewood Flossmoor	1025 E. 162nd St.	South Holland	60473
Homewood-Flossmoor Star		Homewood	60430
Hyde Park Herald	5240 S. Harper	Chicago	60615
Irving Park News	2319 N. Milwaukee Ave.	Chicago	60647
Jefferson-Mayfair Times	7519 N. Ashland Ave.	Chicago	60626
Jefferson-Norwood News	2319 N. Milwaukee Ave.	Chicago	60647
Jefferson Park Leader	3148 N. Central Ave.	Chicago	60634
Jefferson Park Passage	6004 W. Belmont Ave.	Chicago	60634
Judicature	200 W. Monroe	Chicago	60606
Kane County Herald	P. O. Box 10041	Chicago	60610
La Grange-La Grange Park Sun	500 East Ave.	La Grange	60525
Lansing Pointer Economist	1025 E. 162nd St.	South Holland	60473
Lake Forest Lake Forestar	1232 Central Ave.	Wilmette	60091
Lawndale News	2711 W. Cermak Rd.	Chicago	60608
Leyden Star-Sentinel	130-D Broadway	Melrose Park	60160
Libertyville Review	1232 Central Ave.	Wilmette	60091
Lincoln-Belmont Booster	1647 W. Belmont Ave.	Chicago	60657
Lincoln Park-Lake View Booster	1647 W. Belmont Ave.	Chicago	60657
Lincolnwood Life	5158 Main St.	Skokie	60077
Logan Square News	2319 N. Milwaukee Ave.	Chicago	60647
Logan Square Times	4242 N. Harlem Ave.	Norridge	60634
Markham Star/Tribune		Markham	60426
Matteson Richton Park Star		Matteson	60443
Mayfair-Irving Park Passage	6004 W. Belmont Ave.	Chicago	60634
Mayfair Leader	3148 N. Central Ave.	Chicago	60634
Mayfair News	2319 N. Milwaukee Ave.	Chicago	60647
Maywood Herald	1232 Central Ave.	Wilmette	60091
Melrose Park Herald	1232 Central Ave.	Wilmette	60091
Midlothian-Bremen Messenger	3840 W. 147th St.	Midlothian	60445
Midlothian Southtown	5959 S. Harlem Ave.	Chicago	60638
Midlothian Star Herald		Midlothian	60445
Southwest Messenger Press	3840 W. 147th St.	Midlothian	60445
Mid-West Herald and Near West Side Herald	2711 W. Cermak Rd.	Chicago	60608

Mont Clare News	2319 N. Milwaukee Ave.	Chicago	60647
Mont Clare Post	2400 N. Harlem Ave.	Elmwood Park	60635
Morton Grove Champion	1232 Central Ave.	Wilmette	60091
Morton Grove Life	5158 Main St.	Skokie	60077
Mt. Greenwood Express	3840 W. 147th St.	Midlothian	60445
Mundelein Review	1232 Central Ave.	Wilmette	60091
Near North News	26 E. Huron St.	Chicago	60611
New Crusader	6429 M. L. King Dr.	Chicago	60637
News	P. O. Box 7008	Westchester	60153
Niles Life	5158 Main St.	Skokie	60077
Niles Spectator	1232 Central Ave.	Wilmette	60091
Northbrook Star	1232 Central Ave.	Wilmette	60091
North Center-Irving Park Booster	1647 W. Belmont Ave.	Chicago	60657
Northcenter News	2319 N. Milwaukee Ave.	Chicago	60647
Northlake Post	2400 N. Harlem Ave.	Elmwood Park	60635
Northlake Times	4242 N. Harlem Ave.	Norridge	60634
North Loop News	800 N. Clark St.	Chicago	60610
North Town News	7519 N. Ashland Ave.	Chicago	60634
Northwest	2319 N. Milwaukee Ave.	Chicago	60647
Northwest Herald	2711 W. Cermak Rd.	Chicago	60608
North West Leader	3148 N. Central Ave.	Chicago	60634
North West News	2319 N. Milwaukee Ave.	Chicago	60647
North West Suburban	2319 N. Milwaukee Ave.	Chicago	60647
Northwest Sunday Times	4242 N. Harlem Ave.	Norridge	60634
Northwest Times	4242 N. Harlem Ave.	Norridge	60634
Norwood Park-Edison Park Passage	6004 W. Belmont Ave.	Chicago	60634
Oak Forest Southtown Economist	5959 S. Harlem Ave.	Chicago	60638
Oak Forest Star Herald	15859 S. Cicero Ave.	Chicago	60452
Oak Lawn Independent	3840 W. 147th St.	Midlothian	60445
Oak Park Oak Leaves	1232 Central Ave.	Wilmette	60091
Oak Park Weekend World	1232 Central Ave.	Wilmette	60091
Observer	6040 S. Harper St.	Chicago	60637
Orland Messsenger	3840 W. 147th St.	Midlothian	60445
Orland Park Southtown Economist	5959 S. Harlem Ave.	Chicago	60638
Palos Citizen	3840 W. 147th St.	Midlothian	60445
Palos Heights Star Herald		Palos Heights	60463
Palos Park Star Herald		Palos Heights	60463
Palos Southtown Economist	5959 S. Harlem Ave.	Chicago	60638
Park Forest Star	132 Plaza	Park Forest	60466
Park Ridge Advocate	1232 Central Ave.	Wilmette	60091
Portage Park Leader	3148 N. Central Ave.	Chicago	60634
Portage Park Passage	6004 W. Belmont Ave.	Chicago	60034
Portage Park Times	4242 N. Harlem Ave.	Norridge	60634
Proviso Star-Sentinel	130-D Broadway	Melrose Park	60160
Proviso Times	4242 N. Harlem Ave.	Norridge	60634
Ravenswood-Lincolnite	7519 N. Ashland Ave.	Chicago	60626
Ravenswood News	7519 N. Ashland Ave.	Chicago	60626
Regional News	12243 S. Harlem Ave.	Palos Heights	60463
Reporter	4941 N. Milwaukee Ave.	Chicago	60630
Riverdale Pointer Economist	1025 E. 162nd St.	South Holland	60473
River Grove Messenger	1232 Central Ave.	Wilmette	60091
River Grove Post	2400 N. Harlem Ave.	Elmwood Park	60635
River Grove Times	4242 N. Harlem Ave.	Norridge	60634
Rogers Park-Edgewater News	7519 N. Ashland Ave.	Chicago	60626
Rosemont Suburban Times	1000 Executive Way	Des Plaines	60018
Schiller Park Independent	1232 Central Ave.	Wilmette	60091
Schiller Park Post	2400 N. Harlem Ave.	Elmwood Park	60635
Schiller Park Times	4242 N. Harlem Ave.	Norridge	60634
Sentinel	323 S. Franklin St.	Chicago	60606
Skokie Life	5158 Main St.	Skokie	60077
Skokie Review	1232 Central Ave.	Wilmette	60091

South Holland Pointer	1025 E. 162nd St.	South Holland	60473
Economist			
South Holland Star-Tribune		South Holland	60473
Southtown Economist	5959 S. Harlem Ave.	Chicago	60638
Chicago Edition			
South Shore Scene	7134 S. Jeffery	Chicago	60649
Southwest News-Herald	6225 S. Kedzie Ave.	Chicago	60629
Suburban	1000 Executive Way	Des Plaines	60018
Suburban Leader	3148 N. Central Ave.	Chicago	60634
Suburban Times	1000 Executive Way	Des Plaines	60018
Sunday Life	4242 N. Harlem Ave.	Norridge	60634
Sunday Star	4242 N. Harlem Ave.	Norridge	60634
Sun-Journal	18127 William St.	Lansing	60438
Sun-Standard	12814 S. Western	Blue Island	60406
Sun-Times	401 N. Wabash	Chicago	60611
Tinley Park, Southtown	5959 S. Harlem Ave.	Chicago	60638
Tinley Park Star Herald		Tinley Park	60477
Tribune	435 N. Michigan Ave.	Chicago	60611
Uptown News	7519 N. Ashland Ave.	Chicago	60626
Vernon Review	1232 Central Ave.	Wilmette	60091
Weekend Booster	1647 W. Belmont Ave.	Chicago	60657
West Belmont Leader	3148 N. Central Ave.	Chicago	60634
Western Springs Sun	500 East Ave.	La Grange	60525
West Proviso Herald	1232 Central Ave.	Wilmette	60091
West Side Times	2711 W. Cermak Rd.	Chicago	60608
West Suburban Times	2319 N. Milwaukee Ave.	Chicago	60647
West Town Herald	2711 W. Cermak Rd.	Chicago	60608
Wilmette Life	1232 Central Ave.	Wilmette	60091
Wilmette Talk	1232 Central Ave.	Wilmette	60091
Worth-Palos Reporter	10139 S. Harlem Ave.	Chicago Ridge	60415

Crawford

Crawford Press	105 S. Main St.	Hutsonville	62433
Herald		Hutsonville	62433
Register	P. O. Box 98	Palestine	62451

Cumberland

Democrat		Toledo	62468
New	P. O. Box 250	Neoga	62447
Press	106 E. Cumberland	Greenup	62428

De Kalb

Chronicle	P. O. Box 587	De Kalb	60115
Genoa-Kingston Kirkland			
News	686 Park Ave., W	Genoa	60135
Midweek	121 Industrial Dr.	De Kalb	60115
Review	141 Lincoln Ave.	Hinckley	60520
Sycamore News	215 S. Sacramento	Sycamore	60178
Tri County Today	P. O. Box 72	Sandwich	60548

De Witt

Farmer City Journal	115 W. Green	Farmer City	61842
Journal	117 W. Main St.	Clinton	61727

Douglas

Journal	P. O. Box 159	Tuscola	61953
News	5-7 S. Main St.	Villa Grove	61956
Review	115 W. Sale St.	Tuscola	61953

Du Page

Addison Press	112 S. York St.	Elmhurst	60126
Bloomingdale Press	112 S. York St.	Elmhurst	60126
Burr Ridge Doings	10 E. Hinsdale Ave.	Hinsdale	60521
Carol Stream Press	112 S. York St.	Elmhurst	60126
Clarendon Hills Doings	10 E. Hinsdale Ave.	Hinsdale	60521
Du Page Doings	10 E. Hinsdale Ave.	Hinsdale	60521
Elmhurst Press	112 S. York St.	Elmhurst	60126
Examiner	120 Church St.	Winfield	60190
Glendale Heights Press	112 S. York St.	Elmhurst	60126
Glen Ellyn Times Press	112 S. York St.	Elmhurst	60126
Hanover Park Township Times	P. O. Box 94248	Schaumburg	60194
Hinsdale Doings	10 E. Hinsdale Ave.	Hinsdale	60521
Journal	P. O. Box 360	Wheaton	60187
Lisle Township Sun	4742 Main St.	Lisle	60532
Lombardian	613 S. Main St.	Lombard	60148
Lombard Spectator	112 S. York St.	Elmhurst	60126
Oak Brook Doings	10 E. Hinsdale Ave.	Hinsdale	60521
Oak Brook Press	112 S. York St.	Elmhurst	60126
Roselle Record	P. O. Box 94248	Schaumburg	60194
Suburban Trib	765 N. York Rd.	Hinsdale	60521
Two Star Record	P. O. Box 94248	Schaumburg	60194
Villa Park Argus	112 S. York St.	Elmhurst	60126
Villa Park Review	613 S. Main St.	Lombard	60148
Voice of Addison	800 E. Higgens Rd.	Schaumburg	60195
Voice of Bartlett	800 E. Higgins Rd.	Schaumburg	60195
Voice of Bensenville	800 E. Higgins Rd.	Schaumburg	60195
Voice of Bloomingdale	800 E. Higgins Rd.	Schaumburg	60195
Voice of Carol Stream	800 E. Higgins Rd.	Schaumburg	60195
Voice of Elk Grove Village	800 E. Higgins Rd.	Schaumburg	60195
Voice of Glendale Heights	800 E. Higgins Rd.	Schaumburg	60195
Voice of Hanover Park	800 E. Higgins Rd.	Schaumburg	60195
Voice of Hoffman Estates	800 E. Higgins Rd.	Schaumburg	60195
Voice of Itasca	800 E. Higgins Rd.	Schaumburg	60195
Voice of Roselle/Medinah	800 E. Higgins Rd.	Schaumburg	60195
Voice of Schaumburg	800 E. Higgins Rd.	Schaumburg	60195
Wall Street Journal	400 A. R. Schuman Dr.	Naperville	60566
Press	124 Fremont St.	West Chicago	60185
West Cook County Press	112 S. York St.	Elmhurst	60126
Wheaton Times Press	112 S. York St.	Elmhurst	60126

Edgar

Beacon-News	218 N. Main St.	Paris	61944

Edwards

Advocate	Box 427	West Salem	62476
Journal-Register	19 W. Main St.	Albion	62806

Effingham

Daily News	201 N. Banker St.	Effingham	62401
Journal	P. O. Box 38	Beecher City	62414
Press and Dieterich Special Gazette	P. O. Box 667	Teutopolis	62467

Fayette

Banner	419 N. Main St.	St. Elmo	62458
News	P. O. Box H	Farina	62838
Record	218 N. Market St.	Paxton	60957
News-Journal	217 S. Superior St.	Ramsey	62080
Leader Union	229 S. Fifth St.	Vandalia	62471

Ford

Courier	110 N. Sangamon Ave.	Gibson City	60936
Journal	54 W. Peoria	Piper City	60959
Loda Times	218 N. Market	Paxton	60957
Record	218 N. Market	Paxton	60957

Franklin

American	111 S. Emma St.	West Frankfort	62896
News	111-113 E. Church	Benton	62812
Progress	P. O. Box A	Christopher	62822

Fulton

Astoria South Fulton Argus	P. O. Box 427	Astoria	61501
Fulton Democrat	219 W. Market	Havana	62644
Journal	S. Side Square	Cuba	61427
Ledger	53 W. Elm St.	Canton	61520
Times		London Mills	61544

Gallatin

Gallatin County Democrat	Shawneetown	62984
Ridgway News	Ridgway	62979

Greene

Argus	P. O. Box 323	Greenfield	62044
Gazette-Patriot	P. O. Box 231	Carrollton	62016
North Greene News	112 E. Sherman	White Hall	62092

Grundy

Chronicle	Box 218	Gardner	60424
Courant	273 S. Broadway	Coal City	60416
Herald	124 E. Washington St.	Morris	60450

Hamilton

Mc Leansboro Times-Leader	Box 479	Mc Leansboro	62859

Hancock

Eagle	P. O. Box 257	Augusta	62311
Enterprise	Box 455	Dallas City	62330
Hancock County Journal Pilot	P. O. Box 478	Carthage	62321
Hancock County Quill	P. O. Box 128	Stronghurst	61480

Hardin

Hardin Co. Independent	P. O. Box 328	Elizabethtown	62931

Henderson

Henderson County Quill	P. O. Box 128	Stronghurst	61480
Oquawka Current		Oquawka	61469

Henry

Atkinson-Annawan News	P. O. Box 601	Atkinson	61235
Chronicle	119 W. Exchange St.	Cambridge	61238
News	Box GG	Galva	61434
Republic	108 W. First St.	Geneseo	61254
Star-Courier	105 E. Central Blvd.	Kewanee	61443
Times	P. O. Box 601	Orion	61273

Iroquois

Advocate	487 S. Main	Clifton	60927
Herald-News	18 S. Axtel Ave.	Milford	60953
Illiana Spirit	1492 E. Walnut	Watseka	60970
Leader-Review	101 W. Locust St.	Fairbury	61739
News/Independent	119 W. Garfield	Cissna Park	60924
Star		Gilman	60938
Times-Republic	1491 E. Walnut	Watseka	60970

Jackson

Southern Illinoisan	710 N. Illinois	Carbondale	62901

Jasper

Press-Mentor	P. O. Box 151	Newton	62448
Register-News		Mt. Vernon	62864

Jefferson

Register News	112 N. 9th	Mt. Vernon	62824

Jersey

Democrat-News	519 S. State	Jerseyville	62052

Jo Daviess

Gazette-Advertiser	109 S. Main St.	Galena	61036
Herald-News	P. O. Box 35	Stockton	61085
News	240 N. Main St.	Elizabeth	61028
Register	141 Sinsinawa Ave.	East Dubuque	61025
Sentinel-Leader	163 E. Main St.	Warren	61087

Johnson

Times		Vienna	62995

Kane

Batavia Chronicle	P. O. Box 157	Batavia	60510
Beacon-News	101 S. River St.	Aurora	60506
Cardunal Free Press	250 Williams Rd.	Carpentersville	60110
Courier News	300 Lake St.	Elgin	60120
Elgin Herald	250 Williams Rd.	Carpentersville	60110
Hampshire Register	121 A. Keyes Ave.	Hampshire	60140
Herald	P. O. Box L	Elburn	60119
Republican	17 N. First St.	Geneva	60134
St. Charles Chronicle	2601 E. Main St.	St. Charles	60174

Kankakee

Bourbonnais Herald	536 N. Convent Ave.	Bourbonnais	60914
Bradley Press	536 N. Convent Ave.	Bourbonnais	60914
Herscher Press	Box 159	Dwight	60420
Journal	8 Dearborn Sq.	Kankakee	60901
Kankakee Star News	536 N. Convent Ave.	Bourbonnais	60914
News	65 W. First St.	Manteno	60950
Progress-Reporter	110 W. River St.	Momence	60954
Record	Dixie Hwy.	St. Anne	60964
Reddick-Essex Courier	204 E. Chippewa St.	Dwight	60420

Kendall

Kendall County Record	222 Bridge St.	Yorkville	60560
Ledger-Sentinel	68 S. Main St.	Oswego	
Record	304 S. Bill	Plano	60545

Knox

Journal	P. O. Box 98	Knoxville	61448
Post	80 S. Cherry St.	Galesburg	61401
Register-Mail	140 S. Prairie St.	Galesburg	61401
Williamsfield Times	116 S. Magnolia	Williamsfield	61529
Wrova Reporter	Box 471	Woodhull	61490
Yates City Banner	116 S. Magnolia	Elmwood	61529

Lake

Antioch News	952 Main	Antioch	60002
Antioch Reporter	952 Main	Antioch	60002
Barrington Courier Review	200 James	Barrington	60010
Bi-State Reporter	30 S. Whitney St.	Grayslake	60030
Deerfield News Advertiser	1899 Second St.	Highland Park	60035
Ft. Sheridan Tower	30 S. Whitney St.	Grayslake	60030
Fox Lake Press	30 S. Whitney	Grayslake	60030
Fremont Patriot	30 S. Whitney	Grayslake	60030
Frontier Enterprise	35 Genesee St.	Lake Zurich	60047
Glencoe News Advertiser	1899 Second St.	Highland Park	60035
Glenview News Advertiser	1899 Second St.	Highland Park	60035
Great Lakes Bulletin	30 S. Whitney St.	Grayslake	60030
Gurnee Press	30 S. Whitney St.	Grayslake	60030
Highland Park News Advertiser	1899 Second St.	Highland Park	60035
Highlander	P. O. Box 397	Barrington	60010
Lake Forest News Advertiser	1899 Second St.	Highland Park	60035
Lake Villa Record	30 Whitney St.	Grayslake	60030
Mundelein Herald	P. O. Box 639	Mundelein	60060
News-Sun	100 W. Madison St.	Waukegan	60085
Northbrook News Advertiser	1899 Second St.	Highland Park	60035
North Chicago Tribune	30 S. Whitney St.	Grayslake	60030
Round Lake News	30 S. Whitney St.	Grayslake	60030
Times	30 S. Whitney St.	Grayslake	60030
Vernon Town Crier	P. O. Box 52	Prairie View	60069
Vernon Township News Advertiser	1899 Second St.	Highland Park	60035
Warren-Newport Press	30 S. Whitney St.	Grayslake	60030
Wauconda Leader	30 S. Whitney St.	Grayslake	60030
Wilmette News Advertiser	1899 Second St.	Highland Park	60035
Winnetka News Advertiser	1899 Second St.	Highland Park	60035
Zion-Benton News	2719 Elisha Ave.	Zion	60099

La Salle

Leader		Earlville	60518
News		Tonica	61370
News-Tribune	426 Second St.	La Salle	61301
Times	110 W. Jefferson	Ottawa	61350
Times-Press	122 S. Bloomington St.	Streator	61364
Town & Country	Box 279	Ottawa	61350

Lawrence

Lawrence County News	1209 State St.	Lawrenceville	62439
Leader-Times	218 Main St.	Bridgeport	62417
Press	216 S. Christy	Sumner	62417
Record	P. O. Box 559	Lawrenceville	62439

Lee

Gazette	521 Main St.	Ashton	61006
News	219 E. Main St.	Amboy	61310
Telegraph	113-115 S. Peoria Ave.	Dixon	61021

Livingston

Blade	101 W. Locust St.	Fairbury	61739
Chatsworth Plaindealer	101 W. Locust St.	Fairbury	61739
Chronicle-Headlight - Enquirer	127 Hack St.	Cullom	60929
Emington Joker	204 E. Chippewa St.	Dwight	60420
Home Times		Flanagan	61740
Leader	318 N. Main St.	Pontiac	61764
News	113 Krack St.	Forrest	61741
Star & Herald	204 E. Chippewa	Dwight	60420
Times	Box 159	Dwight	60420

Logan

Courier	Mc Lean and Pulaski	Lincoln	62656
Times-News	209 S. Washington St.	Mount Pulaski	62548

Mc Donough

Chronicle		Colchester	62326
Journal	Box 597	Macomb	61455

Mc Henry

Barrington Banner	P. O. Box 209	Cary	60013
Beacon News	113 E. Prairie St.	Marengo	60152
Cary Grove Clarion	P. O. Box 209	Cary	60013
Herald	7803 Pyott Rd.	Crystal Lake	60014
Herald	201 S. Ayer St.	Harvard	60033
Mc Henry County Citizen	3812 W. Elm St.	Mc Henry	60050
News and Mc Henry County Guide	404 Virginia St.	Crystal Lake	60014
Plaindealer	3812 W. Elm St.	Mc Henry	60050
Republican News	104 S. State St.	Marengo	60152
Sentinel	109 S. Jefferson	Woodstock	60098

Mc Lean

Clipper-Times & Lexington Unit Journal	217 Green St.	Chenoa	61726
Gazette	Lincoln St.	Saybrook	61770
Gridley News	101 West Locust St.	Fairbury	61739
Journal, Free Press, and News	207 E. Center	Le Roy	61752
Pantagraph	301 W. Washington St.	Bloomington	61701
Star	105 S. Buchanan	Heyworth	61745

Macon

Herald and Review	P. O. Box 311	Decatur	62525
Leader	P. O. Box E	Blue Mound	62513
Prairie Post	Box 428	Maroa	61756
Region News	130 Wildwood Dr.	Mount Zion	62549
Voice of the Black Comm.	3180 N. Woodford St.	Decatur	62526

Macoupin

Area News	112-16 W. Chestnut St.	Gillespie	62033
Gazette	174 W. Center St.	Girard	62640
Gazette-News	P. O. Box Z	Bunker Hill	62014
Macoupin County Enquirer	125 E. Main St.	Carlinville	62626
Northwestern News	37 E. State	Palmyra	62674
Recorder	169 W. Jackson St.	Virden	62690
Star-Times	108 W. Main St.	Staunton	62088

Madison

Alton Citizen	329 Belle	Alton	62002
Bethalton American	329 Belle	Alton	62002
Collinsville Journal	201 N. Morrison	Collinsville	62234
Herald	113 E. Clay St.	Collinsville	62234
Intelligencer	117 N. 2nd St.	Edwardsville	62025
Journal	1990 Troy Rd.	Edwardsville	62025
News-Leader	822 Broadway	Highland	62249
Press-Record	1815 Delmar Ave.	Granite City	62040
Telegraph	111 E. Broadway	Alton	62002
Wood River Journal	329 Belle	Alton	62002

Marion

Express	P. O. Box 220	Kinmundy	62854
Register	110 NE 1st St.	Sandoval	62882
Sentinel	232 E. Broadway	Centralia	62801
Times-Commoner	120 S. Broadway	Salem	62881

Marshall

Home Journal	204 S. Washington St.	Lacon	61540
News-Republican	303 Edward	Henry	61537
Wenona Index	Box 190	Henry	61537

Mason

Mason County Democrat	217 W. Market	Havana	62644

Massac

Planet	101 W. 7th St.	Metropolis	62960

Menard

Observer	P. O. Box 100	Petersburg	62675
Menard County Review	P. O. Box 100	Petersburg	62675

Mercer

Times-Record	113-115 S. College Ave.	Aledo	61231

Monroe

Monroe County Clarion	212 W. Locust	Columbia	62236
Star	212 W. Locust	Columbia	62236
Republic Times	P. O. Box 147	Waterloo	62298

Montgomery

Free Press-Progress	123 E. State	Nokomis	62075
Hillsboro & Montgomery Co. News	P. O. Box 250	Hillsboro	62049
Journal	431 S. Main St.	Hillsboro	62049
News	327 E. Broad St.	Raymond	62560
News-Herald	112 E. Ryder St.	Litchfield	62056
Panhandle Press	P. O. Box 141	Farmersville	62533

194

Morgan

Courier		Jacksonville	62650
Journal		Jacksonville	62650
Journal	130 S. Pearl	Waverly	62692
Journal-Courier		Jacksonville	62650
Times	P. O. Box 186	Franklin	62638

Moultrie

Findlay Enterprise	P. O. Box A	Sullivan	61951
News Progress	P. O. Box A	Sullivan	61951

Ogle

Journal	Box 237	Forreston	61030
Leader	401 N. Main	Rochelle	61068
Mt. Morris Times	5 E. Front St.	Mt. Morris	61054
News	401 N. Main	Rochelle	61068
Ogle County Life	217 Washington	Oregon	61061
Republican-Reporter	126 N. 3rd St.	Oregon	61061
Tri-County Press	113 N. Franklin	Polo	61064

Peoria

Advertiser	116 S. Magnolia	Elmwood	61529
Bulletin	1016 N. Second St.	Chillicothe	61523
Farmington Bugle	116 S. Magnolia	Elmwood	61529
Gazette	116 S. Magnolia	Elmwood	61529
Gazette	401 Main St.	Glasford	61533
Hanna City-Trivoli Index	401 Main St.	Glasford	61533
Heights Herald	1310 E. Seiberling Ave.	Peoria Heights	61614
Journal Star	1 News Plaza	Peoria	61643
Observer	5717 N. Humboldt	Peoria	61614
Peoria Daily Record	631 Main St.	Peoria	61602
Princeville Telephone	102 N. 7th St.	Wyoming	60491

Perry

Perry County Advocate	318 W. Parker	Pinckneyville	62274

Piatt

Herald	107 N. Main St.	Atwood	61913
News	217 E. South St.	Cerro Gordo	61818
Piatt County Journal	503 Bridge St.	Monticello	61856

Pike

Pike County News	P. O. Box 155	Barry	62312
Pike Press	115 W. Jefferson	Pittsfield	62363

Pope

Herald-Enterprise	Main St.	Golconda	62938

Pulaski

Pulaski Enterprise	315 First St.	Mounds	62964

Putnum

Putnum County Record	305 S. Mc Coy	Granville	61326
Spring Valley Gazette	123 W. St. Paul	Spring Valley	61362

Randolph

Ledger	114 W. Broadway	Steeleville	62288
News-Plaindealer	116 W. Main	Sparta	62286
North County News	122-124 S. Main	Red Bud	62278
Time	Box 711	Menard	62259

Richland

Daily Mail	P. O. Box 340	Olney	62450

Rock Island

Argus	1724 Fourth Ave.	Rock Island	61201
Daily Dispatch	1621 2nd Ave.	Rock Island	61201
Dispatch	1720 Fifth Ave.	Moline	61265
Globe		Port Byron	61275
Milan Mirror	404 W. 3rd St.	Milan	61264
Quad City Times	124 E 2nd St.	Davenport	52801
Rock Island News	1812 3rd Ave.	Rock Island	61201
Silvas News	816 15th Ave.	E. Moline	61244

St. Clair

Advertiser	309 W. Louis St.	Lebanon	62254
Belleville Journal	6 N. Church	Belleville	62220
Cahokia-Dupo Herald	1256 Camp Jackson Rd.	Cahokia	62206
Centreville News	3800 Mc Casland	E. St. Louis	62205
Clinton County Journal	6 N. Church	Belleville	62220
E. St. Louis Monitor	1501 State St.	E. St. Louis	62205
E. St. Louis News	2007 W. 50th	Fairview Heights	62203
Fairview Heights	2007 W. Highway 50	Fairview Heights	62203
Globe Democrat	23 S. First	Belleville	62220
Journal-Press	R. R. 1, Box 303	New Athens	62264
Herald	314 E. Church	Mascoutah	62258
News-Democrat	120 S. Illinois	Belleville	62222
Progress	612 E. State St.	O'Fallon	62269
St. Clair County Herald	P. O. Box C	Mascoutah	62258
Tribune	10850 Lincoln Trail	Fairview Heights	62208
Tribune	10 S. Monroe	Freeburg	62243

Saline

Journal	1200 Locust St.	Eldorado	62930
Register	35 S. Vine St.	Harrisburg	62946

Sangamon

Chatham Clarion	110 N. 5th St.	Auburn	62615
Citizen	110 N. 5th St.	Auburn	62615
County Line Observer		Illiopolis	62539
Divernon News	110 N. Fifth St.	Auburn	62615
Illinois Times	P. O. Box 3524	Springfield	62708
New Berlin Bee	Box 2	Pleasant Plains	62677
Post	110 N. 5th St.	Auburn	62615
Press	Box 2	Pleasant Plains	62677
Sentinel		Illiopolis	62539
State Journal-Register	313 S. 6th St.	Springfield	62701

Schuyler

Times	110 E. Lafayette St.	Rushville	62681

Scott

Times	4 S. Hill St.	Winchester	62694

Shelby

Clipper	130 S. Pine St.	Stewardson	62463
Union	100 W. Main	Shelbyville	62565

Stark

Post-Herald	102 N. 7th St.	Wyoming	60491
Republican	P. O. Box 190	Bradford	61421
Stark County News	120 E. Main	Toulon	61483

Stephenson

Journal-Standard	27 S. State St.	Freeport	61032

Tazewell

Courier	186 E. Washington	Morton	61550
Courier	Box 10	Washington	61571
East Peoria Courier	100 Detroit Ave.	Morton	61550
Pekin Today	100 Detroit Ave.	Morton	61550
Spirit Today	100 Detroit Ave.	Morton	61550
Times	314 Locust St.	Delavan	61734
Times	20 S. 4th	Pekin	61554
Tazewell News	100 Detroit Ave.	Morton	61550
Tazewell Reporter	101 Washington Sq.	Washington	61571
Tazewell South Today	100 Detroit Ave.	Morton	61550
Taz-Wood North	101 Washington Sq.	Washington	61571
Washington Reporter	100 Detroit Ave.	Morton	61550

Union

Gazette-Democrat	P. O. Box 529	Anna	62906
Tri-County Record	130 Front St.	Dongola	62926

Vermilion

Chronicle	206 First Ave.	Hoopeston	60942
Commercial News	17 W. North St.	Danville	61833
Middlefork Journal	P. O. Box 157	Potomac	61865

Wabash

Republican-Register	117 E. Fourth St.	Mt. Carmel	62863

Warren

Abingdon Argus	P. O. Box 128	Roseville	61473
Avon Sentinel	P. O. Box 128	Roseville	61473
Independent	P. O. Box 128	Roseville	61473
Review Atlas	400 S. Main	Monmouth	61462

Washington

News	Box 316	Ashley	62808
News	130 W. St. Louis St.	Nashville	62263
Times	P. O. Box 68	Okawville	62271

Wayne

Wayne County Press	213 E. Main	Fairfield	62837

White

Carmi Times	323 E. Main	Carmi	62821
Mercury-Independent	P. O. Box 220	Grayville	62844

Whiteside

Echo	342 Washington St.	Prophetstown	61277
Erie Review		Erie	61250

Whiteside

Gazette	312 Second Ave.	Sterling	61081
Journal	P. O. Box 30	Fulton	61252
Rock Valley Review	106 W. Second St.	Rock Falls	61071
Whiteside News Sentinel	100 E. Main St.	Morrison	61270

Will

Advocate		Wilmington	60481
Beacon	759 Luther Dr.	Romeoville	60441
Braidwood Index	111 S. Water St.	Wilmington	60481
Coal City Express	111 S. Water St.	Wilmington	60481
Crete-Park Forest S. Star		Crete	60417
Enterprise	519 Lockport St.	Plainfield	60544
Frankfort-Star Herald	20 S. Rt. 45	Frankfort	60423
Herald-News	300 Caterpillar Dr.	Joliet	60436
Journal	Main St.	Braidwood	60408
Manhattan Elwood Express	111 S. Water St.	Wilmington	60481
Wilmington Express	111 S. Water St.	Wilmington	60481
Wilmington Free Press	111 S. Water St.	Wilmington	60481

Williamson

Republican	111-115 Franklin Ave.	Marion	62959
Spokesman	106 W. Cherry	Herrin	62948

Winnebago

Chronical	605 W. State	Rockford	61101
Durand Gazette	406 Center St.	Durand	61024
Midwest Observer	303 N. Main	Rockford	61101
Northern Ogle Tempo	406 Center St.	Durand	61024
Pecatonica News	406 Center St.	Durand	61024
Post	518 Merrill Ave.	Rockford	61101
Register Star	97 E. State St.	Rockford	61105
Rockford Journal	121 Ashley Ave.	Rockford	61102
Rocton Herald	406 Center St.	Durand	61024
Winnebago News	406 Center St.	Durand	61024

Woodford

Herald	214 E. Partridge	Metamora	61548
Leader		Washburn	61570
News-Dispatch	144 W. 5th St.	Minone	61760
Review	105 E. Broad	Roanoke	61561
Woodford Co. Journal	108 S. Main	Eureka	61530

SECTION III

PEOPLE WHO HELP

PROFESSIONAL SEARCH HELP

Independent Search Consultants

Independent Search Consultants is a national
association of professional consultants and record
searchers who offer very specialized services. ISC
consultants are highly trained, and their expertise
in adoption-related searches in unequalled. The
following consultants have expertise in the State
of Illinois.

Gayle Beckstead
2180 Clover Street
Simi Valley, CA   93065
(805) 526-2289

Mary Lou Kozub
2027 Finch Court
Simi Valley, CA   93063
(805) 583-4306

Mary Ann Niebuhr
4221 Tomscot Trail
Madison, WI   53704
(608) 241-0445

Karen Tinkham
P. O. Box 1432
Litchfield, AZ   85340

Teresa Tobin
2308 Algonquin Parkway
Rolling Meadows, IL   60008

SEARCH AND SUPPORT GROUPS

Adoption Research Forum
Post Office Box 2517
Chicago, IL 60690

Adoption Option
Partridge B
325 S. 8th
Quincy, IL 62301

Alliance for Adoption
  Reunions
63 West 540 Lake Drive
Clarendon Hills, IL 60514

ALMA Chapter
Box 87
Bloomington, IL 61701

ALMA Chapter
P. O. Box 59345
Chicago, IL 60659

ALMA Chapter
Box 74
Lebanon, IL 62254

ALMA Chpater
711 North Lakeside Drive
Vernon Hills, IL 60061

Concerned United
  Birthparents
156 W. Burton
Chicago, IL 60610

Concerned United
  Birthparents
1101 Grant Place
Urbana, IL 61801

Hidden Birthright
Box 1651
Springfield, IL 62705

Search Research
Box 48
Chicago Ridge, IL 60415

Truthseekers in Adoption
Box 286
Roscoe, IL 61073

Yesterdays Children
Box 1554
Evanston, IL 60204

GENEALOGICAL AND HISTORICAL SOCIETIES

Adams

Great River Genealogical	Quincy Library	Quincy	62302

Carroll

Carroll Co. Genealogical	P. O. Box 347	Savanna	61074

Champaign

Champaign Co. Genealogical	201 S. Race	Urbana	61801

Clark

Clark Co. Genealogical	P. O. Box 153	Marshall	62441

Clinton

Clinton Co. Historical	P. O. Box 82	Aviston	62216

Coles

Coles Co. Historical	P. O. Box 538	Charleston	61920
Coles Co. IL Genealogical	P. O. Box 225	Charleston	61920
Coles Co. of IL Genealogical	Rt. 1, Box 141	Toledo	62468

Cook

Chicago Genealogical	P. O. Box 1160	Chicago	60690
Chicago Historical	North Ave./Clark St.	Chicago	60614
Des Plaines Historical	Box 225	Des Plaines	60017
Dunton Genealogical	500 North Dunton	Arlington Hgts.	60004
Fort La Motte Genea./Hist.	La Motte Library	Palestine	62451
North Suburban Genealogical	768 Oak St.	Winnetka	60093
Northwest Suburban Council of Genealogists	P. O. Box AC	Mt. Prospect	60056
Polish Genealogical	984 Milwaukee Ave.	Chicago	60622
Poplar Creek Genealogical	P. O. Box 248	Streamwood	60103
South Suburban Genea./Hist.	P. O. Box 96	South Holland	60473
Swedish Pioneer Historical	5125 N. Spaulding	Chicago	60625
Thornton Township Historical	154 East 154th St.	Harvey	60426

Crawford

Crawford Co. IL Genealogical	P. O. Box 110	Robinson	62454

Cumberland

Cumberland Co. Genealogical	Rt. 1, Box 141	Toledo	62468

De Witt

De Witt Co. Genealogical	Box 325	Clinton	61727

Douglas

Douglas Co. IL Genealogical	Box 50	Camargo	61919

Du Page

Du Page Co. Genealogical	P. O. Box 133	Lomard	60148
Elmhurst Genealogical Group	P. O. Box 84	Elmhurst	60126

Edwards

Edwards Co. Historical	P. O. Box 205	Albion	62806

Effingham

Effingham Co. Genealogical	P. O. Box 1166	Effingham	62401

Fayette

Fayette Co. Genealogical	Box 177	Vandalia	62471

Fulton

Fulton Co. Hist./Genea.	45 N. Park Dr.	Canton	61520

Greene

Greene Co. Hist./Genea.	P. O. Box 137	Carrollton	62016

Grundy

Grundy Co. Historical	827 E. Benton St.	Morris	60450

Hancock

Tri-Co. Genealogical	P. O. Box 355	Augusta	62311

Henry

Henry Historical/Genealogical	610 North St.	Henry	61537

Iroquois

Iroquois Co. Genealogical	103 W. Cherry St.	Watseka	60970

Jackson

Jackson Co. Historical	Box 7	Murphysboro	62966

Jefferson

Mt. Vernon Genealogical	101 South 7th	Mt. Vernon	62864

Jo Daviess

Galena Historical Museum	211 1/2 S. Bench	Galena	61036

Kane

Aurora Historical	305 Cedar St.	Aurora	60504
Batavia Historical	West Main St.	Batavia	60510
Elgin Genealogical	1035 Hill Ave.	Elgin	60120
Elgin Historical	444 Park St.	Elgin	60120
Geneva Historical	Wheeler Pk/Stevens St.	Geneva	60134
Kane Co. Genealogical	1133 S. 6th St.	St. Charles	60174
Kane Co. Genealogical	P. O. Box 504	Geneva	60134
St. Charles Historical	2 E. Main St.	St. Charles	60174

Kankakee

Kankakee Valley Genealogical	304 S. Indiana Ave.	Kankakee	60901

Kendall

Kendall Co. Historical	467 S. Main	Oswego	60543

Knox

Knox Co. Genealogical	P. O. Box 13	Galesburg	61401

Lake

Lake Co. Genealogical	413 N. Milwaukee Ave.	Libertyville	60048
Zion Genealogical	2600 Emmaus Ave.	Zion	60099

La Salle

Genealogical Guide - La Salle	P. O. Box 278	Utica	61373

Lee County

Lee Co. Historical		Dixon	61021

Livingston

Odell Historical/Genealogical	P. O. Box 82	Odell	60460

Logan

Logan Co. Genealogical	P. O. Box 283	Lincoln	62656

Macon

Decatur Genealogical	P. O. Box 2205	Decatur	62526

Macoupin

Staunton Area Genealogical	Box 95	Staunton	62088

Madison

Madison Co. Genealogical	P. O. Box 89	Troy	62294

Marion

Marion Co. Genea./Hist.	P. O. Box 342	Salem	62881

Marshall

Marshall Co. Genea./Hist.	506 N. High St.	Lacon	61540

Mason

Mason Co. Genealogical	Box 246	Havana	62644

Massac

Massac Co. Historical	4th & Market St.	Metropolis	62960

Mc Donough

Mc Donough Co. Genealogical	P. O. Box 202	Macomb	61455

Mc Henry

Mc Henry Co. Genealogical	1011 Green St.	Mc Henry	60050

Mc Lean

Bloomington-Normal Genea.	P. O. Box 488	Normal	61761
IL Mennonite Hist./Genea.	918 S. University	Normal	61761
Lexington Genea./Hist.	318 W. Main St.	Lexington	61753

Mercer

Mercer Co. Historical		Aledo	61231

Monroe

Monroe Co. Historical		Waterloo	62208

Montgomery

Montgomery Co. Genealgoical	P. O. Box 212	Litchfield	62056
Montgomery Co. Historical	904 S. Main	Hillsboro	62049

Morgan

Jacksonville Genea./Hist.	P. O. Box 21	Jacksonville	62651
Waverly Genealogical/Historical		Waverly	62692

Moultrie

Moultrie Co. Hist./Genea.	P. O. Box MM	Sullivan	61951

Ogle

Ogle Co. Genealogical	P. O. Box 183	Oregon	61061

Peoria

IL Terminal Railroad Hist.	IL Central College	East Peoria	61635
Peoria Genealogical	P. O. Box 1489	Peoria	61602

Piatt

Piatt Co. Hist./Genea.	R. R. 1, Box 30	White Heath	61884

Pike

Pipe Co. Genealogical	P. O. Box 104	Pleasant Hill	62366

Pope

Pope Co. Historical		Golconda	62938

Richland

Richland Co. Genealogical	Box 202	Olney	62450

Rock Island

Blackhawk Genealogical	P. O. Box 912	Rock Island	61201
Rock Island Co. Historical	822 11th St.	Moline	61265

St. Clair

Mascoutah Historical		Mascoutah	62258
St. Clair Co. Genealogical	P. O. Box 431	Belleville	62221

Sangamon

Illinois State Archives	Archives Building	Springfield	61706
Illinois State Genealogical	P. O. Box 2225	Springfield	62705
Illinois State Hist. Library	Old State Capitol	Springfield	62706
Sangamon Co. Genealogical	P. O. Box 1829	Springfield	62705

Schuyler

Schuyler-Brown Hist./Genea.	P. O. Box 96	Rushville	62681
Schuyler Co. Hist./Genea.	P. O. Box 96	Rushville	62681

Shelby

Shelby Co. Hist./Genea.	P. O. Box 287	Shelbyville	62565

Stephenson

Stephenson Co. Historical	110 Coates Place	Freeport	61032

Tazewell

Tazewell Co. Genealogical	P. O. Box 312	Pekin	61554

Union

Union Co. Genea./Hist.	101 E. Spring St.	Anna	62906

Vermilion

Illiana Genealogical Historical	P. O. Box 207	Danville	61834

Warren

Warren Co. Genealogical	P. O. Box 240	Monmouth	61462
Warren Co. Historical		Roseville	61473

Washington

Marissa Historical/Genealogical	P. O. Box 27	Marissa	62257

White

White Co. Historical		Carmi	62821

Whiteside

Whiteside Co. Genealogists	Box 154	Sterling	61081

Will

Frankfort Area Genealogical	2000 East St. Louis	West Frankfort	62896

Williamson

Genealogical Soc. Southern IL	John A. Logan College	Carterville	62918
Southern Illinois Genealogical	607 N. Logan St.	Marion	62959
Williamson Co. Historical	105 South Van Buren	Marion	62959

Winnebago

North Central IL Genealogical	P. O. Box 1071	Rockford	61105

REFERENCES

AHA Guide (American Hospital Association, Chicago, IL) 1981

Jayne Askin, SEARCH: A Handbook for Adoptees and Birthparents (Harper & Row, New York, New York) 1982

Ayer Directory of Publications (Ayer Press) Annual

George B. Everton, Handy Book for Genealogists, 5th ed. (Everton Publishing Company, Logan, Utah) 1960

Hammond Citation World Atlas (Hammond Inc., Maplewood, New Jersey) 1982

Reg Niles, Adoption Agencies, Orphanages, and Maternity Homes (Phileas Deigh Corporation, Garden City, New York) 1981

Reg Niles, The Searchbook for Adult Adoptees (Phileas Deigh Corporation, Garden City, New York) 1978

Mary Jo Rillera, The Adoption Searchbook, (Tri-adoption Publications, Huntington Beach, California) 1981

Patricia Sanders, Searching in California (ISC Publications, Inc., Costa Mesa, California) 1982

INDEX

(Order blank may be photocopied)

ORDER BLANK

Please send me the following books:

____ copies of SEARCHING IN ILLINOIS, at $12.95
each.

____ copies of SEARCHING IN FLORIDA, at $10.95
each.

____ copies of SEARCHING IN CALIFORNIA, at $11.95
each.

NAME _____

ADDRESS _____

CITY _____STATE _____ZIP_____

Total amount enclosed $_____ . (California
residents add 6% sales tax.) ISC Publications
will pay postage. Please mail book order and
check or money order to:

ISC PUBLICATIONS
P. O. Box 10857
Costa Mesa, CA 92627